Dear Everybody

A WOMAN'S JOURNEY FROM PARK AVENUE
TO A LABRADOR TRAPLINE

ANNE BUDGELL

BOULDER PUBLICATIONS

Library and Archives Canada Cataloguing in Publication

Budgell, Anne, 1950-
    Dear everybody : a woman's journey from Park Avenue to a Labrador trapline / Anne
Budgell.

Includes bibliographical references.
Issued also in electronic format.
ISBN 978-1-927099-17-9

    1. Budgell, Anne, 1950-. 2. Trappers--Newfoundland and Labrador--Labrador--
Biography. 3. Socialites--New York (State)--New York--Biography. 4. Labrador (N.L.)--
Biography. I. Title.

FC2193.3.B83A3 2013   971.8'205092   C2013-900345-2

Published by Boulder Publications
Portugal Cove-St. Philip's, Newfoundland and Labrador
www.boulderpublications.ca

© 2013 Anne Budgell

Copy editor: Iona Bulgin
Design and layout: John Andrews

Printed in Canada

Newfoundland   We acknowledge the financial support of the Government of Newfoundland
Labrador   and Labrador through the Department of Tourism, Culture and Recreation.

We acknowledge the financial support for our publishing program by the Government of
Canada and the Department of Canadian Heritage through the Canada Book Fund.

For Ruby and George

NOTES ON THE TEXT,
PHOTOGRAPHS, AND MAPS

I n Barbara Mundy Groves's papers, there are 75 letters written by her between 1935 and 1948. She saved two diaries from long cruises to Europe with family members in 1926 and 1929, a brief diary of her trip from Boston to St. Anthony in 1935, a tiny diary written in North West River, 1944-1946, and her trapline diary of more than 300 pages, 1947-1949. Typographical errors such as misspellings, redundant quotation marks, and transposed letters have been silently corrected in the excerpts from these papers.

•••

All photographs in this book, except those of Barbara, were taken by her. She brought a camera to Labrador and took photos in North West River, on Grand (Churchill) River, and on the trapline. Barbara took photos on the river as she walked along the boulder-covered shore, nervously watching the men pole and track the heavy canoes against the current. She sent her film to be processed in New York and the prints came back with negatives in sleeves. It was possible to date and locate most of the photos in this book by comparing them with photos in an album donated by her family to the Heritage Museum in North West River. Barbara's collection also included colour slides made from pictures shot during her two winters on the trapline, which she captioned.

•••

Amongst the papers of Barbara Mundy Groves, a hand-drawn map made by Russell Groves, probably in the late 1940s, shows the location of his trapping paths. The western end of Winokapau, Wilfred Baikie's tilt on the north shore, and Fox Island are all clearly marked, as are Grand River, Elizabeth River, and Fig River. Two other features are named: Fanny's Island in Fig River and a lake Russell named Barbara Lake. If names are known for any of the hundreds of lakes, brooks, islands, streams, and rivers, they do not appear on his map or present-day official maps. (Many places were named by Innu people, but those names have not made it to official maps. Fig River is Kakupiu-shipu; in English, Porcupine Lake River.)

Russell's map shows enough features to make it possible to transpose his drawing to a topographical map, but it is an informed guess at best. Fig River on the official government map of today is not exactly where he had his trapline. Russell's Fig River is unnamed on modern maps and widens into a lake that connects to the "official" Fig River. He conflated the parts that were merely portages to be passed over and expanded the areas where he had traps or tilts (cabins). Lines for his portages and trapping paths could be extrapolated because he drew the rivers and lakes he paddled or walked over, illustrating significant islands, small rivers, brooks, and points of land.

Russell drew dots around the perimeter of the Fig River system and larger lakes. These are places where he put traps. He wrote "BH" to indicate beaver houses. He located each of his tilts and the main "House." Notes in Barbara's handwriting add some details. It took one day to walk from the House to Lower Tilt, North Path took two days, South Path four days. The Winter Portage walk from Winokapau to the Lower Tilt took one day. The words "cat," "fox," "marten," "mink," and "otter" were written where those animals were likely to be found.

Place names for the Lake Melville map presented a different challenge. Is it Molioch, Mulliauk, Moliak, or one of the four other spellings found in old documents? Eldred Allen, the Geographic Identification Specialist with the Nunatsiavut Government, Department of Lands and Natural Resources, tried to help. He asked Inuit elders in Rigolet, who told him they weren't sure. Everyone preferred "Moliak" and that is the spelling used in this book and on some current maps. River and place names were taken from official maps but numerous other spellings exist for Sebaskachu, Kenemich, Kenamu, Nascopie, and Winokapau. They are all derived from Innu names. The excellent website www.innuplaces.ca identifies hundreds of places in Labrador and translates names. There are some mysteries, like Mulligan, known to the Innu as Maunakan. Nobody knows if the name originated with English or Innu speakers.

The map of the Grand (Churchill) River shows what it looked like in 1946, when Barbara and Russell did their first trip upriver together, with Nora Groves and John Blake. The river has changed since 1971, the amount of water flow moderated by the development of the Upper Churchill hydroelectric project. The flooded area of western Labrador, Smallwood Reservoir, is a prominent feature on modern maps. The river will change again with the development of the Lower Churchill Project. When the new dam is built at Muskrat Falls in Phase One, a massive reservoir of 107 square kilometres will flood the river valley for 60 kilometres between the falls and Gull Island. Phase Two calls for a dam 99 metres high to be constructed at Gull Island, creating an even larger reservoir of 200 square kilometres in area, filling the valley for a distance of 225 kilometres.* The river rapids, both feared and respected by the trappers, will be gone forever.

—Anne Budgell

---

* *Lower Churchill Hydroelectric Generation Project* ..., November 30, 2006, a document prepared by Newfoundland and Labrador Hydro as required by federal and provincial environmental assessment regulations.

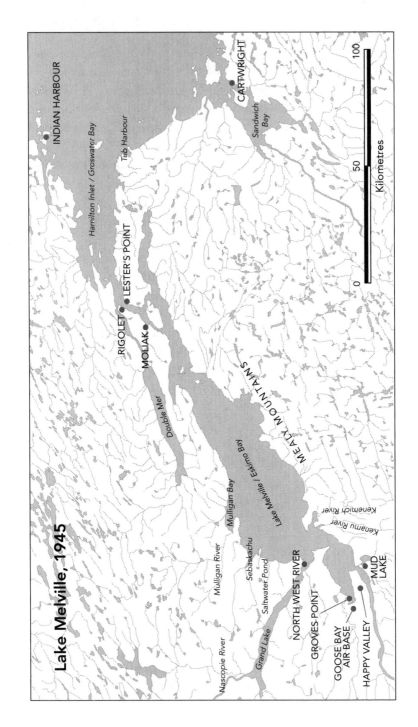

Lake Melville, 1945

INDIAN HARBOUR

CARTWRIGHT

Sandwich Bay

Hamilton Inlet / Groswater Bay

Tub Harbour

LESTER'S POINT

RIGOLET

MOLIAK

Double Mer

MEALY MOUNTAINS

Lake Melville / Eskimo Bay

Mulligan Bay

Kenemich River

Mulligan River

Sebaskachu

Kenamu River

Saltwater Pond

NORTH WEST RIVER

MUD LAKE

Nascopie River

GROVES POINT

Grand Lake

GOOSE BAY AIR BASE

HAPPY VALLEY

0   50   100

Kilometres

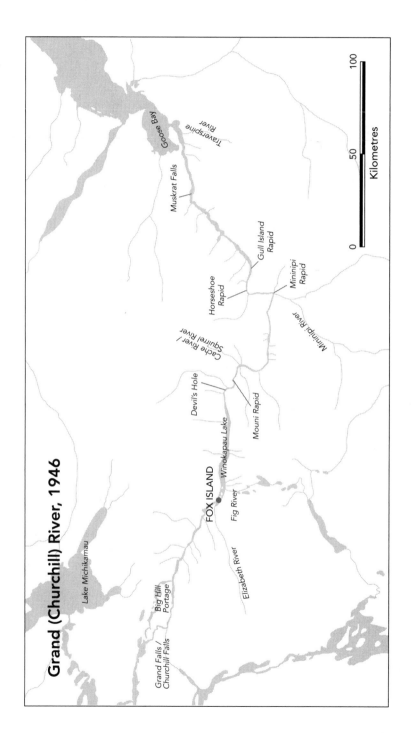

Grand (Churchill) River, 1946

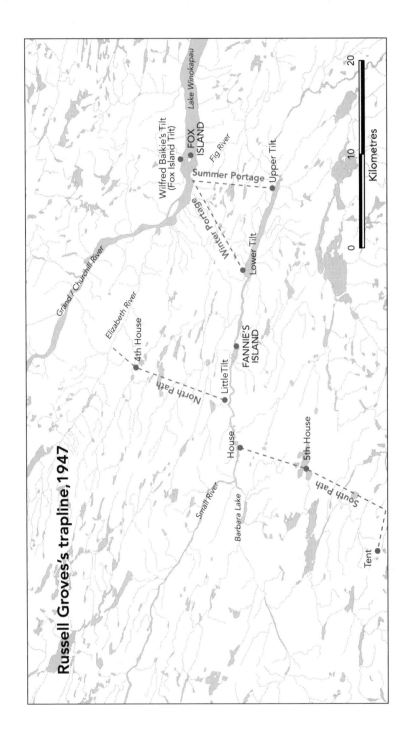

Russell Groves's trapline, 1947

Lake Winokapau

Wilfred Baikie's Tilt
(Fox Island Tilt)

FOX ISLAND

Fig River

Summer Portage

Upper Tilt

Winter Portage

Lower Tilt

Grand / Churchill River

Elizabeth River

4th House

North Path

Little Tilt

FANNIE'S ISLAND

House

5th House

South Path

Small River

Barbara Lake

Tent

Kilometres

0   10   20

ACKNOWLEDGEMENTS

I started writing this book when I retired, after working more than 30 years in CBC radio and television newsrooms. It was a good change, away from deadlines and the rush of getting a daily radio show on the air. I had the luxury of taking all the time I needed to do research—something that never happened in my working life—which helped me fill out the story of Barbara's life in New York and her first years in Labrador. While research and writing are solitary activities, getting the book done turned out to be very much a collaborative effort. Some people deserve special thanks.

Librarian David Hoffman at the New York Public Library installed me in a quiet corner and set me up with their latest Internet searching tool. Thanks to him I found Barbara's engagement notice of 1944. David Taylor, at the Library of Congress in Washington, D.C., answered several of my queries and sent Grenfell Mission and Mundy/Havemeyer family tidbits my way. In Labrador, Sgt. (ret.) Max Peddle of the Military Museum at CFB Goose Bay, Aimee Chaulk and Jill Larkham at *Them Days* magazine and archives, and Ernie McLean of the Labrador Heritage Society Museum in North West River guided me to useful materials. In St. John's, I received assistance from Joan Ritcey and the wonderful staff at the Centre for Newfoundland Studies in Memorial University's Queen Elizabeth II Library. Archivist Melanie Tucker and staff at The Rooms Provincial Archives directed me to the vast collection of Grenfell materials housed there. Gordon Barnes at the Railway Coastal Museum helped me properly identify the skipper of the *Prospero*.

I owe a debt of gratitude to the Writers' Alliance of Newfoundland and Labrador. I used their manuscript evaluation service and was fortunate to have Marjorie Doyle read and comment on my early efforts. She had another go at the growing manuscript when WANL chose me for their mentorship program. As an accomplished writer of non-fiction, Marjorie was the perfect mentor, balancing constructively critical with encouraging comments. My former CBC colleague, Ron Crocker, also read the manuscript and gave me many helpful notes and suggestions. Both he and Marjorie buoyed me up with their appreciation of the story of the privileged New Yorker transported to a trapline. Terence Ollerhead, for years the managing editor of *The International History Review*, gave me an important nudge in the right direction at the beginning of the writing process.

Members of the Mundy and Bryant families in the United States generously shared documents, photos, and letters. Thanks go to Peter and Jackie Mundy, who hosted me at their home in West Boothbay Harbor, Maine, while we sifted through boxes of memorabilia. Anthony Bryant dug up his father's recollection of his financial adventures, and Ted Mundy sent me explanations of branches of the family tree. I was glad to get a first-person account of another wop's experience when I visited Barbara's friend, Priscilla Randolph (Randy) Toland Page, at her summer home in York, Maine.

I learned a lot in my interviews with people from Labrador, friends and relatives of Barbara and Russell. Florence Michelin, Bella Shouse, Sylvia Blake, Jessie Michelin, Sheila Paddon, John Paddon, Shirley Hefler, Derrick (Dick) Chaulk, Morris Chaulk, Ruth Voisey, and Phyllis Groves Lacoursiere were all glad to help. Lloyd Montague assisted with the Groves-Montague family history. Henry Acreman sent me the book his mother, Celesta, had written about her time as a Grenfell nurse and with the "Industrial." Jean Crane had stories of living in the Mission dormitories. My mother, Ruby Budgell, has told me stories all my life about working in the dorms, at the hospital, and on the base, and what it was like to grow up in North West River. Gerald Dyson and my uncle, Dick Budgell, told me about the construction of the base at Goose Bay. Dick Budgell worked for many years at Churchill Falls and helped me understand the river and how trappers used it, but when I canoed down the river with Joe Goudie in 2012, I really saw what Barbara saw.

I paddled past Fox Island and the south shore of Winokapau, where she and Russell started their portage for the trapping paths. Thanks again to Joe for inviting me to join the group. It was a wonderful experience.

My friends Marjorie Groves and Don Kerr shared their home in British Columbia, allowing me to be "writer-in-residence." Marjorie's father, Russell, lived next door until he died in March 2007 and loved to see anyone from "home," especially if they arrived with frozen seal-flipper pie or partridgeberry jam. After a day of transcribing letters and diaries, I always had questions for him and a single question usually prompted multiple yarns. We spent many hours at the dinner table.

It has taken years to get to this point, and when there was no guarantee it would ever come to anything, for trusting me with her parents' story, and a thousand other favours and encouragement along the way, my greatest gratitude goes to Marjorie.

PROLOGUE

In the winter of 2003, I was visiting my friends Marjorie Groves and Don Kerr in British Columbia when Marjorie mentioned she didn't know what she was going to do with all her mother's papers. Her mother, Barbara Mundy Groves, died in 1994, leaving numerous letters, diaries, stacks of clippings, notebooks, and other ephemera. I asked if I could take a look, and spent the next couple of days fully absorbed, cast back in time to 1944 when Barbara left Manhattan for the tiny community of North West River, Labrador, to work with the International Grenfell Association, usually called the Grenfell Mission or simply "the Mission." By 1946 she was in love with a fur trapper, and the next year she married him. I was spellbound when I read what she had written about Labrador, not just because it was an inside peek at a time and place that figured so prominently in my own family history but because she did things most women, even Labrador women, did not do.

Parts of the story I had heard from the time I was a child. My mother, Ruby McLean Budgell, herself the daughter of a fur trapper, had grown up in North West River and knew Barbara and her husband, Russell Groves. I'll never forget my mother taking me to lunch at the Groves home when Marjorie and I were both about six years old. The small house was like everyone else's, with a wood-burning stove, hand pump for water, and kerosene lamps, but also with fine things not common in the community: mahogany furniture, Persian rugs, and pictures on the wall. The chicken noodle soup was served in pretty china bowls, set on a linen tablecloth. It wasn't only outside appearances; Barbara Groves sounded like someone on the radio, speaking with authority and not the local dialect. No trouble to tell she was from "away."

I knew people came to Labrador from the United States and England as volunteers with the Mission, and a few stayed. What I didn't know until I delved into the papers was that, after Barbara and Russell married in 1947, she spent two full winters with him on his trapline near Fig River, deep in the Labrador interior. The whole story was preserved in a leather-bound journal. Barbara had been enchanted by the romantic thought of a winter completely alone with the man she loved and, some days, there was nothing romantic about it at all. The bread was baked, clothes washed and mended, floor of the cabin "rebrushed" with fresh spruce boughs when Russell returned from a full day walking in snowshoes, checking his traps in frigid, windy weather. His clothes were thrown off and he would fall asleep exhausted, leaving Barbara tearfully wondering what she was doing there. In the early months, the couple had not found their rhythm. Surviving in the wild, during that first winter, was as much about learning to live together as it was about hunting and trapping.

By the autumn of 1947, when Barbara and Russell were preparing to go upriver, she had already written much about life in North West River in letters to family and friends. Although the letters to her mother are newsy and affectionate, I wondered if perhaps one reason Barbara went to Labrador was to get away from her. The demure content of her letters to "Dearest Mother," compared with the tidbits in her diary about all-night dances and midnight canoe excursions, indicates she did not want to give any opportunity for criticism or correction. In all the family correspondence that was kept, there is only one letter written by Mrs. Mundy and it reveals that she was determined to supervise Barbara's social life, where men were involved. Barbara was 25 years old when the letter was written and almost 34 when she left New York for North West River, long past time to be out of her mother's house and on her own, married or not.

Barbara also wrote to "Everybody," Mission pals who had been volunteers in Labrador or Newfoundland. Those letters were typed using carbon paper to make multiple copies and she usually kept one for herself. She was a great observer, a writer with an ear for a good yarn, stories her correspondents would find entertaining. She was also perhaps unconsciously trained in the style of writing she read in *Among the Deep-Sea Fishers*; the popular quarterly journal of the International Grenfell

Association (IGA) often published articles written by adventurous volunteers. She was a friend and great admirer of the author and former Mission volunteer Elliott Merrick and frequently referred to two of his books in her own writing. *True North*, his story of a winter spent in the bush with a fur trapper, had no small influence on Barbara. She used Merrick's *Northern Nurse* as a helpful guide to people and life in North West River.

Barbara's trapline diary covered the years 1947-1949 but she kept diaries at other significant times in her life. One details the Mundy family's tour of Britain and continental Europe in 1926, another was kept during a two-month cruise from New York to northern Europe in 1929. When she was accepted as a volunteer with the Mission in St. Anthony, Newfoundland, in 1935, she started a journal on the day she left New York. On arrival in Labrador in 1944, she started a diary, keeping brief notes about events. She saved every scrap of paper for nearly 70 years, but nothing about life in Manhattan. Perhaps it was too humdrum, too boring, when compared with conquering river rapids or riding on a komatik pulled by a team of dogs. Fortunately for me, the social life of someone from her circle in New York was well covered by the society page editors of the *New York Times*. Her name was listed among those in attendance at dinner dances, fashion shows for charity, or meetings to plan a benefit opera performance. Her committee work for the Needlework Guild of America and the IGA was often mentioned in *Among the Deep-Sea Fishers*. Sifting through society notes yields evidence that she was busy, but she wasn't always happy. She plainly says it in one letter to her mother—she had been lonelier when surrounded by millions than she ever was in North West River, where a stroll through the community would bring greetings from several people. In Labrador, she found satisfying work and good friends, and she fell in love.

Marjorie told me her mother sometimes talked about writing a book. I wish I could tell Mrs. Groves (she was never "Barbara" to me) how much I have enjoyed working with her, my ever-present collaborator, and I hope she would approve of what I have done with her material. It's all because her daughter agreed—after we had both read the trapline diary—that it was a great story and had to be told.

Chapter One

THE UNBEATEN PATH

*Over dangerous footing or up a few rickety steps he also
goes first and then leans over and offers her his hand. Under
all ordinary circumstances, indoors or out, the gentleman
precedes her only if the way is dangerous or uncertain.*

—Emily Post, *Etiquette*

Alone in a small canvas tent, top covered with fresh snow, pitched in a hollow among the trees on the shore of Fig River, Barbara Mundy Groves filled an enamel basin with hot water. It felt good to wash her face and hands and even better to apply lipstick to wind-dried lips. She dug among her things to find a pencil stub and a compact black leather-bound book with lined blue pages, cold fingers writing the date, Friday, October 24, 1947.

*Here am I with everything I've ever wanted—a husband to love &
do things for who would return that love, a house of my own, a life I've
always longed for, living in a country & in a way I love—everything about
it is what I've wanted <u>all</u> my life & yet I've failed in it all. I'm not making
R happy, I'm not happy myself as a result & I can't seem to learn the things
that I must to live here & be a proper wife here.* (Diary: October 24, 1947)

Nothing in Barbara's privileged life—growing up in Manhattan, attending boarding school and college—had prepared her in the slightest for what she was doing, with the possible exception of her much-improved sewing skills, which had already come in handy. (At least she was competent at something.) She and her new husband, Russell Groves, have travelled for almost a month by canoe and foot, from North West

River, a village in the middle of Labrador, to his fur trapping grounds deep in the interior, near the border of Quebec. They have paddled and poled up the rapid water of the Grand River, taken long and arduous portages many times to avoid dangerous spots, heavily burdened by all they will need to spend a winter in the wilderness. Packed in with the tent, traps, axes, and kettles were hundreds of pounds of flour, oatmeal, split peas, fatback pork, tea, sugar, and the cake she had baked for Christmas.

When they departed the community on the shore of Lake Melville, they were in company with the Grand River and "Height of Land" trappers, the men who go farthest upriver. One by one their companions dropped off at their own trapping places, until they reached the south shore of Lake Winokapau—Lake Winnie—and then it was their turn.

Russell, Barbara, and their dog, Spot, left the others and set out for Russell's trapping grounds on Fig River. The tent she is warming in is at one of his many camps. It will be at least another week before they reach the main "house," a log tilt (cabin) located at the centre of the trapping paths. For the first time since they married in August, there will be no neighbours, no friends, and no relatives dropping by. It is what she has been waiting for. She wrote: "the next few months are to be just ours & ours alone"—a romantic thought, but if she was honest, a frightening one too. What would she do if anything happened to Russell?

Before Barbara married Russell, she had spent two years in Labrador, managing the Grenfell Mission's Industrial Shop and living in the comfortable staff quarters of the Mission hospital in North West River. She enjoyed her job and had helped out at the hospital when needed. There had never been more than a single nurse at the hospital and no doctor during wartime, so her assistance was appreciated. As busy as she was, she always found time to go canoeing, snowshoeing, hiking, or hunting with a small rifle. She and her friends had paddled the nearby lakes and rivers, tramped all over the countryside picking berries and setting rabbit snares, no outing complete without a boil-up. After four weeks on the river, she had lost count of the boil-ups.

Barbara had written her mother, sister, and friends dozens of letters since arriving in North West River, describing life in a community where the men were gone for months at a time, while the women raised families by themselves all winter. Her long, chatty letters were written during quiet times in her cozy bedroom in the staff quarters, warmed by a small Franklin stove, or typed in her office at the Industrial Shop. She was following in the footsteps of many Mission workers over the years, volunteers who had come to stay for a while, doing worthwhile work but usually returning home to the United States or Britain. *Among the Deep-Sea Fishers* was full of stories of plucky Vassar girls who spent the summer working in the clothing store or the hospital at Mission headquarters in St. Anthony, and daredevil Harvard boys who crewed on the hospital ship sailing up and down the coast. Like them, Barbara had never imagined staying in Labrador after her contract was finished, but now here she was, Mrs. Russell Groves, filthy, exhausted, cold, and hungry, in a snow-capped tent in the middle of nowhere with a fur trapper husband who was probably sorry he had brought her there. If ever her adventures made it to the pages of *Among the Deep-Sea Fishers*, she would insist that she not be described as "plucky."

The leather-bound diary had been a wedding gift, which she optimistically titled *Life Begins at 37*, after the popular self-help book *Life Begins at Forty*. Her first entry, on August 12, was written in New York as she said goodbye to her family and friends and prepared to go back to Labrador to get married: "Goodbyes a bit choky, but not moist. Hope Ma will live 'till I can come back to tell her all is well with R & me." Her mother's health problems might have kept her there but she desperately wanted to marry Russell and, anyway, her sister, Harriet, was in New York with her mother. As soon as she was back in Labrador, she knew she was home: "That's the way I feel about it, & there's no doubt in my mind that I love R & his country very much indeed. May it never change."

Those were her words on August 16. Only two months later her entries had a more anxious tone. Were all husbands as taciturn as Russell? Or was it just the Labrador way? Thank goodness she had the diary. It was her closest confidante, taking the place of her best friends and nearest relatives, women she wouldn't be able to speak with for months. She may have expected to write a breezy account of sights seen, progress on the river, the weather, the animals killed and eaten, but as weeks went by, she came to depend on organizing her thoughts and feelings and releasing them on paper, when she could summon enough energy to scrawl a few notes. Some nights, after they made camp, fixed supper, and hung their wet clothes up to dry, the diary was put aside until morning.

Every day was a physical test—she had expected that—but also an emotional trial. Why was Russell critical so often? She wanted to be a help to her husband but, just a few weeks into a long winter, felt she was a useless burden. As hard as she tried, it wasn't good enough.

Everything I do seems to be wrong. Some things I can laugh about to myself as they were just little things I thot would be thoughtful to do, but they definitely were not wanted. Others I'm just supposed to know how to do & I don't. R is discouraged & disgusted with me, I'm afraid. (Diary: October 16, 1947)

Freshening up with warm water and soap was comforting. She was glad Russell wasn't there to point out her frequent bathing was a waste of water and fuel. She could just imagine what he'd say if he saw her applying lipstick in a tent on the trapline. That would be another "first" to add to the already long list.

My first paddle in over a year (and my first all-day paddle I ever had) has left me aching—although not as completely so as my first wash day! I'm not doing very well—almost frozen before 1st boil and so bad at steering R threatened "to go home"—he was serious about it too. I'd rather die first & I'll do it successfully if it kills me. In the afternoon he explained what I should do instead of taking it for granted I remembered or knew already. If he'll only continue to do that I'll be all right. But I know so little I can't even ask what to do in different cases until I've done the wrong thing & then it's too late. I guess it's hard for him to believe anyone can be so ignorant of things that are just part of him. These last five weeks have been full of "firsts" for me—among them: just the ordinary everyday housekeeping & cleaning; washing clothes, etc.; baking bread; keeping a fire on; getting used to no plumbing for any length of time; trying to win Phyllis' [Russell's daughter] affection; etc. etc.—to say nothing of a first husband. It's been quite a dose, but I've lived thru' it. Just getting used to a husband would almost have been enuf in so short a time! (Diary: October 3, 1947)

More than once, Russell threatened to turn around and take her back to North West River. In his experience, competence on the river assured you arrived alive, with your food supply secure and dry; failure could endanger your life, or even take it. He had come up the river every year since he was 12, had been trapping alone since he was 15, and didn't have much patience with mistakes. He was the only trapper with a wife in the country that winter, a wife more familiar with hailing a cab on Park Avenue than canoeing a Labrador river. Paddling the fully loaded canoes over calm, deep water was the easy part. Getting all their supplies carried to the trapping path, over hills, around rapids and shallow places, was slave labour. She worried about how it was for Russell on the portages, carrying more than he usually did, all the extra on account of her: "for each mile we advance R walks about 16." She had done as much as she could, feeling stronger after four weeks of daily practice, and was relieved to know they were nearly at the main tilt without suffering any major disasters. That day, Russell continued to portage their supplies, without help from her.

In the aft. R went for a load. I wanted to go too but he seemed to want to be alone, so I went for a walk alone too, probably did us good! I never could find my way about without him—could barely make out yesterday's track when shown to me and <u>never</u>, never could find one myself like that. Went as far as the top of the hill with R & then tried to find my own way about & not very successful—didn't dare go too far afield. Sat on top of the hill & looked at Fig River—it was cold, a kind of day that would be dreary to many—not me tho'—the water was dark & loppy and I had that same feeling—how wonderful to be off like this away from everything & everybody with someone you care for. (Diary: October 24, 1947)

In the quiet, darkening forest, she recalled the repeated cautions from relatives and friends in New York and North West River. How many times had she been told she didn't know what she was getting herself into? That it wasn't a life for a woman, especially one whose previous wilderness experience was Audubon Nature Camp. Even those who wished her well probably expected her to fail miserably. Just the thought of it made her even more determined to prove that her decision to marry Russell and go with him for the winter was the right one.

I finally went out and looked at the snow & trees & river & tried to put more pleasant thots in my mind. R is everything to me now & all I have to live for & things must be well between us; we must meet each other half way & make our marriage what we both expected—I think we both expected it. I know I did—I suppose maybe loving him as much as I did— and do—made me dream dreams that will never come true. Gosh—how I have thought almost every minute of the day & night for two years now of our being together & planning together & really building a life together that would be complete in every way. I knew it was a gamble & I guess he did too—but I wanted it so terribly that I <u>had</u> to take it & I've <u>got</u> to win. I realize more & more how much I do love R & to have things as they are now is agonizing. I don't pray very often & I guess the two <u>real</u> prayers of my life were for and about R. They were answered so maybe now again 'twill be: Make things right for us—make us as happy as we were. When he went away a year ago, just the touch of his hand as we said good-bye settled things for me then. I <u>knew</u> we loved each other & that I had to come back to him. Don't let either of us ever have regrets that I did. (Diary: October 24, 1947)

A supper of "delicious beaver" and the snow making it almost like fairyland calmed her and she hoped for a restful sleep after a "nightmarish jumble of weird dreams" the previous night. Perhaps the worst was behind them, now that they were on their own at Fig River. She had paddled many miles, tried to keep up with the men and do her share of carrying. She had stuck it out and it had been the hardest thing she'd ever done in her life. Russell was wonderfully patient some days but occasionally frustrated by her inexperience. She knew that any close call scared him and he would probably be on edge until they reached his main "house" and settled in for the winter. The greatest comfort to her was the knowledge that every night, whether in a canvas tent or a log tilt, they would be together and the trials of the day would fade.

I've been happy tho'—and am not sorry I came back. If only I don't fail tho' along the way. I just <u>can't</u>. Last night the moon came out clear and lovely. It was a <u>heavenly</u> night in <u>every</u> way for me. I hope it was for R. (Diary: October 3, 1947)

At 37, she was with a man she loved deeply, but more than that, she had left behind everything familiar and easy to join him for life. By rights, she should have married a Wall Street executive and be living in an apartment on the Upper East Side. She should be busy with the opera benefit committee, lunching with friends at Delmonico's, her children in boarding school, servants doing the housework. A "cruise" was a trip to France, not across the bay to Mud Lake. She had come so close to being that woman, like her mother, following the prescribed course, doing what was expected, taking the beaten path. You wouldn't find many beaten paths around Fig River, she had noticed, and if you wanted bread made or clothes washed and mended, you had better put the cap on your lipstick, get out of your sleeping bag, and do it.

Chapter Two

SUGAR BARONS AND RAILROAD KINGS

Too many of us are likely to assume a rich man a gentleman.
No qualification could be further from the truth, since the
quality of a gentleman is necessarily measured by what he
is and never by what he has.

—Emily Post, *Etiquette*

In the wild country of Labrador, Barbara had plenty of time to think about where she was and what she had left behind. There were no distractions there, just endless repetitive carrying and hauling of all their supplies and food, on their backs or by canoe. She could well imagine what her father would say about such a primitive mode of transportation.

Floyd Woodruff Mundy was a senior partner at Oliphant & Co. and the editor of the annual publication *Mundy's Earning Power of Railroads*. After 40 years in the business, what he didn't know about the financial condition of railroads in the United States and Canada wasn't worth knowing. He had a well-deserved reputation for his conservative approach to investment, perhaps shaped by a shocking event in his early days with the firm.

The story of the murder of one of the city's most prominent businessmen filled the front page of the *New York Times* on December 21, 1907, under the bold headline, "Ruined Speculator Kills J.H. Oliphant." The killer, Dr. Charles Geiger of Beaufort, South Carolina, had been a client of the brokerage firm for more than two years. Witnesses said he spent the morning quarrelling bitterly with Oliphant about his loss of

$75,000, pleading for a loan so he could get back into the market. He already owed the firm $5,000 and Oliphant refused the loan. They broke to have lunch, returned to the office at 20 Broad Street, next to the Stock Exchange, when Geiger took out a pistol, shot Oliphant in the stomach and himself in the head. Barbara's father was working in an adjoining office, heard the shots, rushed in, and attended to his gravely wounded employer. A horse-drawn ambulance took Oliphant to hospital, where he died. Mundy was made managing partner 10 days later and stayed with the firm for his whole career.[1]

Following his graduation from Cornell in 1898, Floyd Mundy could have chosen to work anywhere. He married his childhood friend and neighbour, Harriet Bryant, and they lived in their home city of Chicago for a short time and then moved east, to a house in Montclair, New Jersey, and a position for him in the financial district of New York. An ambitious young man with an analytical mind, Floyd saw ways to apply his abilities to the growing railroad industry. And he had another advantage in the city—members of his mother's family were on the famous list of Four Hundred, the inner circle of those who counted in New York society, along with the Astors, Roosevelts, DuPonts, and Vanderbilts.

Floyd's mother, Annie Havemeyer Mundy, had been dead since 1934, but Barbara could easily conjure up her formidable grandmother, the matriarch her sister, Harriet, called a "great grey battleship," an imposing woman usually dressed in grey or black, a widow since 1918. Grandma Annie never tired of telling people she had been born a New York Havemeyer; her family was famous for owning most of the country's sugar refineries and also for some old political notoriety. Her father, Albert, was president of Havemeyer and Co. when she was a girl. Her uncle William was mayor of New York City three times between 1845 and 1872. She was 23 the year he died in office. Annie and her husband, Norris Mundy, lived in Chicago while Norris ran the regional office for the sugar company. When he retired in 1913, they returned to New York, much to Annie's relief, and lived in an apartment on Park Avenue.

For Barbara's mother, Harriet Blanchard Bryant Mundy, who had no family in the city, the extended Mundy-Havemeyer clan was intimidating. She knew they would provide her entrée into society, but she was not inclined to bow down to them either, even though a few probably thought her hometown of Chicago was practically the wild west. Fully briefed by her mother-in-law on the eminent stature of the family she had married into, Harriet had always told her girls they were members of the Daughters of the American Revolution thanks to the Bryants, not the Havemeyers, classed as latecomers to America, in her books. As far as she was concerned, the Bryant name was as prominent in Chicago as Havemeyer was in New York, allowing for some failures, along with successes, in business. Her father, John J. Bryant Sr., had been a director of the Chicago Board of Trade, a grain trader, and, by all accounts, a gentle, sweet man. In his turbulent professional life, he made and lost fortunes. On one very bad day, June 17, 1887, his loss of $25,000 in wheat trading merited a note in the *New York Times*. His son Henry remembered the good days when "spans of beautiful horses and retinues of servants would come home, and a false standard of living was set for the whole family." In the famous "bull panic" of 1901, Henry recalled how his father was ruined when creditors "decided they wanted their money quick." Without funds to pay tuition, young Henry dropped out of college with less than $2 in his pocket.[2]

Harriet's wedding to Floyd Mundy that year was a small ceremony at home, although her parents gave her a huge double-drawer chest of monogrammed sterling silver flatware. Bryant eventually recovered and when his youngest daughter, Mary, was married, he could afford to pay for a very large wedding.

The Bryants and Mundys were neighbours in the upper-middle-class enclave of Riverside, just 10 miles from the Loop, encircling downtown Chicago's business district. It was a new community, one of the first "railroad" suburbs in the United States. Riverside residents enjoyed modern municipal works and services, easy railway access to the city, new churches, a golf club, and shops, and lived in houses designed by some of the country's leading architects. The two families shared meals and news about each other's children. Their oldest sons, Floyd Mundy and John J. Bryant Jr., graduated from Cornell and worked as investment brokers with the same firm. By the time Floyd and Harriet married, the families had been close for years. Harriet's brother, John Jr., would run the Chicago office of Oliphant & Co. and serve as president of the Chicago Stock Exchange in the 1920s.

The Mundys were from Watertown, upstate New York, a good distance from high society and membership in the Four Hundred, but solidly established in the smaller city's business and civic life. Norris's father, Pearson Mundy, worked hard and married well, choosing Maria Donner Woodruff, one of five attractive daughters of Norris Woodruff, a railroad director, merchant, and banker in Watertown. Pearson and Maria Mundy eventually were very well off and later, quite wealthy, thanks to a generous bequest from the husband of Maria's sister, Emma. When railway entrepreneur Henry Keep died, Emma was left with millions and each sister-in-law, including Maria, received $100,000, a considerable fortune in 1869.[3] Rich bequests of cash and jewelry periodically blessed the senior Mundys, and then the younger generations, as their wealthy relatives passed away.[4]

After an unexpected inheritance in 1908, Floyd and Harriet purchased and furnished a larger house in Montclair, New Jersey. When Barbara was born in 1910, the household included six-year-old Floyd Jr., four-year-old Harriet, a Scottish governess, an English chambermaid, and a Norwegian cook.[5] They lived in the suburban home on South Mountain Avenue until Barbara was eight. Floyd Mundy sold the big house in 1918, according to the family story, without even telling his wife; it had something to do with the difficulties of getting furnace coal during the war. He came home one day with the news they'd be moving to an apartment above Hotel LaSalle on East 60th. For the children the move from the suburbs to the city made little difference. They would be away at boarding school or college most of the time and in the summer they'd go to camp or the house he rented in Camden, Maine. For him, it would be much more convenient, not having to commute 40 minutes by train to the financial district. He was absorbed in his career, and his wife, Harriet, with household staff to cook, clean, and mind the children, could devote her time to shopping, or more worthy activities.

After 10 years on East 60th Street, the Mundy family's move to a larger, new apartment at 1009 Park Avenue was announced in the *Times*'

"Notes of Social Activities."[6] It was the year before Barbara graduated from Miss Madeira's, her boarding school near Washington, D.C. Her sister was still at Vassar and her brother, Floyd Jr., had finished at Cornell and was engaged to marry Margaret (Peggy) Raye. Floyd Mundy was one of the first tenants in the Bing & Bing development designed by Emery Roth and Mott Schmidt. Roth was famous for designing the Ritz Tower, the San Remo, and the Beresford, all stately, spacious apartments in the new Art Deco style. The family had the entire tenth floor, nearly 5,000 square feet, with the vestibule from the elevator opening into a very large (29 x 10 feet) gallery in the centre. Tradesmen and servants would use a separate service elevator. Four large bedchambers were for the family, with three modern bathrooms (Harriet and Barbara shared one), and roomy closets. The kitchen and pantry were located at the back, connected to the servants' quarters, almost a separate apartment, with four small bedrooms, a servant's hall, and a bathroom.

Eleven large windows in the main rooms overlooked Park Avenue and the intersection with 84th Street. It was only a few blocks to the Metropolitan Museum of Art, walking distance to Central Park, near their church on Madison Avenue, and the shops on Fifth. At first Barbara's mother thought perhaps it was too far north on the Upper East Side, but Floyd was convinced these were going to be some of the most sought-after addresses in Manhattan. In the end, everyone agreed that 1009 Park Avenue, they always called it "Thousand Nine," was quite suitable. Barbara's father was pleased they would be near his widowed mother.

Floyd Mundy's conservative approach to business was paying off. The family was comfortable and secure at home in Manhattan. They enjoyed summer holidays in Maine or Glacier National Park in Montana. In the winter they went skiing or to resorts like the Homestead Hotel in Hot Springs, Virginia. Like her brother and sister, Barbara attended a good private school and then college, with the benefit of travel within the United States and cruises to Europe on their holidays. On June 11, 1926, the entire Mundy family sailed to Southampton, England, on the SS *Homeric* and then took a summer-long motor tour of the continent. For Barbara's sixteenth birthday on July 1, her parents gave her a string of pearls.

The women of the family cruised again in 1929, after Barbara's graduation from boarding school, aboard the SS *Carinthia* of the Raymond Whitcomb Line. Her father, brother, and Floyd's fiancée, Peggy, saw them off: "we with hankies and Floyd with his hat had a grand time wig-wagging to each other. An aeroplane flew low over us." They departed late in June, and returned on August 9, after stopping in Iceland, Norway, Sweden, Finland, Denmark, France, and England. For this cruise, she kept notes in a beautiful logbook, its cover decorated by a gilded design of two sea horses nose to nose and "Miss Barbara Mundy" embossed in gold letters. She noted that she played all the deck sports, met some attractive men, and had a good time dancing.[7]

In September 1929, Barbara left New York to attend Connecticut College for Women in New London. Her sister had a social work position at Madison Avenue Presbyterian Church. Floyd Jr. got married, despite Grandma Annie Mundy's expressed disapproval of his fiancée as a woman from a family "without a pedigree," hardly fair to Peggy, whose seafaring ancestors had been in America at least as long as the Havemeyers.

Two months after the Mundy women returned from their Scandinavian cruise, the stock market crashed. Events had been building to the crisis, after a week of the market almost crashing every day, a near collapse in March, and severe price dips in September. The wild stock market speculation drove share values far beyond their real worth and, when prices weakened, people panicked and sold, causing a cascade of declining values. On "Black Tuesday," October 29, more than 16 million shares were bought and sold. The slide continued every day and, by mid-November, the market had lost $26 billion, about a third of its value. As shocking as it was, it didn't keep people from buying back into the market. Stocks regained some of their value by April 1930. This economic upheaval was unprecedented, but it was first seen as an isolated event. It wasn't yet being called The Great Depression and President Herbert Hoover was still touting the strength of the American economy.

Despite the extraordinary number of bank failures and the market collapse, editors of the *New York Times* determined the major news story of 1929 was Admiral Richard Byrd's aerial survey of the South Pole.[8] Barbara would have agreed with their decision. For millions of Americans in the 1930s, the heroic deeds of Byrd, Charles Lindbergh, Amelia Earhart, and all the other daring aviators were a welcome distraction from the daily news of financial disaster. Barbara was fascinated by their exploits, setting records for the first crossing of a continent or an ocean, or the quickest time across. She amassed a thick file of clippings about their accomplishments and purchased large photos of Byrd in his fur clothes, the huts and tents of camp "Little America" showing its three radio towers, dogsleds, and aircraft parked on snowdrifts. Barbara was there, and had her camera with her, when Byrd and his crew paraded down Broadway upon their return to New York on June 19, 1930. She saved an envelope postmarked "Dublin, New Hampshire," dated August 6, 1930, a lightning bolt emblem superimposed over the words *Byrd Antarctic Expedition* in the top left corner. The typed letter, signed by her hero, thanked her for the photos she had sent him of his arrival in New York.

Another man she admired greatly, and one of the most popular lecturers in the United States, was the medical missionary Dr. Wilfred Grenfell, properly addressed as Sir Wilfred since receiving a knighthood from the king in 1927. His listeners, sometimes in assemblies of up to 3,000, were enchanted by stories of his adventures, bringing medical care to the isolated fishing communities of the northwest Atlantic. In the early days his talks were illustrated with magic lantern slides, and later with motion pictures, showing a young burn victim being treated or a crippled boy with a donated crutch. Prominently featured would be the hospitals, orphanages, ships, and clinics built and operated with money donated by his friends and supporters, some of the most successful business people in the United States, delighted to rub shoulders with the charismatic doctor. After hearing him, admirers could browse tables full of his books and displays of carved ivories, hooked rugs, handwoven goods, and other articles made by the women and disabled men of Labrador. Grenfell's books were on Barbara's shelves and copies of *Among the Deep-Sea Fishers*, the magazine about the work of his

Mission, were scattered on the coffee table in the living room.

By the end of 1931, it would take more than the exploits of handsome explorers and rugged missionaries to divert attention from the nearly 2,300 American banks that had failed. Barbara's father, cautious as always, aligned himself with one of the solvent ones. Floyd Mundy was made a director of the Excelsior Savings Bank in 1932 and it survived through those difficult years and for many years beyond that.[9] So many people were out of work that the National Child Labor Committee made the radical suggestion that children under age 16 should be required to attend school. Two million children in the workforce made it even more difficult for newly unemployed adults to find a job.[10] Five hundred women applied daily at the Work Bureau's central office on Fifth Avenue. A reporter interviewed five young women in a dire situation, sharing one room, two with jobs and three unemployed. They had pawned most of their belongings, keeping one good dress to wear to job interviews.[11]

Life for Barbara and her college chums was happily remote from the growing unemployment lines. Two months after the stock market crash, she came home to attend a dinner dance at the Ritz-Carlton hotel, held by Nancy Rodman, who had made her debut in society the previous season.[12] Barbara enjoyed her singing part in the student production of *The Mikado*, added to her autograph collection, improved her French, and read poetry. There was another summer transatlantic cruise and a tour in France in 1932. She was one of the few students who had a car, very handy for outings and for going home to New York on weekends. In her yearbook, two girlfriends wrote appreciative notes about the grand rides they had taken in her car.[13]

For their graduation portraits, the young women were photographed against a dark background wearing black, collarless V-neck blouses. In the text beside Barbara's photo, the yearbook editors had written that she "generally appears to be on her way to execute some mission of great importance. She is one of the few among us who enjoys collecting funds and keeping accounts." Barbara had been taught how to manage her money correctly, although she had never shown much interest in how money was made, perhaps as a result of growing up in a household where there was always plenty of it and it wasn't much discussed.

The spring of 1933 was a poor time to be entering the workforce, with one in four Americans unemployed. Floyd Mundy discouraged Barbara and her sister from taking paying positions when so many people needed one. He could afford to support them and anyone could see it would be ridiculous to move from the large family apartment on Park Avenue, not only because there was plenty of room. The proper place for single young women was at home, with their parents; even their brother had lived at home until he married. There were no employment prohibitions on Floyd Jr., who was admitted to the Oliphant firm in 1931.[14]

Barbara understood her father's reasoning, at least the part about taking a job away from someone who needed to earn a living, and it was impossible to argue with him. After graduation she found herself back in New York City with time on her hands. It was quite a change from her college days with classes to attend, papers to write, club activities, and road trips with the girls to keep her busy. She was young, energetic, and educated, and would surely find something more to do than buff her nails and attend luncheons. No doubt her parents believed their daughters would be with them for a few more years at most, until they married and moved to homes of their own, but what was expected to be a brief interlude between college and marriage turned into a decade of dependence, and the beginning of a lifelong connection with a medical mission dedicated to helping people in cold, remote Labrador.

Chapter Three

THE FARTHEST NORTH ENTERPRISE OF MERCY

We know that times are pretty bad
For all of us; the stores have had
To stock a cheaper grade of furs
Than Labrador exports as hers.
(The rabbits that supply our meals
Cost less than foxes, bears and seals;
And Imitations artful aid
Turns sea-weed into marmalade.)
But though such skins we cannot buy
We cannot let the trappers die.

—A.G.G., "The Boston Fair"

Women fortunate enough to be shopping for furs during the Depression could salve their consciences somewhat with their membership in organizations like the International Grenfell Association (IGA). It was one of the favourite charities of society women in New York, drawn by the stories Dr. Wilfred Grenfell told about the destitute, hungry, and poorly clothed people of Newfoundland and Labrador. New members were always welcome on the large committees for events such as the opera benefit. The planning meetings were pleasant social gatherings, often held in the homes of the more prominent members, or over lunch in a good restaurant. Members served on committees according to their age and marital status. Young, unmarried women began on the Debutante subcommittee and graduated to Junior rank. Married women were identified as matrons, and the older, richer ones were usually granted titles of director, co-chairwoman, or patroness.

Barbara's mother, Harriet, was pleased to be listed as a patroness and had reserved an opera box for the Mission's benefit performance of Verdi's *La Forza del Destino* in 1930.[1] In addition to being a principal source of revenue for the Mission, the opera event was an enjoyable way to help the unfortunate residents of the desolate north.[2] Seats for the opera sold well that year, perhaps due to the terrible news that the Mission's hospital in Battle Harbour had been destroyed by fire. The disaster prompted an editorial in the *New York Times* on November 7, referring to the Mission as the "Farthest North enterprise of mercy, which has become in a degree an American institution, since so many young Americans have a part in it."[3]

The editorial writer had called it correctly. The Mission was a United-States-based charity, dependent on American philanthropy and volunteers. Its head office was in New York. Its founder, Grenfell, spent summers in Newfoundland and Labrador and winters on the lecture circuit in the United States, Canada, and Britain, touring from his home base in Vermont. The medical mission to summer fishermen that he began in 1892 had grown by 1927 into a charitable foundation that operated four year-round hospitals—one in the Labrador interior at North West River, one at Battle Harbour on the south Labrador coast, one in Harrington Harbour on the Canadian (Quebec) coast, and the largest, a modern, new one in St. Anthony, Newfoundland. Six nursing stations served smaller communities, and there were two boarding schools. The Mission had a small fleet of vessels, including the hospital ship, *Strathcona* (after 1922, *Strathcona II*).[4]

While the impression may have been created that Grenfell's charitable work embraced only Labrador, the medical Mission was initially concentrated on the northern tip of the island of Newfoundland, the southern part of the Labrador coast, and the settlements of Labrador's Hamilton Inlet. The coast north of Hamilton Inlet was the domain of the German and English missionaries who belonged to the United Brethren, also called Moravians.[5] They had been labouring in the much farther north more than 100 years before Grenfell arrived, and became increasingly irritated by him and the hero-worshipping attention he received in the United States.[6] Unlike the IGA, they did not have a handsome celebrity leader drawing crowds at public appearances, selling thousands of books telling of his adventures among Arctic fishermen. Like the Mission though, the Moravians published a quarterly journal, *Periodical Accounts*, with stories of their work, including photos of Labrador and Alaskan Inuit families, helped by donations from the United States and England.

The Mission provided medical and social services in its territory without much financial contribution or interference from the Newfoundland government, except for a waiver of duties on imported goods. In 1905, a small grant of $500 a year was given to each Mission hospital.[7] In the years of his tenure, the first decade of the twentieth century, Newfoundland premier Robert Bond was under assault by certain commentators for any grants to Grenfell, especially while duties were not being paid. One of his most strident critics, with unfettered access to the Letters to the Editor pages in the daily newspapers, was Roman Catholic archbishop M.F. Howley, who described the Mission as pauperizing and degrading. Howley wondered why Grenfell wasn't working nearer his English home, "among these swarming millions of wretched sufferers, instead of wasting his efforts among the few hundreds of hardy, healthy inhabitants on Labrador?"[8] Grenfell's descriptions of destitution and near starvation in Labrador cast shame on the merchants and traders who had business interests there and some wanted no favours or special treatment given to him.[9] Whatever small amounts were being paid to the Mission stopped in June 1932 when the financially strapped Newfoundland government discontinued all help to the hospitals and nursing stations.[10] The bankrupt government was replaced by a British-appointed Commission in 1934 and the relationship with the Mission was put on the agenda. With no money to spend, a bureaucratic solution to the funding problem for the Mission was found when the Commission of Government offered it a subsidy equal to the amount of duty paid on imported goods, an exercise in bookkeeping meant to silence critics.[11]

The work of the Mission could not have been done without the money raised by the IGA in the United States. Between 1934 and 1938, when the grant from the Newfoundland government was never greater than $6,000, American donations topped $67,000.[12] Mission revenue came from wealthy philanthropists, sales of handicrafts such as hooked mats, the efforts of high society women at events like the annual opera benefit in New York, the free labour provided by summer volunteers, and the take at the door when Grenfell gave a public talk. The fundraising strategy was to stage well-organized events in large halls, directing appeals to a specially invited group of what Grenfell called "the best people." He gave 80 talks on his tour in the United Kingdom in autumn 1928, sometimes two a day.[13] In 1929, he toured the United States and Canada, giving two dozen speeches in cities from east to west.[14] He filled large rooms, like Carnegie Hall in New York, Symphony Hall in Boston, and Massey Hall in Toronto. A one-night event could yield as much as $19,000.[15] The talks about poverty in distant, northern places did not continue to enthrall Americans, especially during the Depression. A decline in net return from lectures was "viewed with alarm" by Mission accountants in 1938.[16]

In his glory days, Grenfell had a polished repertoire of stories that had worked for years, triggering donations and inspiring volunteers to come forward and do as well or better than the Princeton boys who "spent the summer giving us the excavation" for an orphanage in St. Anthony, and the "boys from Yale University [who] came and put a dam across a valley, which has given running water all the year 'round ever since."[17] Many had accepted the challenge, spending a summer in Mission service, dining out later on anecdotes about their northern experiences and close association with one of the most-admired men of the day. For some families, "it became a rite of passage, a family tradition."[18]

The Mission had an impressive list of volunteer alumni, the sons and daughters of wealthy, influential American families, many listed in *Who's Who*.[19] Volunteers were nicknamed "wops" (and sometimes "wopesses" for the women) because they worked without pay; Grenfell always emphasized it was not connected with the derogatory term for Italian immigrants. Some who went as young medical students later ran hospitals. Others became prominent in American politics, like Henry Cabot Lodge and Cyrus R. Vance. Brothers Laurance and David, sons of tycoon John D. Rockefeller, spent the summer of 1929 as crew on *Maraval*, one of the Mission's boats.[20] Inventor and businessman Clarence Birdseye, credited with developing the American frozen food industry, went to Labrador as a Grenfell volunteer in 1912. He returned to the coast as manager of a fox farm and lived there for five years. Birdseye always said it was on the coast of Labrador that he observed people freezing fish straight out of the water and adapted their method to start a new, revolutionary industry.[21]

Anyone who attended a lecture, or read one of his books or articles, was justified in thinking Grenfell and his legions of wops worked only in Labrador. His book titles never mentioned Newfoundland—*Forty Years for Labrador, The Romance of Labrador, Down North on the Labrador, A Labrador Doctor, Grenfell of Labrador, Tales of the Labrador, A Labrador Logbook*—and whether he said "down north" or "on the Labrador," he understood those terms to include Newfoundland. He told members of the Empire Club in 1921 that he had arrived in Toronto from the "wild lands of Labrador … having come straight up from the Coast by the *Manoa*, which is the new service that has been inaugurated this last year between Labrador and the mainland," perhaps confusing any audience members who were aware that Labrador *is* on the mainland.[22] He spent his summers sailing the hospital ship *Strathcona* from one fishing station to another on the southern coast of Labrador and the northern peninsula of Newfoundland; it was the only way to travel in that part of the world. That Newfoundland was an island and Labrador the mainland was irrelevant: it was all "the Coast."

Grenfell knew his audiences would not care or wonder about any fine distinctions between Labrador and Newfoundland, and, although he acknowledged that the people saw themselves as different from each other, he was much amused by that. He regaled the Empire Club audience: "Labrador and Newfoundland are different. The average Newfoundlander does not like to be mixed with Labrador. I often hear a Newfoundlander say, 'Oh, you mix us up with the Labrador,' and the Labrador men say, 'Oh, for God's sake don't mix us up with the Newfoundlander."[23] He persisted in mixing them up, probably because he had learned, after giving hundreds of talks and interviews, that Labrador, with its Inuit and Arctic associations, had more drawing power with his American audiences than Newfoundland, with its codfish and fishermen. Fishermen in Maine and Massachusetts were much like those in Newfoundland. Publicity photos and book dust jackets showed Grenfell wearing fur mitts, with enormous snowshoes under his arm, the very picture of a northern explorer, although in wintertime he was usually in the United States. Grenfell had never wintered in Labrador. The last winter he spent in St. Anthony, Newfoundland, was 1918-1919 but he went there every summer for 15 years longer.

The Mundy family's involvement with the Mission solidified after Barbara's sister Harriet's summer as a wop. In 1928, she worked with the Industrial Department at Indian Harbour, a fishing station on the Labrador coast at the entrance to Hamilton Inlet.[24] Harriet returned from her summer service even more enthused about the work of the Mission and its dedicated leader. Her copy of Grenfell's inspirational book, *What Christ Means to Me*, was inscribed by him, with a pencil sketch of *Strathcona* on the inside cover, depicting a tiny vessel trailing a plume of smoke, tilting on a huge wave and dwarfed by a menacing iceberg nearby. In her copy of *Yourself and Your Body*, a health book with illustrations by Grenfell, he drew another of his favourite sketch motifs, a lone husky dog, howling at the moon.

That summer Harriet worked with staff members Annie Baikie, a competent young Labrador woman who had been "away" for training,[25] and an intrepid Australian nurse, Kate Austen, who later married American wop Elliott Merrick. With a degree in English from Yale, Merrick taught school in North West River from 1929 until 1931. He was a writer as well as a teacher, and his first book, *True North*, published in 1933, inspired many young people to volunteer with the Mission. His account of the winter he and Kate spent with trapper John Michelin made the frozen Labrador wilderness seem like a perfectly fine, if physically trying, place to be. His book *Northern Nurse* was a bestseller when it came out in 1942. Based on Kate's experiences, it gave insight into the work of a Mission nurse, the people, and life in North

West River. Barbara and Harriet saw the Merricks frequently at Mission functions and knew them well enough to call him "Bud" and her "Austy."

In the spring of 1931, Harriet assisted at a special four-week-long sale of handicrafts at a storefront on Madison Avenue. Over $3,000 was raised, including $375 from the sale of two polar bear skins.[26] At the preview, by invitation only, motion pictures of the Far North were shown, and also photos taken by another former wop and Mission Board member, Varick Frissell, famous for his film "The Viking."[27] Frissell tragically lost his life only days before the sale, in a ship explosion off the coast of Newfoundland. The Mundy girls may have known Frissell—his mother was on committees with them. He was a Yale graduate who went to Labrador with the Mission in 1922, returning to explore and make films on Grand River. Grenfell considered Frissell a shining example of a wop who believed in the work of the Mission, inspiring a fundraising effort at Yale to build a new school in North West River.[28]

With their committee work and attendance at fundraising social events, Harriet and Barbara had many opportunities to meet another famous Mission supporter, one with authentic Arctic credentials. Newfoundland Captain Robert (Bob) Bartlett, the skipper of the *Roosevelt*, Admiral Robert Peary's polar exploration vessel, was a member of the Mission's governing board. In 1932, he gave a talk to opera committee members, telling them of his intention to go back to the Arctic to erect a monument to Peary.[29] The committee was organizing a benefit performance of *La Bohème* for December 8 and preparing for the opening of a new Grenfell Labrador Industries shop on Fourth Avenue.[30]

In 1933, Harriet helped organize the Mission booth at the New York Flower Show "for the purpose of interesting visitors in the subject of gardens in Labrador." The volunteers were drilled on Grenfell's message that nutrition in the "barren northland" would be much improved by vegetable gardens.[31] Having spent a summer in rocky Indian Harbour, Harriet could certainly vouch for that.

Hardly a notice about Mission committee activities went in the newspaper without a mention of the Misses Mundy. The family name also shows up frequently in the "Alumni News" column of *Among the Deep-Sea Fishers*. The Mundys met Sir Wilfred and Lady Grenfell numerous times, at the annual Alumni Dinners or sales of work, and had often heard him lecture, repeating his refrain about the bitter poverty "on the Labrador."

It was likely when they lived in Montclair, New Jersey, that the Mundy family was first introduced to the Needlework Guild of America, a women's organization that partnered with the Mission. The name perhaps conjured up knitting or embroidery circles, but these women sewed and distributed new clothing to the needy. The Guild had originated in England in 1882, founded by Lady Giana Wolverton, who prevailed upon her society friends to clothe orphaned children. She believed "the wealthy and titled were often bored, discontented, frustrated"—women with time and money to spare. She called upon her friends to sew and donate two identical new articles of clothing for a child, "one to wear and one to wash," plain garments of calico or flannel with neat seams and small stitches.[32]

The Guild idea crossed the ocean in 1885. In 1890, the New York City branch was established and, within a year, 40 sections contributed 4,500 articles of clothing to the poor.[33] The many hundreds of volunteer women were the wives, mothers, and daughters of the social and business elite of the country and knew exactly how to set up an organization properly. By 1900, there were 311 branches, further subdivided into sections. When San Francisco was destroyed by an earthquake in 1906, the Guild sent clothing and money. Household linens and clothing were sent to France during the First World War. In New York, they sent clothing to the babies' ward at Bellevue Hospital, the Home for Discharged Convicts, the Home for Destitute Blind, and, eventually, the Grenfell Association of America.[34] By the 1940s, the Guild had 564 branches and claimed to be one of the largest women's organizations in the United States.[35]

The Guild's relationship with the Mission began after a Guild member read an article in *Outlook* magazine in 1908. Anna Tatnall recalled being so greatly impressed by what she read of the Mission that she "started at once to knit mufflers."[36] Tatnall was directed to Emma White of the New York IGA office, who easily recruited her with stories of unfortunate fisherfolk "stranded on that bleak coast with almost nothing in the way of either food or clothing." Research done, Tatnall presented her case to the National Board of the Guild and, in 1908, the Board created "the extra-special New England-Labrador branch, for the purpose of assisting the Grenfell Mission in Labrador."[37] A second branch, "Labrador Coast-to-Coast," was organized in 1929, and, in 1944, the two branches would be folded into one Labrador branch. Starting in July 1933, a Guild column about the activities of the organization's Labrador branches was featured regularly in *Among the Deep-Sea Fishers*.

Barbara's sister, Harriet, as treasurer of the Labrador Coast-to-Coast branch in New York, was probably among the crowd who filled the Madison Avenue Presbyterian Church on a day in late April 1931. Several hundred Guild members heard Grenfell's speech about the Labrador people, who were facing one of the "bitterest seasons in their history." He was soon to leave for another summer sailing the coast in his hospital ship and urged the women to continue contributing clothing to the Mission as "many natives are almost naked and any kind of wearing apparel will be most welcome."[38] Barbara became fully involved with the Guild and the Mission after her college graduation and return to New York. She quickly progressed to chair the Guild's Junior Committee. In 1934, she received a handwritten letter from Grenfell after she had submitted her report of activities that year. She shared the somewhat rambling contents with the other members. Grenfell was nearly 70 by then, and the letter was reminiscent of his speeches: "I do hope that all your workers are rejoicing as they think of the hungry fed—the naked clothed—(which frees money for food)—by THEM. Better days are ahead for the fishermen & their families. We have a 'Commission' government honest & capable, like Pres. F. Roosevelt, giving back hope to our long robbed and discouraged seamen."[39] He had gotten himself into hot water several times for criticizing the Newfoundland government and merchants for their neglect of the northern fishing settlements and had high hopes for the Commission of Government, appointed by Britain to resolve Newfoundland's debt issues. Grenfell always thought the simple solution to Newfoundland's financial problems was confederation with Canada, not a popular idea in St. John's.

In April 1935, Barbara helped plan a spring event with Sir Wilfred as their guest. He gave an illustrated lecture at Grand Central Art Galleries, with a display and sale of craft items "made by the fishermen" from Labrador.[40] A few days later, Grenfell spoke at a special lunch at Sherry's restaurant held by the Labrador Coast-to-Coast branch of the Guild and attended by more than 300 women. Perhaps it was after hearing Grenfell and speaking with him that Barbara decided to volunteer to go north. She would travel to the places she had heard and read so much about and see for herself if the work done by American volunteers was needed and appreciated.

Chapter Four

ST. ANTHONY WOPESS 1935

Whatever led you to come North, so far as we are concerned, it is the simple fact that you came and helped in the way you could that makes us want to thank you. If it gave you pleasure, as I sincerely hope it did, I am doubly thankful, for that is one more nail in the coffin of the pessimist, whose fault is that he is not gay enough himself to realize that the only lasting fun in life comes from what we contribute to it.

—Letter to Barbara Mundy from
Sir Wilfred Grenfell, October 24, 1935

D ivorce was not uncommon in New York society, but it was a jolt for the family when, after 33 years of marriage, Floyd Mundy left his wife and married his secretary. Barbara's mother was Mrs. Floyd W. Mundy in every public setting—including her listing in the *Social Register*, which some people used instead of the telephone book—now she was Mrs. Blanchard Mundy. Barbara knew how much it hurt her mother and how strange it was to see what had been *her* name in the newspaper society notes whenever her ex-husband and his new wife gave a supper dance at the Mount Washington hotel, which they often did.

In November 1933, the autumn after Barbara graduated from college, Mrs. Mundy asked her daughters to go with her to Reno, Nevada, while she established the necessary six weeks residency period for a divorce. They thought they had managed it with some discretion but just days after the court order was issued details were published in the *New*

York Times. January 5, 1934 was a difficult day for Barbara's mother. The story was short but had an appalling headline—"Award to Mrs. Mundy" and underneath, "Broker's Wife Gets Allowance in Nevada Divorce Action"—as if she were a fortune-seeking flapper who had married above her station, not a devoted wife and mother of long standing. Now everyone knew the marriage was over and that she received $2,250 a month "temporary allowance."[1] In Mrs. Mundy's world a good address, the right clubs, and a wealthy husband were credentials and proof of her standing. To suddenly lose her place and find herself on a train to Reno was a swift and bitter comedown, although Mrs. Mundy was among many New York socialites who opted to travel to Nevada because of its lenient divorce laws.[2] Barbara was 23 when the divorce happened, hardly a child, and suddenly her secure place in the world had been disturbed. It was difficult to imagine her father secretly courting a woman; he was a gruff and sometimes stern man, not just in business but also with his children. Not a single photo in the family album showed him smiling. In all the pictures taken at celebrations and holiday gatherings, he looked serious, with his brow tensed and mouth turned down, even at the wheel of a sailboat on a sunny day.

The sisters couldn't help but wonder how long the affair had been going on before their father moved from Thousand Nine to the University Club on 54th Street. He had never tried to explain himself to his daughters, and Barbara and Harriet sided with their mother. Their home was with her on Park Avenue. It was different for Floyd Jr., who had followed his father's path to Cornell University and then directly to the firm. Could their brother have known of the affair with the secretary? How awkward too for Uncle Jay; Barbara's uncle, John J. Bryant Jr., worked for the same firm as her father, although in the Chicago office. Uncle Jay would be loyal to his sister but yet he'd have to maintain a professional relationship with his ex-brother-in-law. Perhaps Uncle Jay had offered advice while his sister was taking her divorce action. He'd have had a good idea of what Floyd Sr. was worth and what he earned at Oliphant & Co. Maybe he had encouraged her to take a long cruise the next summer, when she and Harriet sailed on Canadian Pacific's *Duchess of Bedford* to England, Scotland, Ireland, and Wales. Barbara could have gone with them, but she had other plans. Her application to the Grenfell Mission had been accepted and she was assigned to St. Anthony. As her sister had done, she would be a wop and work without pay.

It was an excellent decision for Barbara to go away that summer, not only because of her parents' divorce but also because of the thoroughly enjoyable time she had in her job with the Mission and the other wops. The American volunteers got to know each other during their long journey to St. Anthony, a cruise well documented in Barbara's diary. They sailed on June 26 from Boston. A photo of the departing group of 11 young men and women, on the vessel *Newfoundland* of the Furness Line, appeared in the Boston *Herald* the next day, the smiling women all wearing hats, and three sporting large corsages.[3] Among the wops were two who would become her good friends: Josephine (Jo) Colgate, from Llewellyn Park, New Jersey, and Elisabeth (Bette) Hamilton, from Milton, Massachusetts. Bette and Jo were experienced Mission volunteers, going for a third summer as clothing store assistants.

Upon arrival in St. John's, Newfoundland, on July 1, the group booked into the Newfoundland Hotel and spent three days sightseeing. They saw the new movie *The Wedding Night*, starring Gary Cooper, drank ice cream sodas, toured Marine Drive, and picnicked on Signal Hill. They were considering going north on the coastal steamer *Kyle* but decided on the *Prospero*, a government mail and freight ship, with Captain Thomas Hounsell from Newtown, Bonavista Bay. The vessel departed St. John's on July 4 at 10 a.m., making the historic port of Trinity that afternoon and Catalina by night. They stopped at Fogo the next day, and later Twillingate, where Barbara went ashore and mailed some letters. *Prospero* visited Exploits and Pilley's Island, "where [they] anchored for night—too dark to enter as it's rocky and very narrow." The ship passed "Horse Islands where Varick Frissell was lost and into LaScie, many empty cans left here to be filled with cod liver oil." A wonderful tea was served, including cod tongues, salmon, and fried capelin. Encounters with "greenish-bluish-white" icebergs were worthy of several entries in her brief log of the trip and her letters to family.[4]

The icebergs were perfectly glorious—a great many and very large; we counted 41 at one time, and it was not a clear day ... As we were waiting we could see an iceberg move rapidly on the horizon—I didn't know they could go so fast. (Letter: July 10, 1935)

It was exciting to travel through the icefields, just as Admiral Byrd and Captain Bartlett had described in their books. They hadn't exaggerated. Some icebergs were as high as skyscrapers and could be heard creaking and cracking apart. The trip north required careful vigilance by the crew, and the American girls were delighted to assist.

We helped the 2 lookouts, 2nd mate & Capt. look for bergs. Much excitement when Capt. suddenly said "hard a port," we skimmed by a nice piece of ice. Down for a "mug-up" after our watch. Up again to find a clear night, and crescent moon shining on the waters. (Diary: July 5, 1935)

On they went to Coachman's Cove, Fleur de Lys, Sop's Arm—where some surveyors left the ship—then Jackson's Arm, Hooping Harbour, Englee, Grey Island, and Conche. They saw "beautiful bergs—16 large ones in front, not counting those elsewhere or the many small ones." Barbara started writing letters as soon as she boarded the ship in Boston and asked her mother to save them, "as a sort of diary." On July 10, on Mission letterhead, she partly handwrote and partly typed a letter to her mother and Harriet, which eventually reached them at Roche's Hotel in Glengariff, Ireland, describing the cruise north.

For the first three days we had a charming woman at our table—she had a little grace of her own which was a delightful beginning to each meal—it was "were you sea-sick?" After she left we had a walrus looking tea agent who asked us at the first meal we had with him if we knew what he had in a tiny bottle which looked like an ex-perfume bottle. We both scrutinized it carefully but had no ideas on the subject, pebbles were the best we could do. He then informed us that they were "my 157 gallstones removed about ten weeks ago"!! Fortunately for us the meal was over or we would have had hysterics right in front of him. (Letter: July 10, 1935)

It was a full coastal Newfoundland tour, as the *Prospero* made scheduled stops at every possible port, even those with no wharf to tie up to. The young women swarmed the ship and charmed the skipper, taking full advantage of his good nature.

Jo and I managed to go ashore in every mail boat so we saw the towns if they could be called such. Until our last day the harbors were very deep,

winding and quite wooded shores, then it became more barren, quite like Nantucket, I thot. I can see how people love it so that they stay the winter. Our new Capt.—Hounsell—was terribly nice. Of course, we had the run of the ship, and were on the bridge most of the time. When it cleared we had our steamer chairs on top of the pilot house! We wanted our pictures taken there and we asked the Capt. if he thot someone would take them for us. He said, "I think I could manage it myself." So he did. It was a scream. He had apparently never held a camera before. First he pointed the lens at himself and then at the sky. Finally we straightened him out or hope we did and he suggested he go down on the foc'sle head to take it. We had wanted him to but thot it might be beneath his dignity, so were greatly relieved. He went and a lot of sailors were busy at the time getting things out of the hold. The poor man had a bad time locating us and when he did the boom was in the way so he ordered the bos'n to move it. I think they all thot he was nuts. We hope the picture comes out after all the trouble it caused.
(Letter: July 10, 1935)

Late on July 8, they reached St. Anthony, the headquarters for the Mission. Unlike the fishing communities the new wops had viewed on their trip north, St. Anthony was a town with many impressive structures. It had a concrete block hospital, built by local labour, which had opened in January 1927, with beds for 75 patients though it often held many more. Grenfell described it as a "modern steel-framed building, fitted with electric light, central heating, modern plumbing etc."[5] The Children's Home (orphanage) was a plain, three-story brick structure with many windows. A greenhouse was attached to the old wooden hospital, and here seeds were germinated for vegetable plants to sell to anyone who had gardens all along the coast. At the cove, the Mission's slipway and dry dock facilities kept the *Strathcona* well maintained and there fishermen could repair their boats. *Strathcona* spent most of the summer on the water, with staff not only dispensing medical services but also collecting handicraft goods, distributing clothing, settling legal matters (Grenfell was a Justice of the Peace), and sometimes giving people passage to the next community.[6] The Industrial Shop contained looms for weaving and tools for carving. Other buildings housed carpentry and machine shops, an electrical plant, a tannery, and a tinsmith's shop.[7] For Mission supporters from London, New York, or Boston, who had gathered clothing or raised funds, seeing the activity at St. Anthony was assurance that their volunteer work made a worthwhile contribution.

As soon as the wops landed, they settled into accommodations, some at Blackburn Cottage, some at the Inn, and some at the orphanage, paying $1 per day for room and board, "which it is claimed more than covers the cost."[8] Sir Wilfred was once asked by a young volunteer why they had to pay for board and lodging while they worked without pay, and Grenfell told him, "patients and orphans would not be warm this winter otherwise—there is no money to supply all their needs." The young man replied, "Enough said," and continued with his work.[9] The eager volunteers of summer 1935 would not have a chance to chat with their hero. Staff and wops were informed that "the Grenfells are definitely not coming back this year. Sir W. has to stay in bed a good part of the time."[10] Grenfell had been suffering from angina attacks and loss of memory. His wife, Anne, who was having her own health problems, was afraid his memory failures would be exaggerated and "the next thing [they] shall hear is that he is losing his mind." She wanted it kept private and asked family members not to tell anyone.[11]

Gertie Peabody was Barbara's roommate at the Inn and she "apparently knows 'everybody.' She went around with Laurance Rockefeller a lot at one time—etc. etc." At first, Barbara was not pleased with the meals of fish, potatoes, turnips, "ad infinitum," but that was her only complaint about the food.[12] Near the end of her time in St. Anthony, after weeks of hearty eating and hiking, she got on the scale and was surprised to report: "Horrible intermission here while I weighed, and found I had gained about 15 lbs.—disgusting thot!" Her reaction was to grab a doughnut and go for another hike.[13]

The food was plain but abundant. Australian nurse Dora Elizabeth Burchill, who spent the summer in Indian Harbour three years later, also mentioned the "twenty ways of serving fish on the Coast." If Mission staff were bored with fresh fish, they were certainly impressed by the baking. Nurse Burchill praised Agnes, the Labrador woman who did the cooking and housekeeping, for she "made loaf bread every week" and also "dried apple or apricot pie, rice pudding with prunes" and spotted dog (also called spotted dick), "a steamed pudding spotted generously with raisins; it is lovely served with molasses boiled to a golden brown frothy sauce."[14]

On July 26, Barbara ventured out for the first time to visit eight Scottish wops at their tent camp; seven of them were engineering students from the University of Glasgow. The young men had arrived at St. Anthony after a full month travelling.[15] Their task that summer was to build a road from St. Anthony to Hare Bay using crushed rock. Barbara remembered their joking about how they would all be 78 years old when the road was completed, at the rate they were going.[16] They were a convivial bunch, adding greatly to her enjoyment of St. Anthony. She grew especially fond of Peter Brown.

On Wednesday it poured & I got all dressed up in rubber boots etc. for a long walk in the rain after supper. Of course it stopped as soon as I had started! I met Barzan—a wonderful great Pyrenees [dog] of Kivi's [nurse Anna Kivimaki] and walked with him. We went up by the tea house along the ridge and found ourselves almost of top of the Scotch camp. I'd never been there, so I hollered and finding Tom (in bed), Evan, & Peter at home. I stayed about an hour. Tom was in the Black Hole & P. & E. & I had a jolly time in the hut. Was fed! Wonderful oat cakes and honey. (Letter: July 26, 1935)

In the summer of 1935, the roster of 80 volunteers assigned in Newfoundland and Labrador included doctors, nurses, medical students, professors, teachers, dentists, secretaries, boat crew, and workers for the offices, industrial shops, clothing stores, or outdoors.[17] (Another 43 were on permanent staff, including 7 doctors, 13 nurses, 9 teachers or principals, 5 orphanage superintendents and housemothers.) Some wops, away from home and parents for the first time, had a tremendous energetic spirit. Many were young, unmarried, and bound to take every opportunity for social gatherings. Barbara hoped they would anyway, and she was not disappointed. She was beginning to understand why Bette and Jo returned summer after summer.

Last Sunday we had a picnic of about twenty-five. The Cluett [Grenfell Mission coastal vessel] wops were in port and it was a grand crowd. They have gone north now for two weeks and our social life has gone down considerably. What with dances on the tour boat, and parties all around we were pretty well exhausted. Bed before midnight was unheard of—and that's something for the "missionaries" of St. Anthony. (Letter: July 27, 1935)

When Dora Burchill arrived at the wharf in St. Anthony in 1938, "an animated group of attractive people stood waving and shouting words of welcome." They were mostly wops, "young men in cream flannels" and "radiant girls in bright summer frocks."[18] During Burchill's time at the nursing station in Indian Harbour she "soon learned to love the fascinating island home that looked so bleak and desolate," perhaps partly because it was not all work for the volunteers and fishers. She described a dance held in the "old disused laundry" attended by "fifty or so men who danced among themselves" and the five women on the island. Music was provided by mouth organ and accordion and "how those men could play." Dancing had to stop by midnight Saturday, as you would not dance on Sunday, but dancers would stop only if they knew the time.[19]

Barbara wasn't terribly busy at the office. She told her brother, Floyd: "Sometimes we work very hard—before boats usually—and other times we have time on our hands which if we are in the office is boring—but in the shops amusing as the S.W.'s [Scottish wops] drop in and help us waste it!"[20] The time being wasted must have been noticed as just a few days later she wrote to her mother and Harriet that she had been given more responsibility, assisting an ophthalmologist from Cincinnati who had been to St. Anthony many times.

To start off with I have a new—or rather two jobs—now! I'm still doing my own, but in addition have become Dr. [Frank D.] Phinney's sec'y for the two weeks he is to be here. However, I think I'll be doing histories, etc. for the interns too. It's lots of fun to be in a hospital again, and it's strange to have everything on such a miniature scale! (Letter: July 31, 1935)

Dr. Charles Curtis was the medical supervisor in charge of operations on the coast; he had lived and worked there for 18 years, winter and summer, and was not as keen as Grenfell to have the Mission overrun with exuberant, fun-loving wops. He complained that doctors did not have the time to supervise them and wanted their numbers reduced.[21] Although Grenfell had retired from his leadership role with the Mission in 1936, retaining the honorary title of Superintendent, he infuriated Curtis by continuing to make decisions and extending invitations to anyone willing to go north. The founder of the Mission was becoming a "nuisance" and Curtis threatened the board that he might leave if changes were not made.[22] Barbara had one experience of his exasperation with volunteers.

Lisping Charles has now yelled at me! I was to work in the hospital, as you know, & the first morning I decided not to stay as there wasn't much to do—as I went to the Industrial building. I heard a Hey yelled and looked around—there was the Chief hanging outside the top of a 2nd story window! And he wanted to know if I wasn't going to work in the hosp. My, he's terribly funny. (Letter: August 3, 1935)

Barbara likely strayed away from the hospital office because her fellow wops with jobs in the clothing store always had something to do. When the Mission ship arrived, bales and boxes of clothing would be unloaded on the wharf and the strongest "American college boys" would carry them to the store to be unpacked. The store in St. Anthony was abuzz with women outfitting their families. Requisitions were filled from the clothing stores in the outlying mission stations and parcels were shipped along the coast on the Mission schooner.[23]

New clothing came from the Needlework Guild, but another essential element was the used clothing donated by IGA branches in the United States, Canada, and Britain. Mission supporters cleared their closets of unwanted garments and bundled them up to go north. Packing and shipping thousands of items occupied many more volunteers and, unfortunately, it wasn't all worth the effort. After several summers' duty in the St. Anthony clothing store, Bette Hamilton reported that they once unpacked a barrel to find it entirely full of "muslin blouses and old ladies' bonnets." They needed heavy, warm flannel shirts, woollen trousers, overalls, and sweaters for men who worked outdoors—perhaps not as abundant as pinstripe waistcoats in the wardrobe closets of their New York City patrons. The clothing store staff actively discouraged donations of thin rayon socks and sleeveless, legless summer underwear.[24]

In the fall and winter months, the St. Anthony clothing store was open on Tuesdays and Fridays and people walked long distances from communities in the surrounding area. Store director Dorothy Thomson counted 500 customers in September 1933. Lines formed by 7 a.m. and competition for certain things, like pants and shoes, was fierce. Clothing store staff found creative ways to use items that were unsuitable to wear. High heeled shoes with pointed toes, "which fit no women," were cut into usable bits. "Prize packs" might contain scraps for a quilt, or two felt hats, at least useful for stopping drafts around windows. An old woollen coat or jacket could be remade to fit a child.[25] Most Newfoundland women were able or expert needleworkers, an essential skill for survival in a remote and ill-supplied place. If donors wondered about the fate of their out-of-style pocketbooks, they might be amused to know the girls of the Children's Home "begged for them" as accessories when they played "tourist lady, in imitation of the beauteous creatures glimpsed during the periodic summer visits of the tourist steamers."[26] Unfortunately, there were no photos published in *Among the Deep-Sea Fishers* of orphan girls proudly flaunting their precious handbags on the wharf at St. Anthony.

Eventually, the IGA had to admit problems with the amount and quality of donated second-hand clothing that found its way to the coast. They needed bedding and warm children's clothing and instead "there is a considerable amount of second-hand clothing sent … that is not fit for distribution and has to be burned. This is a difficult matter to handle as one cannot offend people who are generous, but on the other hand, … clothing came from England and Canada so moth-eaten and ragged that it was useless."[27]

Grenfell often explained the method of dispensing the used and new clothing: "As the Government allows this charity in free of taxation, none may be, or ever is, sold for cash. It must be given out, for work preferably, freely if necessary."[28] He always proudly described "our clothing store, run on strictly scientific charity lines," a system which "maintains their independence, as work of some kind is always returned wherever possible."[29] It was a barter system without negotiation; prices were set by the IGA. One Labrador man's recollection was prefaced by the comment "I'll tell you a short story but I don't know if you will like it." Arthur Rich said Grenfell "would go around tellin' everybody out in other countries that the Labrador people was bad off, so they was, and they'd get a lot of clothing. But he never give us none of that clothes, you had to cut wood and they'd give you $4.00 for a hundred of wood."[30]

It was not Grenfell's fault, but the popular impression amongst American donors was that the new and used clothing was given freely to all who needed it. The confusion was understandable, because other American branches of the Guild distributed clothing to the needy as gifts, with no payment or labour required, but in Newfoundland and Labrador, clothing was a medium of exchange. Items would be purchased with credits for work done; for amounts of fish caught, firewood cut, or berries gathered; for handmade items, including hooked mats, wall hangings, footstool and chair covers, carved wooden bookends, sewn grass baskets, Eskimo dolls, scarves, napkin rings, embroidered card table covers, purses, knitting bags, and a multitude of other things. Men who dug ditches or repaired roads for the Mission in the summer of 1932 were paid with $1,200 worth of clothing, 20,000 pounds of beans, 18,000 pounds of ground wheat, 18,000 pounds of brown flour, and 1,000 pounds of white sugar.[31] It was how Grenfell encouraged self-sufficiency, even in people who were ill or handicapped with few options to work for pay. If you couldn't fish or cut wood, you could sew or carve.

The "Industrial" department of the Mission started with weaving, taught by American occupational therapist Jessie Luther, who was recruited by Grenfell in 1906. Those interested learned how at the Loom Room in St. Anthony. Newfoundland women had not always been weavers but they were accomplished and clever mat hookers. Their homes all had homemade floor mats, hooked during the cold winter months from rags and scraps, onto old flour or sugar bags tightly held in a simple wooden frame. Rug hooking evolved into a cottage industry, with patterns by Luther, artist and designer Rhoda Dawson, and Grenfell; materials (flannelette, silk, wool, and burlap ["brin"]) and patterns supplied by the Mission. These hooked mats in attractive folk-inspired patterns became a Mission trademark.[32]

Labrador or northern imagery dominated in the designs of the handicrafts produced for sale in Mission shops. Grenfell's drawings were used for many of the popular mats, depicting winter scenes with dog teams and polar bears. The wording on the labels affixed to the hooked mats was a matter of some discussion in the Industrial Department. Grenfell wanted labels to say *Made in Labrador*, although most of the mats were made in Newfoundland. Lady Grenfell agreed *Made in Labrador* had better publicity value so they decided the label should say *Grenfell Labrador Industries, Made in Newfoundland and Labrador*.[33] There were no untruths in it and Labrador was mentioned twice.

Over 3,000 mats were hooked in 1929, revenue from sales was $63,000, and mat hookers received $3 per mat on average, for about two weeks' work.[34] It could be said that by being paid so little for their labour, mat hookers were as generous to the Mission as anyone in the United States who donated money or clothing. That opinion was rarely expressed, although one anonymous songwriter, reportedly a man from Pinware River who lost his job at the Mission, found a way of airing a grievance:

> Come all ye poor women who work night and day
> Making mats for the Mission for three dollars pay,
> But to tell you the truth, the way it do seem,
> You'll get the milk skimmed and de relations de cream.
> The boxes and bales from St. Anthony come;
> The relations and friends take the best of it home.
> The manager says, "Take the best for yourselves,
> And what is left over I'll put on the shelves."[35]

There was nothing to be gained by complaining publicly about the Mission, especially if you wanted to shop at the Clothing Store or haul your boat up on the slipway. Without the Mission, there would have been no medical services in the area. The Newfoundland government was absent, other than visits by Newfoundland Rangers, who were responsible for giving out the meager "dole." The Mission had built hospitals, nursing stations, schools, and orphanages. The Industrial Department made it possible for women to earn a few dollars by hooking mats and doing needlework in the wintertime. Patients in the hospital recovering from tuberculosis were learning woodworking and weaving. Young people from the coast had been sent away to be educated and returned home as nurses, teachers, or tradesmen. No other part of Newfoundland or Labrador could claim such socially progressive work being done.

Later in the summer of 1935, the American, English, and Scottish wops in St. Anthony talked about how they would travel home. Barbara mused about heading across the ocean for some shopping, a far cry from scrounging in the bins of the Mission's clothing store.

One can get to Europe from here for less than $50—gee, I'm almost tempted to go in October and meet Ma in Paris for a couple of weeks to buy winter clothes! I know Ma wants to do that & if she had my charming company she might! The way over is the way the S.W.'s, Betty Ham, Marg [Marguerite Fuller], etc. came over. Oh dear, I've got my wandering bug again. (Letter: July 31, 1935)

On August 2, everyone attended a dance held by "the Newfoundland boys," which was "fun, but as usual very energetic." The dance rated just a few words in a letter home, but an outing with Peter Brown a week later was a short story in itself.

This last week has been too pleasant for words. In the first place, without the use of even an aspirin I've been most hale & hearty—a tiny bit tired this A.M. perhaps from double paddling last night. On Monday night, Peter took me out in his little blue, collapsible canvas canoe with sails. It was <u>more</u> fun. We sailed gaily out of the harbor, and the Bight and to Cape St. Anthony. There was a delicious swell, and we could actually feel the water underneath, & the boat would take the shape of the water. We wanted to land, but it was too difficult as the boat, being canvas, had to be lifted quite out of the water. The rocks were slippery, and not shelved and the swell was too great. P got out, and I was about to when a large wave came along, and as the tide was coming in, and there was quite a suck we decided it was too dangerous. So Peter started to get into the boat when another wave came and he fell in, up to his waist. I managed to hold on to the rock, and disentangled him & the paddle & all was well but for a moment I thot the boat was going over. We tried several other places, but gave it up and came home, paddling some of the way. The sunset had been *perfectly glorious with clouds, and then a half moon came up. P had his harmonica, and we sang & he played. It was simply grand—all but the puddle I was sitting in. The boat is only about 17 feet long & his long legs were on either side of me and his soaking trousers managed to ooze a large puddle! I finally took my shirt off and sat on it—my knitted one—ooh! We had a swell evening, decidedly the best since I've been here.* (Letter: August 9, 1935)

Peter was getting ready to go home to Scotland, and Barbara was sorry to see him go, but they had made enough of a connection to plan to see each other again.

This week has been grand and I shall miss Peter and our silly but grand times! He and Betty Fyfe have asked Peggy and me to stay with them next summer. Oh, next summer is going to be swell. (Letter: August 9, 1935)

With Peter and the other Scottish wops gone, the parties wound down. Barbara's letters were about sewing, reading the new book *Life with Father* aloud, or listening to music on the Victrola in front of the fire. She and the other Americans stayed well into the fall.

I walked out to the near point with Marguerite. I'd never been there. It's lovely—great rocks, and surf pounding. I wish I'd found it sooner to enjoy. We lay on the rocks and talked of the summer and how grand it had been. And would another summer—all very different—ruin this by comparison and associations. Everyone says this has been a unique summer in every way—good times, congenial crowd, etc. It's so different here that other things and people aren't missed—even those with whom we've had such happy times. But, when we get home, I wonder if we won't miss it all terribly then? Oh, I hope not. Somehow I want this summer to be kept intact and unspoiled by anything. (Letter: October 4, 1935)

By October 12, world events had intruded slightly into everyone's awareness. Radio broadcasts told about the Italian dictator, Benito Mussolini, invading Abyssinia. The Italian Air Force had bombed Adowa and tens of thousands of Italian infantry were occupying the country. Meanwhile in Germany, the chancellor and Reich president, Adolph Hitler, was openly rearming the country, in violation of the Versailles Treaty. Another war in Europe was looming as a very real possibility, so far away from peaceful Newfoundland.

We read a while after supper & then to the Curtis's for <u>war news</u>. I stayed a bit after the others left, then came home, changed my shoes and went up to Fishing Head. It was a beautifully clear moonlight night & I felt I just had to go up again. I wasn't too disappointed when no one seemed eager to join me. So I went up alone. It was glorious. Altho' it was clear there seemed to be a slight mistiness about everything. Looking toward Cremeliere [a fishing settlement 4 miles west of St. Anthony] was lovely. The darkness of the cliffs, a path of moonlight on the water and the distant land on the other side of the Bay. Everything was so silent and still. I lay up there on a soft bed of moss for about half an hour. I was glad to be there, and glad to be alone. I wish I could have been able to drink it all in. (Letter: October 12, 1935)

Days away from heading back to New York, Barbara began to dread departure: "I realize only too clearly that the time is nearing—almost here—when I get back to civilization. It's going to be awful to be so confined and so unfree again."[36] She revisited all her favourite places and packed her things, waiting for word from Captain Kenneth Iversen of the *Cluett*[37] about when they would leave. On Tuesday, October 15, she wrote her mother from Flower's Cove, en route to Charlottetown, Prince Edward Island, where they would clear Canadian Customs and Immigration, describing events of the day before.

I worked in the A.M. and just after lunch we heard we would probably go between 7 & 8 if the moon came up. It had clouded—the second beautiful morning to go that way. So I packed hurriedly & tore up to the tea house to finished my panorama picture and back to supper—Garth there—hoping we'd stay a while longer. But no, about 7:15 she blew and we went down—the orphans giving us a good send-off. And so we left St. Anthony in full moonlight but mackerel sky. And that was my last look—a very nice one. Stayed on deck until we left—F.H. [Fishing Head] behind and then to bed. Rhoda [Dawson] in bed and Jo & I bunked together. We rolled, it smelled, the other three passengers sang. <u>We</u> survived tho'. Woke up at Red Bay—saw Minnie Pike, and then crossed the Straits to here. It was bleak, <u>very</u> cold, and even hailed. We got here just before lunch and gosh it was good! Chicken! (Letter: October 15, 1935)

In the last letter saved from the summer of 1935, written to Barbara's sister, Harriet, from on board the *Cluett*, she sounds happy and hopeful that perhaps something more may come from her time spent with Peter Brown.

There's one thing about this summer—and particularly the last part of it. It can't make me unhappy because it was so perfect. Whatever happens in the future I can always remember it was a very perfect, <u>very</u> happy and complete episode. And if this proves to be just an episode—as it probably will—here's hoping that another comes along just as grand but that will not have to be just an episode but will continue on and on.

It's hard to believe I'm actually on my way home. I feel as if I were just off on a jaunt and would go back—very soon. I wonder if I will ever go back? Gosh, I hope so. (Letter: October 16, 1935)

She had earned her stripes as a Grenfell wop and hoped to return someday. As they sailed out of sight of Newfoundland, she began to miss it. Barbara had got the place in her blood.

Today has been too perfect for words. Gloriously clear and smoother. We've had all sails up all day. You've never seen such a perfect day—it's a shame that our trip is over. We had breakfast in bed—very luxurious—and spent the entire day aft on top of the wheelhouse. Read this morning and reminisced this afternoon. It's funny what trivialities have really meant so much! We've been in sight of Magdalen Is. & Cape Breton most of the day. At sunset or a bit before we sighted P.E.I. and <u>many</u> schooners—a beautiful sight. The land is red, cliffs, green trees, very fertile. It's pretty, but somehow the ruggedness and grandeur of Nfld. is really more appealing. This might be anyplace; the other is unique. There were about a dozen or more schooners—full sail—going out. And tonight is beautiful. Have just come in from sitting up in the bow. I'm going to miss the expanse of sea and sky. I just felt as if I should sit there forever and drink it all in. But it's so very beautiful it makes one sad. (Letter: October 16, 1935)

The summer had been a fulfilling and welcome respite, but soon she would be back at Thousand Nine, once again under the watchful eye of her mother. Mrs. Mundy took her role as chaperone seriously, as was revealed in a letter she wrote to Barbara's grandmother, Matilda Bryant, in Chicago, before Barbara got home from St. Anthony.

The children have been shocked & deeply hurt by their father's marriage but I will greatly appreciate your not speaking of that ever to members of the family. Please Mother respect my wishes in this. I would like to make you a visit and since I am entirely alone this would be the best time to do it as I cannot leave strange maids in the apartment nor can I come after B gets home—too many beaux to be chaperoned. To be sure I let them alone but want to be here just the same.[38]

The winter ahead would be so different from summer and fall in St. Anthony, where you could set out on foot in any direction for a beautiful coastal or forest walk. Spontaneous dances, picnics, and midnight rambles would be no more, social appointments would be arranged, proper clothing worn, her presence perhaps noted in the society pages. A "mug-up" wouldn't be a casual cup of tea shared with friends in the kitchen or around a campfire. The "Christmas Mug-Up" was a catered fundraiser at the Hotel Barbizon, with Barbara among the many volunteers helping out.[39] Far from hiking freely all over the countryside, or boating at every opportunity with available men like the delightful Peter Brown, she would be under scrutiny by her unhappy mother, who was unwilling to leave her alone in the apartment with "too many beaux."

Chapter Five

THOUSAND NINE, PARK AVENUE

Except on occasions of religious ceremonial, nowhere is greater dignity of manner required than in a box at the opera.

—Emily Post, *Etiquette*

Back at home on Park Avenue, Barbara resumed her life before St. Anthony, with a more prominent role in the Needlework Guild as secretary of the Coast-to-Coast Labrador branch.[1] Some of the much older long-serving members had died, or retired from their positions, and she was officially elected in the autumn of 1935 to the committee of which her sister had formerly been the treasurer. She would serve for nine years, receiving a token annual salary of $240. It was a job she took seriously; her yearly reports were professionally printed pamphlets of more than 20 pages, keeping track of the clothing and cash donations.

The main branch was responsible for collecting, packing, and shipping everything donated from each of 40 Guild sections in 12 different states—hundreds of bundles of clothing and household linens annually. In her official capacity, Barbara exchanged regular letters and reports with Grenfell. He knew she would share the contents with members and wanted to assure them of the need to continue to help those who dwelt in "lonely little cottages" facing "our sub-arctic winters miserably clad." It was getting harder to motivate donors when there was so much poverty all around them at home, so his anecdotes were deliberately heart-wrenching.

One of the earliest patients I attended had her night clothes frozen to the wall when I went to her house, and another, whom I was sending home from our first little hospital, said "But I can't go, Doctor, I haven't any clothes." "You came in clothes," I said. "Yes, but the lady who lent them to me sent for them again after." More than once I have been unable to print group photographs I had taken owing to the lack of clothes on some of the people. (Letter: January 3, 1936)

Grenfell found more for Barbara to do. In the summer, he made "a blunt but fervent request" to her to serve on the executive committee working on the Mission's annual opera benefit.[2] He was diligent about thanking his core group of volunteers and reminding them of the large scope of the work to be done. He wrote next in the fall, again stressing the importance of the work to provide clothing.

Some needy folk require medical care, some little children must be sheltered in our orphanages, others must be given the chance our schools afford, others need a cabbage, others need industrial work; but in order to take advantage of these opportunities, they one and all have to be warmed and clothed. (Letter: October 26, 1936)

That winter Barbara spent some time in Arizona and was looking forward to her summer trip to Scotland for the reunion of St. Anthony wops. Jo Colgate and Bette Hamilton joined her and the others in Edinburgh in August. (Her hope that something might come from the connection with Peter Brown evidently was dashed.) The St. Anthony 1935 women were also among more than 100 Grenfell alumni who attended the annual dinner in October 1936 at the Shelton Hotel in New York.

International politics may have altered plans for further transatlantic cruises but otherwise did not disrupt Barbara's life, which continued in a set pattern of committee work, holidays, and activities with friends. The world was still in economic depression and troubling events in Europe made the headlines nearly every day in the late 1930s. Adolph Hitler had rebuilt the military, invaded Austria, and annexed the Sudetenland portion of Czechoslovakia. In an effort to maintain the tenuous peace, British prime minister Neville Chamberlain signed the Munich Agreement in October 1938 with Germany, France, and Italy, acquiescing to the German annexation of the Sudetenland. Barbara's friends in England and Scotland were anxious about the possibility of another war.

The "Alumni News" column in *Among the Deep-Sea Fishers* served as a notice board for all Mission staff and volunteers, who submitted items to keep their friends up to date about marriages, births, deaths, appointments, illnesses, and vacations taken. Barbara attended another Alumni Dinner in October 1937. Her old boss, Dr. Charles Curtis from St. Anthony, was guest speaker that year. She and Jo Colgate had been to an Audubon Nature Camp in Maine in the summer of 1938 and skied in the Laurentian Mountains in 1939. Barbara was an active committee member with the Social Service Auxiliary for Stony Wold Sanatorium, a tuberculosis hospice for needy women, and helped organize fashion shows and luncheons.[3] She did her duty at the Mission booth at the annual Flower Show and sold tickets to the opera benefit performance of Wagner's *Tannhäuser* planned for January 18, 1939.[4]

While Barbara's volunteer work was done at home in New York, her friends Jo and Bette went to St. Anthony again in 1939, making a side trip to North West River. Jo had a movie camera with her and "showed the excellent colored movies which she took during the past summer" at a Guild meeting in Boston.[5] Barbara spent the summer of 1939 in Camden, Maine, with her mother and Harriet. That was the year Grenfell made his last trip to St. Anthony, but it was as a visitor, not a working doctor. His wife, Anne, had died in 1938, and he brought her ashes to be buried on the hill behind the hospital.[6]

In Europe, the German army invaded Poland in September 1939. Britain declared war, bringing the Dominion of Newfoundland along with it. A week later, Canada also declared war. The United States had a controversial policy of neutrality that would keep them from siding with their traditional allies and out of the war for two more years. Anna Kivimaki, a nurse who had worked at St. Anthony, was editor of *Among the Deep-Sea Fishers* and wanted subscribers to know that their correspondence to Newfoundland would be opened and read: "Letters from Newfoundland come through with large labels on them OPENED BY CENSOR. All mail and telegrams are now routed by way of St. John's for censorship." She said the mail boat was running with blackened portholes and the Mission's amateur radio station in St. Anthony had to stop sending messages.[7] "Alumni News" began to include information about military enlistments and postings, some for the Scottish wops of 1935. Peter Brown had obtained a commission in the Indian Army Ordnance Corps in 1940.[8]

In January, Barbara received a typed letter from Grenfell, sent from The Miami-Battle Creek Sanitarium, where he was resting, with many handwritten corrections and instructions to Barbara to "lick it into shape," possibly for inclusion in her annual Guild report. As was his habit, Grenfell related an illustrative story about what happened to him once when he went through the ice while travelling over a frozen bay to see a patient.

I had reason to hasten to the nearest house on the land, in order to borrow some dry clothing. The cheery fisherman who owned the house at once said as he disappeared into his bedroom "of course he could lend me a dry pair of trousers." When he came out he still insisted on giving them to me, though he was wrapped up in a sheet because it was the only pair he owned. (Letter: January 15, 1940)

He thanked the Guild for its "magnificent total of garments, a new record, sent to us in the past year," even more appreciated since war restrictions had come into effect. To call the total "magnificent" was not the usual "Grenfellian" exaggeration. In her exhaustive report of 1940, Barbara listed over 27,000 items for "the special needs of the hospitals, orphanages, and people of Sir Wilfred Grenfell's Mission." Her accounting started at afghans and aprons and finished with waistcoats, washcloths, and wristlets—an astounding 4,138 pairs of socks, stockings, and bootees; 816 pairs of gloves and mittens; 470 pairs of bloomers; 212 pairs of trousers; 1,816 sweaters; 19 corsets and girdles; and 83 neckties. The shipment also contained diapers, belts, pillowcases, handkerchiefs, shoes, and hats. She congratulated the sections on doing a good job that year of getting their donations in promptly for the first shipment to go north by the *Cluett* in May. Since war had been declared, the Mission vessel was the only way to ship to Newfoundland, and if they missed its departure, there would be no clothing for the coast.[9]

It would take more than war in Europe to disrupt the activities of New York high society's female volunteer force. In February 1940, Barbara attended a meeting at the Fifth Avenue mansion home of Mrs. Andrew Carnegie, honourary chair of the Grenfell Association's opera benefit committee. Mrs. Lewis Fox Frissell (mother of the late Varick Frissell) was "executive chairman in charge of all arrangements," and Barbara was a member of the large Junior committee, along with Grenfell's daughter, Rosamond. The Metropolitan Opera performance of *Parsifal* was booked for March 20 and much work had to be done to ensure full attendance.[10]

The Mission's faithful followers had known for several years that Grenfell's health was poor, although he seemed in good form at his 75th birthday celebration in February, and in March he attended the Needlework Guild's annual meeting in New Orleans. In May, he was at the head table for the annual alumni dinner at the Murray Hill Hotel. Barbara was among the 137 guests. Tony Paddon from North West River, who was studying medicine on Long Island, was Master of Ceremonies. All speakers paid tribute to Tony's father, Dr. Harry Paddon, who had served the Mission in Labrador since 1912, and died suddenly on Christmas Eve 1939, leaving the hospital in North West River without a doctor. Grenfell deeply felt the loss of his friend and colleague, and wrote a heartfelt tribute to Paddon, saying he was "everywhere beloved and respected."[11]

Grenfell told Barbara in his January letter that he hoped he would be able to visit the coast that summer, but when the time came, he wasn't well enough to travel. In June, she received her last letter from him, again thanking Guild members for their efforts, "an increase of nearly 2000 garments is really preaching the gospel."[12] Few of the inner circle were surprised when he died in Vermont on October 9, 1940. He had been in steady decline since his wife's passing in December 1938.

"Wilfred Grenfell of Labrador Dead" was the front-page headline the next day.[13] In Barbara's opinion, Grenfell had been a truly admirable person, ranked with men like Dr. Albert Schweitzer.[14] Grenfell had saved hundreds of lives and put his own life in danger many times to do his work. His Mission had built hospitals, clinics, schools, and industrial shops. His example had inspired many to donate and volunteer. That year, Barbara's annual report lamented the loss; she was worried about how Grenfell's death would affect involvement in the Guild and the Mission. He would be missed greatly, and they would probably never again have such a charismatic and devoted leader.

Barbara encouraged members to contact anyone who had signed the guest book at the Grenfell-Mission-themed café, *Dog-Team Tavern*, in Vermont, in the hope of creating "some spark of interest that can be kept alive through giving to our work." She was determined that the work of the Mission, at least the part she was responsible for, would go on, urging members to donate an even greater number of garments in 1941.[15] Barbara kept up her effort to maintain Guild membership and morale, though it was becoming apparent that interest in the organization was waning. Many members didn't know how to sew, or didn't want to sew, and would rather donate the cash value of two garments or buy something to bring to a meeting. Those attending the annual general meetings in Philadelphia were told that branches had "evaporated into space" and the national executive was worried about the "wasting condition" of the Needlework Guild of America.[16]

Cecil Ashdown, the IGA's executive director, had taken on the task of correspondence between the Mission and the Guild after Grenfell's death. In 1942, from his winter home in Bermuda, he wrote Barbara, who was spending a few weeks at the Soreno Hotel in St. Petersburg, Florida, to thank her for the annual report: "only those of us who have been to the Coast know what value this work is to people who live in these chilly regions."[17] Chilly regions, including New York in winter, were mainly avoided by Ashdown, but at least he had visited the coast in summer, and he had the best of intentions. It would be hard to measure up to Grenfell when it came to motivating volunteers.

Mission executives noted that fundraising was becoming more difficult, membership numbers were dropping, and the commitment of staff and wops had diminished in the years since their aging and ailing leader had been unable to make public appearances.[18] The Yale School in North West River, once blessed with more volunteers than needed, had a serious shortage of staff since the outbreak of war.[19] The Mission was forced to look to Americans "almost entirely" to fill vacancies. The American Neutrality Act restricted Americans from working as crew on "belligerent" vessels, which included the Mission ships registered in Newfoundland, but American wops were allowed to work onshore.[20]

The volunteer shortage only worsened when American neutrality ended late in 1941. On December 8, the United States declared war on Japan after the surprise attack on American naval vessels in Pearl Harbor, Hawaii, the day before. On December 11, Japan's allies, Germany and Italy, declared war on the United States, and President Franklin Roosevelt responded with a declaration of war against them. More than 10 years of economic stagnation were suddenly over as the country mobilized to fight on two fronts. Thousands joined the military and thousands more flocked to factories. Anyone who wanted a job could have one and everyone who could work, male or female, was encouraged to do so. Those who might have volunteered for the Mission were now occupied at home or overseas.

Barbara was doing her bit to help the war effort by working at New York Memorial Hospital as a nurse's aide. She kept up her duties as a member of the Mission's opera benefit committee. In November, after nine years as Labrador branch secretary for the Guild, she was elected vice-president.[21] She still lived with her mother on Park Avenue, the full-floor apartment large enough to afford each of them privacy; Barbara's separate phone number was listed in their entry in the Social Register. She was useful and contributed in her public life, but events in her private life are vague for those years. No clues about a special man are given in the papers she saved, but there was a man, and they were getting serious about each other. Many in her group were marrying; she and Bette Hamilton had attended Jo Colgate's wedding in West Orange, New Jersey, in October 1943. That autumn, Barbara had every reason to believe she would be the next to send invitations to a wedding. Her engagement was announced in the newspaper in early January 1944:

Mrs. Blanchard Mundy of New York has announced the engagement of her daughter, Barbara B., to Leland H. Burt of Wilmington, Del., son of the late Mr. and Mrs. Chauncey H.

Burt. Miss Mundy, daughter also of Floyd W. Mundy of this city, was graduated from Miss Madeira's School in Washington and from Connecticut College for Women. Her fiancé was graduated from Phillips Exeter Academy and from the Sheffield School of Yale University. His previous marriage ended in divorce in 1940.[22]

At 33 years old, Barbara wanted nothing more than a home of her own. She prepared for marriage by studying housekeeping as she had literature and poetry, by reading, listening carefully, and keeping good notes. She learned to use the Décor-Graph, a modern approach to home interior design, with a kit of graph paper and cardboard furniture. It was fun to imagine what her first home would be like.

Kitchen should be light, airy, bright & colorful. White is nice but hard to keep clean. Waxing linoleum protects it and battleship linoleum is best. Be sure to choose standard *equipment and make sure the refrigerator is insulated.*[23]

Barbara had grown up with servants doing all the housework, usually when she wasn't around to see them do it. She had never washed dishes, cleaned floors, or done laundry. That winter, she took classes in cooking, baking, and cleaning. She filled a spiral notebook with recipes and useful tips, dating from January 4, the day her engagement announcement went in the newspaper, to January 25. Her home economics instructor discussed the qualities of various butter substitutes—Nucoa, Dixie, or Parkay—and what to do with dried beef. The instructor showed them creative ways to make an appetizing meal with wartime rations. On January 7, they made bread. (Little did she know how important that lesson would be.) She had grown up eating meals prepared by a cook, and now was making careful notes on how to stretch a food budget, although, admittedly, it would be a budget for a household where menus were planned and groceries delivered to the door: "Menus should be made out for a week at a time. Get what you need and no more! Buy foods in season and check on the food when delivered. If you are entitled to bone—take it!"

The spiral notebook of recipes and housekeeping tips was saved, but nothing was left to explain why the engagement failed. By March 24, Cecil Ashdown had written her a letter of recommendation for the Labrador job and she was committed to spending six months in North West River. Family members naturally speculated on the broken engagement. Her brother Floyd's son Pete, who was 13 at the time, always believed his grandmother was responsible and somehow broke it up.[24] Another cousin spoke about Mrs. Mundy hiring a private detective, who convinced her Leland Burt was after Barbara's money, but that was gossip repeated years later.

The observant reader of the newspaper engagement notice would find two allusions to divorce in one brief paragraph. Why had her mother felt it necessary to include the information about Leland's previous marriage? Using the phrase "daughter also of" brought attention to her parents' acrimonious divorce. Barbara and Leland had not set an approximate date for the wedding and that was another ominous sign. The details remain unknown, but the result was clear: in the end, Barbara did not marry Leland Burt.

Barbara was determined that leaving the city was the right decision and she was tired of conversations with her mother and sister and brother, who all seemed to think they knew better than she did. In her 30s, no longer engaged, a tad too handy to spinster territory for comfort, she was tired of being listed in *Society Notes* purgatory between the "debutantes of recent seasons" and the "young matrons" of the day. What a relief it would be to put New York far behind. The trappers of North West River weren't scanning the newspaper, gleaning tidbits such as who attended a dinner dance unescorted or whose former fiancé was seen out and about, and that was perfectly fine with her.

Chapter Six

DOWN ON THE LABRADOR

Then of course, they had to take wives of the natives of this country. There were very few white men here, much less women ...

—Lydia Campbell, December 6, 1894

W hile railroad executives and sugar barons were making fortunes in the United States, there were no such industrialists in Labrador. A sparsely populated place, occupying the full Atlantic coastline from 52 degrees to 60 degrees north latitude, Labrador had been a prime objective for missionaries, explorers, fur traders, fishers, seal hunters, and whalers for hundreds of years, although mainly neglected by distant colonial administrators in Newfoundland for just as long.

The economy was based on fish and fur; merchants sailed schooners to their premises every summer from Newfoundland, and Hudson's Bay Company (HBC) traders worked at posts sprinkled north, south, and inland. Labrador was home year-round to a few thousand people, but thousands more came every summer from the bays of the northeast coast of Newfoundland to the rich northern fishing grounds, living either in makeshift shacks onshore or aboard schooners. They would spend months catching, splitting, salting, and drying cod that would be packed on board their vessels and brought to market in Newfoundland in the fall, then shipped to Europe or the Caribbean. The resident population were Inuit (Eskimos), living mainly in communities north of Hamilton Inlet (also known as Eskimo Bay, Invuktoke to the Inuit);

Innu (Indians), nomadic hunting people who travelled the interior; and the people who called themselves settlers, descendants of immigrants from Europe intermarried with the aboriginal people.

Although equally descended from aboriginal ancestors, Labrador "settlers" usually identified themselves by their French, Scottish, or English forefathers, pioneers revered by their descendants for their ability to adapt in a harsh place. Family stories often depicted matrilineal ancestors as uncivilized until they married an Englishman. Women were sometimes mentioned in the few existing written records, but not always by name. HBC agents, or factors, were primarily concerned with business transactions; men trading with HBC would get priority in the daily writings, although attendance was sometimes recorded at social gatherings like Christmas and Easter. Marriages, deaths, and the names of men passing through for a night were noted, but wives, female children, and servant girls were unnamed attachments to them.

Most of the women who married or had children with the men who had settled in Eskimo Bay were at least part Inuit. It was the most southerly winter settlement area for Inuit in the world. Evidence of old houses and burial cairns could be found at all the good fishing, hunting and camping places on the peninsulas and islands in the Narrows between Groswater Bay and Lake Melville.[1] In the first HBC journals kept at Rigolet, the names of numerous Inuit families appear over and over, spellings changing all the time, including Chickwas (Sikwas, Chiquake, Chickwalk, Shiwak), Tooktoosina, Puniac (Ponniuk), Shuglo (Shougelou), Oucoupiouk, Couniouk, Deer, and Palliser, named after a Newfoundland governor.[2]

HBC trader William H.A. Davies counted fewer than 150 people in the district in 1840; 15 to 20 worked for the trading companies; of the 45 planters, "eight are white men, the remainder half-breed Eskimaux." According to Davies, "a great portion of this class is now composed of the offspring of the former planters with the Eskimaux women."[3] The newcomers came in at a disadvantage, unused to the weather, the food, the way of making a living, but gradually they instated a new language and economy. They were not without talents; some could read and write, build houses and boats, make barrels and nets. They knew how to use salt for preserving food and how to make beer and wine. They brought songs, dances, stories, and a different way of practicing religion. The fortunate ones found wives.

In 1887, English explorer Randle Holme observed that what he called "pure Eskimos" were numerous in Hamilton Inlet, but not often found farther south. He thought the ones he met were "quite civilised." If he had travelled north to the Moravian mission stations of Hopedale, Makkovik, Nain, Okak, or Hebron, he would have met Inuit who could read and write, some in two languages, and some who played string or brass instruments in the church band. He described North West River and the area around the head of the bay as populated by "a considerable number of families, mostly half-breed Eskimos."[4] These families would have included the descendants of Thomas Groves and Susanna Webb.

Russell Groves's great-great-grandfather was an Englishman who came to Labrador from Bristol early in the nineteenth century, probably to work for a fish merchant or the HBC. Trader Simon MacGillivray described Thomas Groves in 1837 as a "hard dealer but a serviceable man in his way to the Company," when Groves refused to sell fur for the price he was offered. The day before, Groves had sold the Company three "excellent" flats (small rowboats) for £55.[5] The summer before, when selling fish, the trader complained that while they were under many obligations to Groves, he had kept the largest ones for himself. By the time his name began showing up regularly in HBC accounts, he had been in Labrador long enough to be married and start a family. His wife, Susanna Webb (1808-1864), according to family lore, was part Inuit. Thomas and Susanna had at least two sons; the names Joseph and Frederick appear in the HBC journals.

Most resident Labrador families maintained two houses, one inland for the winter and one nearer their salmon or cod fishing places for the summer. Thomas Groves's family wintered at Traverspine, a settlement of a few families at the mouth of Grand River. It was a good place for hunting and trapping, with plenty of tall forest around for fuel and logs for building houses and boats. In summer, the family shifted to Tub Harbour, a fishing station at the entrance to Hamilton Inlet. Probably because of his boatbuilding skills, Groves was the only salmon fisherman selling at Rigolet who wasn't indebted to HBC. In 1836, he and a partner sold a large two-masted boat called *Racehorse* to the Company and his share of the payment was £20.[6]

The Groves name shows up frequently in the Rigolet HBC diary, especially when Thomas was the factor there for a few years, and members of the expanding family came back and forth to visit. There were also sarcastic references to him in the post journal for North West River kept by Chief Trader Henry Connolly in 1863.[7] By his references to "The Lords of Creation, the Blakes and the Groves," it wasn't difficult to tell who had attracted Connolly's disapproval. Connolly jealously guarded the HBC domain, resenting any effort by planters to do business elsewhere. By the 1860s, Thomas Groves had been in Labrador for about 40 years, had his own boat, and, when not employed by HBC, was likely doing some independent trading, which might account for any snide remarks by the HBC trader. After years of service for, and with, HBC, Groves knew well how the company operated. To be one of the only planters not indebted to HBC, and as master of a good boat, he had the independence and ability to travel to other parts of the coast to see if a better deal could be made for his fish and fur.

Thomas and Susanna's son Frederick (born 1829) was 19 or 20 when he married Sarah (Sally) Blake, the daughter of an Orkneyman and a Labrador Inuit woman. They had five sons and four daughters before Frederick's sudden death in 1865. Thomas Groves was factor at Rigolet when he noted in the HBC journal that his son would be buried at Moliak. Some Groves family members must have moved their winter home to the little settlement on the north shore of Lake Melville, judging by how many grave markers were planted there by the mid-nineteenth century. It was closer to their summer salmon fishing place at Lester's Point, across the Narrows from Rigolet, the HBC's main trading and transshipment depot for fish and fur in central Labrador.

In the mid-1870s, one of Thomas's grandsons, Frederick Malcolm, married Mary Ann Webb. They had six children, four sons and two daughters. Their second child, Charles, would be Russell's father. Charles married Elizabeth Montague, daughter of another Orkneyman, John Montague, and Mary Louisa Goudie. From the Goudie branch of the family they could claim Cree ancestry. Mary Louisa's grandmother was a Cree from northern Quebec.[8]

Elizabeth Montague Groves had a short life, heavy with tragedy, none of it remarkable in Labrador. Her mother died when she was eight, and her father drowned when she was 16. She married Charles Groves when she was 17 and died at 27 in 1913. Two-year-old Russell and his older sister, Ida, were raised by their stepmother, Mary Ann (Annie) Michelin, from Mud Lake.

Charlie and Annie Groves had five more children and lived at Groves Point, where the Goose River flows into Goose Bay. Charlie and his older brother, John, each built a house there, just a few minutes walk apart. They were trappers who worked around Grand River. John trapped the Unknown and Grand rivers, Charlie trapped at Horseshoe and Porcupine rapids. In 1937, John told his nephew Russell that he was "finished with this old river" and, from then on, he rented his trapping grounds to Wilfred Baikie, taking a third of what Baikie earned.[9] Groves kept up the cabins, supplying stoves and traps. He had become a businessman; he and his wife, Betsy, operated a store in competition with HBC. Russell would eventually trap a section of his uncle's old trapline, giving him a share of the furs he trapped.

It was characteristic of John and Charlie Groves that they settled away from others, instead of in North West River or Mud Lake. They were not avoiding people; they were always glad to see visitors, and anyone passing along by dog team in the winter would usually stop in. They were, however, determined to be independent and to have as little as possible to do with the HBC. The family legend was that the young brothers once walked to North West River from Groves Point to ask the factor for help when they and their father had not done well with fish and fur, and were refused. John begged for credit for his parents but was given nothing; he then vowed he would never deal with the HBC again.[10] When he was able, John set up his own small store at Groves Point, trading with trappers and Innu. Some Innu families would camp at Groves Point every summer. The Groves children played with Innu children and learned their language. John and his wife, Betsy, were known for being generous hosts and yet very possessive about their property. Berries picked on Groves Point were theirs;[11] a beaver shot off John's wharf was John's.[12]

By Labrador standards, Russell's uncle, John, was a wealthy man. He had his store, a sawmill, and a workshop where he built canoes for sale. John did things differently than other people, perhaps because he had lived and worked in Canada and had seen a bit more of the world. He surrounded his house with boardwalks, one leading to the outhouse. He kept his dogs in a pen with a shelter. There was an office in his house, the walls lined with books, and a wooden desk with carved decoration.[13] He gave more to the church than anyone. The Parish Record showed a donation of $15 in 1932, when an ordinary trapper, like his brother Charlie, gave 50 cents.[14] He competed directly with the HBC. Innu and settler trappers sold him their furs because he paid more: $6 for a marten when HBC was paying $2.50. He brought his furs to St. John's or Montreal to sell, bypassing the HBC in Labrador.[15] Trappers were pleased with the new goods he brought back to trade, including .44-40 rifles (Winchester lever-action repeating rifles), much superior to the old-fashioned muzzleloaders they had been using.[16]

Finnish geographer Väinö Tanner was impressed by John Groves, when Groves rescued him from a swamped motorboat and put him up for a night. (Tanner and a contingent of Scandinavian scientists came to Labrador in 1937 and 1939.) Tanner noted that the Groves home was "specially wealthy," with bearskins covering the floors, a bed made with beautifully embroidered linen, and breakfast of fresh oranges, porridge, bacon, eggs, salmon, tarts, and marmalade.[17]

John was fiercely independent and worked hard for every cent he had. His brother Charlie, Russell's father, was just as independent, worked just as hard, though always as a trapper, salmon fisherman, and homesteader. While John could pay a teacher to educate his two children, Charlie moved his larger family temporarily to North West River, when the children of his second marriage were old enough to attend school. Elliott Merrick and Kate Austen lived in Charlie Groves's vacant house, which also had bearskin rugs and a "treasure" of a big black wood stove from Quebec. It was evident from the rental agreement that Charlie Groves did not share his brother John's moneymaking instinct. Merrick wrote, "Charlie couldn't decide what to charge us for rent, so he gave it up and decided to charge us nothing at all."[18]

Russell Groves was born in 1911, four generations after Thomas Groves arrived from England. He was a typical Hamilton Inlet Labradorian, with English, Scottish, Inuit, and Cree ancestry, part of the new blended population that had evolved in central Labrador, as the European immigrants melded with the aboriginal people. Elliott Merrick wrote admiringly about the "unique race with oddly combined cultures" in whose presence he "felt abashed and very inferior." He said that life for him and his wife, Kate, "will be forever changed because of the three years we once spent with the part-Eskimo people of Hamilton Inlet."[19] He described them as "Scotch Presbyterian in religion, old English in speech and many customs, Eskimo when it comes to seal fishing and dog driving, Indian in their ways of hunting and their skill with canoes." Merrick often said he thought the people, who had so little, were the happiest people he had ever known, but he warned against idealizing their life, saying a good deal of hardship was involved with living there. He cautioned those who thought the people were helpless and bereft, saying he and his wife had gone to Labrador "to help the people" but found themselves "constantly being helped by them."[20]

The place engendered independence. The "unique race" became the majority in the bay and were confident of their position there, a confidence perhaps partly derived from the certain knowledge that everything they owned, they had made or built, and could do so again if need be. No civil or legal authorities were present, except for sporadic summer visits by a magistrate from St. John's, sent mainly to collect duties or settle disputes among skippers and crews of the hundreds of fishing schooners from Newfoundland. Clergy of various denominations had staked out territory, but a visitor in 1933 concluded, "Sectarian differences are a continued source of amusement to the trappers."[21] There had never been a Labrador representative in the Newfoundland House of Assembly. Labradorians had never voted in an election. And until provoked, Newfoundland had never registered any great interest in its northern possession.

It was the activities of a logging company in Hamilton Inlet that finally brought the Labrador boundary issue to the fore in 1902. Quebec authorities complained that loggers cutting timber on the south side of Grand River had no business to be there. The Newfoundland government replied that it was fully entitled to grant the permit. The dispute was batted back and forth until both governments agreed in 1907 to allow the Judicial Committee of the British Privy Council to decide where the boundary should be. Canadian and Newfoundland lawyers, surveyors, and cartographers buttonholed every livyer who could mark an "X" on an affidavit, marshalling evidence to support competing cases.[22] Having been ignored for so long, the fishermen, trappers, and homesteaders took their opportunity to express themselves. Joseph Michelin's affidavit said he had always paid revenue to the Collector of Customs from Newfoundland and never had anything to do with Canada.[23] Not everyone was on Newfoundland's side. Orkneyman Malcolm McLean, a resident of Labrador for 50 years, was "dissatisfied with the present state of things" and swore in his statement that everyone believed "that this country should be held to constitute part of Canada rather than Newfoundland."[24]

Evidence gathering took decades and the legal case would have been irrelevant early in 1925 if Quebec had taken up the offer to buy Labrador. Prime Minister Walter S. Monroe of Newfoundland offered to sell most of Labrador, tentatively asking a price of $30 million and, less than a month later, dropping it to $15 million. Newfoundland wanted to keep a coastal strip 3 miles deep for the sake of the summer fishery. Quebec's premier, who must have thought Canada's position the strongest, had already written to the Newfoundland prime minister suggesting they both wait for the Privy Council decision, losing his chance to accept the unseen lower offer. The decision on March 1, 1927, in Newfoundland's favour determined the boundary would be at the height of land, hundreds of miles from the coast. St. John's editorial writers stirred up excitement about the victory and resource development possibilities and, for a brief time, Labrador was seen as a valuable prize. Not enough of an asset to hold, however, as Prime Minister Sir Richard Squires of a nearly bankrupt Newfoundland attempted again to sell the greatly enlarged Labrador territory to Quebec in 1931. With no keen buyer, the next year the new prime minister, F.C. Alderdice, tried and failed to lease Labrador to a British syndicate for 99 years.[25]

Any further effort to unload Labrador had to be shelved in 1934 when the beleaguered Newfoundland government resigned, relinquishing control of its affairs to a British-appointed Commission. The disposition or development of Labrador was consigned to the distant back burner until after war broke out in 1939 and its strategic location became both an advantage for the allies and a potential opening for the enemy. The people of Labrador, unaccustomed to much official intervention in their lives, were about to be outnumbered by newcomers from the south. Familiar with explorers and adventurers, traders and missionaries, they were soon to meet thousands of Canadian and American construction workers, airmen, and officers. The HBC, the Mission, the few resident clergymen, and visiting magistrates who sailed along the coast in summer would no longer be the undisputed authorities in the land.

Chapter Seven

AIRPORT IN A BERRY PATCH

*We knew that they were goin' to build the Base here and
they did want a few men for surveyin' in the beginning so
I was one of them that got the job. It was beginning to be
a dark outlook for the future if this war was goin' to carry
on like it was, and the price of fur was goin' down, so we
grabbed the chance and took the job.*

—Isaac Rich, "We Grabbed the Chance"

S itting on a train about to depart for Boston, the first leg of her journey to Labrador, Barbara imagined her father remarking on how much income the New York Central Railroad reported last year or how gas rationing for automobiles during the war was reviving the fortunes of the railroads. Floyd Mundy was the acknowledged expert in the industry and well known also for his insistence on full disclosure to his clients, long before regulations required it.[1] Unfortunately, the full disclosure policy was not applied at home, where it might have saved her mother much heartache and embarrassment. Barbara's relationship with her father had been strained by his affair and remarriage. He knew she was leaving the city for a volunteer job in Labrador, but he was not among the crowds at the station that Sunday, May 21, 1944. Her mother and sister sent her off with a corsage of gardenias and candy for the trip.

That morning, the three of them had breakfast in the dining room, Barbara's mother pressing the button on the floor with her foot to summon the maid and muttering once again about the war causing a shortage of servants. Barbara's sister, Harriet, was plainly unhappy that

Barbara was leaving for such a long time, not because she'd miss her so much but because she'd be the one left behind with their mother and her multitude of ailments and complaints. After breakfast, the doorman summoned a car and brought Barbara's duffle and suitcases down to the lobby. Barbara tried to stay focused on her reasons for leaving—she was nearly 34 years old, still living at home, and had just had her heart broken. If ever a change was needed, this was the time, and, besides, it was only for six months.

Cecil Ashdown's letter of recommendation was rather brief, considering her more than nine years of volunteer work.[2] Credit was given for being able, "conscientious and careful in all work she undertakes," but he neglected to mention that Barbara had been elected vice-president of the Needlework Guild just the previous November. The three-sentence letter didn't quite encompass all the record-keeping, report writing, committee meetings attended, and talks given to promote the work of the Guild and its connection to the Mission in Newfoundland and Labrador. It also didn't mention the planning meetings for the annual opera benefit, sales of work, endless teas, lunches, and socials for the New York branch of the IGA. None of that mattered now. The job was hers, and she had a very good reason to leave New York.

The United States had been at war for over two years and Grand Central Terminal was always a confusion of activity. The platforms were swarming with men in uniform kissing their wives or girlfriends goodbye. For Barbara, it was a different farewell. She wasn't going across the ocean to risk her life. She was on her way to Moncton, New Brunswick, to get passage on a Canadian military flight to Goose Bay, Labrador, from where she would travel by boat or dog team to the tiny community of North West River. She smoothed the skirt of her best travelling suit, selected in the hope that it wouldn't wrinkle too quickly. She'd be wearing it until she got to Moncton. Her ticket was for the morning train from New York to Boston, where she would spend a few hours with Bette Hamilton, and then board "The Gull," the overnight train to the eastern Canadian provinces. Bette had become a true Mission insider. After several summers serving as a wop in St. Anthony, she was a member of the Mission board and wrote the Guild column for *Among the Deep-Sea Fishers*. Barbara was preparing herself for the questions she expected to be asked about what she was doing, just a few months after announcing her engagement. She hoped Bette would be supportive of her sudden decision to leave New York to spend six months in Labrador. At least Bette had been to North West River and was familiar with where Barbara would live and work.

Bette met her in Boston as planned: "we had a pleasant visit—my first at the Arnold Arboretum—the lilacs were at their height and the azaleas were pretty good too. She supped me and put me on the train in high style."[3] The two spent several hours together, but Barbara did not report in her diary what they talked about and how she explained her broken engagement. She wrote instead about the overnight train ride, "the bumpiest ever," and about how "seven or eight dizzy Dutch girls en route to Australia via Halifax were put off at the border" by Canadian immigration officials in the middle of the night. In the dining car, she struck up a conversation with an Army nurse named Jean Hilchey, who had spent two years in St. Anthony working in the Mission hospital: "of course, we started in as you can imagine—it was really fun and she had many amusing stories to tell of and on the various others. Her tale of the hysterectomy Dr. Curtis did on one of his pet cows was something—all the attention and more than he'd give a human almost."[4]

Barbara arrived in Moncton by late afternoon and got a room in the Hotel Brunswick across the road from the railway station: "I'm told I'm lucky to get anything—the john is down the hall—pea green in color—the ceiling in my room looks as if it might collapse at any moment—the lobby is appalling and the people therein even more so! The seediest bunch I've ever seen!"[5] It took two days to get a flight to Labrador, during which time she was not impressed by Moncton.

If there's anything to see in the town I certainly haven't seen it! I took a walk around this aft. and tonight movied—I certainly hope I get out on Wednesday! Tomorrow I hope to see the tidal bore come in—heaven knows what I'll do the rest of the time—There is not even a bench in the park to sun oneself on! (Letter: May 22, 1944)

Moncton was the location of No. 8, Service Flying Training School, one of more than 70 flying schools operated in Canada under the British Commonwealth Air Training Plan. Students from the British Commonwealth, many Australians and New Zealanders, began arriving in Canada in 1940, and, by 1942, "Free" French, Norwegians, Belgians, Poles, and Czechs were graduating and being sent into active service. The schools graduated 3,000 a month and, until 1942, those numbers included Americans; 9,000 came north to enlist in the Royal Canadian Air Force (RCAF).[6] The Canadian Army had a large military supply base in Moncton. It was an important terminus for the Canadian National Railroad and war materiel was transshipped from the rail yard to eastern ports on the way to Britain. Troop trains with as many as 25 cars were running through Moncton around the clock, bringing troops to board ships in Halifax.[7]

All you have to do to know there's a war on is to cross the border. Between troop trains & the airforce here it is something. This place is simply alive with the latter—Czechs, French, Dutch, Chinese etc. etc. all in the RAF or RCAF blues … (Letter: May 22, 1944)

The military men knew something big was in the works, judging by the acceleration in the movement of troops and supplies. It was most apparent overseas, in southern England, where since early spring, two million American and a quarter of a million Canadian troops had been marshalled.[8] Clearly, the Allies were preparing for an imminent assault of the continent.

If not for the new military airport, Barbara would have had to travel in U-boat-infested waters by coastal steamer to Goose Bay, and then not until shipping opened in the summer. Instead, the direct flight from Moncton would get her there in mere hours. Flights to Labrador weren't on a fixed schedule though, and her instructions were all very clandestine.

I called about my future as soon as I arrived and may get off tomorrow but I guess not as I've received no word tonight. I'll be called the night before & then it'll be confirmed at 7 A.M. after weather reports are in. They go in the A.M. and after I go to a certain field and ask for a certain squadron it's a military secret, so I guess there won't be much to tell—after my arrival everything is very strictly censored on the spot! Weather north

has been beautiful of late & the man I spoke to here says I'll probably go on
by dog team as the ice is still solid and the 17 mile road is now impassable
it is so broken up. It is used by trucks when in condition. (Letter: May 22,
1944)

When they left Moncton on May 24, Barbara was one of 10
passengers on board an "olive drab" Douglas Dakota DC-3, RCAF
#164 Squadron transport aircraft. Seven others were construction
workers and two were "RCAF boys returning from furlough." She was
thrilled by the flight, nearly four hours flying 8,000 to 9,000 feet above
Prince Edward Island, Anticosti Island, then Quebec and Labrador,
"progressively wilder" with "millions" of rivers, lakes, and ponds, many
still covered in ice. As she would soon learn, the spring ice breakup took
its time in Labrador and travel on land or even by air was sometimes
impossible.[9]

Barbara was flying to Goose Bay airport only three years after the
idea to construct it was hatched. Labrador was identified as a vulnerable
area, an opening that could allow invasion by the Nazis. That fear was
not without foundation. Enemy submarines had become bolder and not
only patrolled the open ocean but also ventured into Newfoundland and
Canadian waters, in the St. Lawrence River, the Gulf of St. Lawrence, the
Strait of Belle Isle, and the Cabot Strait, attacking merchant, military,
and even civilian vessels. Late in 1941, unnerving press reports quoted
Canada's Minister for the Navy, Angus Macdonald, saying U-boats
had been seen from the Newfoundland shore.[10] In March 1942, three
torpedoes were fired at St. John's narrow harbour entrance, one hitting
the rocks below the Fort Amherst lighthouse. In the first months of 1942,
the Germans sank 44 ships in Canadian and Newfoundland waters.[11]
The Canadian Army stationed 600 infantry and artillery soldiers at
Rigolet, Labrador, to keep watch on the narrow opening of Hamilton
Inlet, ready to fire on submarines if necessary. A tiny Canadian Navy
post was 4 miles farther out the bay.[12]

Since the declaration of war by Britain in 1939 and the United States
in 1941, the island of Newfoundland had become a critical strategic
location for Canadian and American military. Both countries had
bases in the vital eastern port of St. John's, less than 2,000 miles from

Scotland, serving a steady rotation of naval and merchant ships. Fishing communities were bulldozed and even cemeteries relocated to make way for an American air and naval base at Argentia, Placentia Bay, and an airfield at Stephenville in western Newfoundland.[13] Canadians built an airport at Torbay, near St. John's, and in 1942 took over control of the Newfoundland Airport, in the centre of the island near Gander Lake, expanding it greatly. The Gander airport was managed by the RCAF, made available also to the British and Americans,[14] and had been used since late 1940 for ferrying aircraft from North American factories to service in Britain.[15]

An airport in Labrador would provide an alternative for the Ferry Command with the advantage of being 200 miles closer than Gander to the United Kingdom, for flights going the Great Circle route via Iceland. To reinforce the case for the new airport, a British propaganda film from 1941, *The 49th Parallel*, released in the United States as *The Invaders*, depicted a desperate German U-boat crew shipwrecked in Hudson's Bay sneaking across enemy territory in Canada, heading for refuge in still neutral United States. Some scenes for the film had been shot at the base in Goose Bay, "in the social room at the hospital several years ago."[16]

Pilots and surveyors for the RCAF started sniffing around Labrador in the summer of 1939. Work to find possible sites began in earnest after a joint meeting of Canadian and American authorities in Ottawa in March 1941. On June 16, Canadian surveyor Eric Fry and an RCAF crew landed their Stranraer flying boat at North West River. Fry "partly" confided in the HBC manager, Jack Keats, about his mission, and as a result saved himself and the crew a lot of wasted time. Keats suggested three possible places, one a "bench-land on the south side of Goose Bay proper." A few days later, with local men Sid Blake and Dan Michelin as guides, they headed for Goose Bay, stopping at the mouth of Terrington Basin to confer with John Groves, who also recommended the flat bench-land "as a good possibility." Enlisting the help of Dan's brother, First World War veteran Robert Michelin, they walked for two hours on a footpath from Robert's home at the mouth of the Traverspine River, arriving at a site of "exceptional quality." Fry was pleased with the expansive dry plateau, 70 feet higher than water level, but near enough to the bay that supplies could be brought ashore. He decided the local name "Robert's Berry Bank" wasn't suitable "for perpetuation," so it became "The Goose Bay Site."[17]

On July 1, Fry saw two American PBY flying boats overhead, doing reconnaissance and taking photographs of the bench-land site. Fry made a beeline to North West River and exchanged information with the Americans. He met Captain Elliott Roosevelt, son of the American president, accompanied by Alexander Forbes, who had done extensive aerial photography and mapping of northern Labrador in the early 1930s under the auspices of the American Geographical Society. Roosevelt had been dispatched to Labrador with exactly the same mission as Fry: to find a suitable site for an airport.[18]

Forbes and Roosevelt seemed just as surprised to see the Canadians as the Canadians were to see them, perhaps because they hadn't gotten there first. Forbes said, "It seemed odd, after the secrecy that had surrounded our project in Washington, to find that here it was a matter of common knowledge among the trappers and traders."[19] The Americans didn't appreciate that in the quiet, enclosed world of the Labrador interior, where the arrival of the first supply ship every spring was enough to bring everyone out of their houses, people were naturally riveted by the sudden landing of several amphibian aircraft loaded with survey teams, especially when the American president's son was among them. For two weeks before the Americans got there, Eric Fry and his men had been exploring potential sites for a port and runways. Every move they made had been observed and widely reported. Roosevelt, Forbes, and their crew were guests of the Mission, staying in the staff quarters at North West River. Whatever kernels of information they dropped at the dinner table were also heard and repeated.

In separate reports to their respective governments, the Canadian and American surveyors agreed that the Goose Bay bench-land site was the best place for a Labrador airport, but there was no shared plan to build it. In his July 6 report to the United States War Department, Roosevelt said he had no faith in the Canadians' ability to build an airport "this year or even to complete it by the end of 1942."[20] While the Americans flew away assuming the task of building the airport would fall to them, the Canadians got on with the job. The building contract was awarded to McNamara Construction in early September and the company immediately chartered HBC vessels *Fort Rigolet* and *Fort Cartwright* and sent them along the coast to recruit workers.[21] Robert Michelin's berry grounds were about to be churned into mud, buried in gravel, and paved over with concrete.

The lure of a regular wage of 35 cents an hour was enough to attract hundreds of men, although trappers and fishermen wondered if they'd be able "to stand being told what to do for six months."[22] They were not encouraged to bring their families, but some came with their families and their dogs. Robert Davis, from Sandwich Bay, recalled the fishery "was a failure," so he and his brother packed up to go. He decided not to bring his dog team, and made a terrible choice: "Rather than leave them around to starve to death, I drowned my whole team of faithful dogs. It was like stabbing a friend in the back."[23] Labrador workers soon learned they were earning much less than those from Canada, who were being paid $1 an hour for the same work, because "the Commission of Government wouldn't allow the Canadian contractors to pay us more than the rates that was going on the Island of Newfoundland, which at that time was 35¢ maximum."[24] Complaints were heard and the hourly rate at Goose Bay increased to 60 cents by spring.[25] Workers on bases in Newfoundland had also complained about the wages, kept low to conform to rates paid at mines and other industries.[26]

When Robert Davis and 14 other men arrived at Goose Bay they saw the Canadian Department of Transport icebreaker *N.B. McLean* "tied up to the sand bank, discharging all kinds of equipment, the like of which most of [them had] never [seen] before." They stepped onto a floating log walkway and were immediately put to work unloading the ship, a timekeeper taking their names. They lived in canvas tents on the roadside, "a North West River tent, a Rigolet tent, a Cartwright tent, and, separate from them all, the tent city of the mainlanders." Davis said the Canadians called them "natives." In the Mess Hall, the "mainlanders" (Canadians), Newfoundlanders, and "natives" sat at separate tables.[27] Some Labrador workers frustrated their bosses in the early days because they "would quit whenever they felt like it. Three men walked three hundred miles to go home to the coast for Christmas. In the summer months they would leave the job at any time to go fishing and they would always stop for tea in the middle of the morning and afternoon."[28]

Russell Groves wasn't among the first of the North West River trappers to get a job at the construction site. He knew he would hate the work and living in tents with gangs of other men, but eventually decided not to go trapping because his wife, Jane, was seriously ill with tuberculosis. One of their two daughters, three-year-old Elizabeth, was sick too. He walked or hitched a boat ride home to North West River as often as he could to see his family, always hoping the next time his wife and little girl would be better.[29] At least his earnings, about $25 a week, would be more than he made in an average winter on the trapline.

McNamara's engineers and surveyors had flown to Goose Bay as soon as the contract was signed and had marked out the roads and runways. From Montreal, eight ships set out at one-week intervals, carrying 17,000 tons of freight, rushing against the deadline of winter ice. Crews worked all day and night to build a temporary dock and just three days after the icebreaker *McLean* sailed into the basin on September 19, low in the water with its load of bulldozers, cranes, and shovels, they were able to get machines ashore.[30]

A road was plowed through the swamp and forest, from the dock to the airport site, surmounting the hurdle of the high bank from water level to the flat ground above. Bulldozers and graders were hauled up to the plateau with block and tackle. The deep sandy soil, overgrown with shallow-rooted spruces and low-growing shrubs, was smoothed over by convoys of bulldozers. By November 16, three winter runways were built, each 7,000 feet long. The first plane arrived early in December, landing on hard packed snow.[31] In April 1942, the gravel and snow-packed runways were used by the RAF Ferry Command for their first "short stage" route flights via Greenland and Iceland. Two Cansos and a Liberator successfully made the proving flight.[32]

A permanent camp for several thousand men was built with timber cut and milled at Goose Bay; "a tree would be growing one day and part of a building the next." Construction records were being broken every day, even with all the tea breaks taken by the workers. When marine navigation opened in 1942, they began paving the permanent runways, first laying down gravel hauled from 21 miles away, over a road built in one month: "Paving operations were conducted with great speed, record runs of 13,000 square yards being completed in a single 12-hour shift. Two complete paving units were employed. The paving work involved the placing of 623,000 square yards of 6-inch concrete, the equivalent of over fifty-three miles of 20-foot roadway."[33]

Elliott Merrick returned to Labrador in 1942 to research the story of the air base construction. McNamara's assistant superintendent, Jackson Clark, gave Merrick a tour, taking him to the edge of the runway where fresh concrete was being laid. Clark extolled the virtues of the location: "sand base, practically level, beautifully drained. If we'd had clay we'd have been up against it in mud-time."[34] By the end of 1942, there were 5,000 service personnel and 3,000 construction workers resident at Goose Bay. As another measure of the size of the place, 4,500 packages of cigarettes were smoked every day.[35]

The wilderness camp became a full-fledged airport with gigantic hangars, paved runways, storage for millions of gallons of fuel, barrack block accommodation, mess halls, officers' and enlisted ranks' clubs, power plants, hospital, laundry, bakery, radio station, recreation huts, and even a Finnish-style sauna. Goose Bay was the largest airfield in the western hemisphere, possibly the largest in the world.[36] One day in the summer of 1943, 87 bombers took off in 89 minutes.[37] USAF records showed that in June 1944 "2,598 aircraft passed through Goose Bay and during the 12-month period ending 30 September 1945, the airport handled 25,000 aircraft."[38] Flying conditions were ideal year-round at Goose Bay, double the number of flying days per month achieved at either Gander or Torbay airports in Newfoundland. The sound of aircraft overhead was constant.[39] Just two years after the surveyors first walked there, the Canadians and Americans each had a functioning base and the plateau overlooking Lake Melville was level under 6 inches of concrete.

When her flight landed, Barbara was met by "Jack Tevenay [Thevenet]—a North West River boy working at the base" and brought to the home of Jackson Clark, who hosted all Grenfell workers passing through.[40] Barbara couldn't put many details of what was going on at Goose Bay in her letters, which would be censored, but her diary entries told how busy the airport was in the days leading up to D-Day and the Normandy invasion on June 6.

Goose Bay is tremendous—largest field in the world. Three runways (6,000 ft. each—1¼ miles). Thirty miles of roads, 3 or 4 construction camps, RCAF, Army on Canadian side and about 1 mile on other side of field is American Army Air Force. Am. & Can. sides quite separate unit— in case of attack. Gun towers all around, bomb dumps, fuel dumps (10-12 million gals. gas per yr. Each Liberator carries 2700 gals. per trip). Even after walking & driving about I didn't see everything! One side unaware of what happens on other! Plenty food, gas, etc. On Friday between 7 and 10 about 75 Liberators (B-24s) took off—directly for Prestwick, Scotland. Took off about 3 mins apart & flew right over us at end of runway, waved as they passed—thrilling to see them head straight out over Bay or toward snow-covered Mealies [mountains] & to know (or hope) they'd all be in Eng. by dawn. Later went to other side of field to see them lined up, ready to take off. (Diary: May 24, 1944)

Lilacs had been blooming in Boston, but in Labrador it was what people called "the time between ice and water," with not enough solid ice on the rivers and bays to support dog teams pulling sleds or airplanes landing on skis, and not enough open water to launch boats or for amphibian aircraft to land on floats. Travel to North West River was out of the question until the ice moved or melted.

I arrived here yesterday, too late to go on by dog-team—it's about two weeks since any contact has been had with N.W. [North West River]. A ranger started off by canoe last night but it'll be a week yet probably before a motor boat can risk it. The ice is out of the immediate bay here, but beyond it's open only near the shoreline. (Letter: May 25, 1944)

Barbara would be in Goose Bay indefinitely, and had time to fully scope out her surroundings, including the hydroponic greenhouse— "beautiful veg in there growing in sand & thriving on vitamin shots of chemicals"—which supplied the military mess halls.[41]

I will say a bit about my stay at the base, or what I can safely. It is a most fascinating place, and altho' I took long walks and drove about there is much I have not seen. It's unbelievable in every way. I did have meals at the three construction camps, the Officers Mess on both Am. and Can. sides. Went to the movies one night, a dance another! Walked on a balmy spring-like day, also in snow and hail, and on Sunday we had a most terrific dust and sand storm. Got rather bored just enjoying the great open spaces and after meeting the Red X [Cross] gals I offered to help them— was glad to see how they worked. The last night I was there I gave out the famous doughnuts and coffee—how those boys went thru' them—Never have I seen so much food disappear so fast—it was delish I must admit. (Letter: June 2, 1944)

The sheer size and constant activity of the place surprised her as she found her way around, with friendly men picking her up wherever she walked: "trucks to jeeps fall all over themselves offering lifts. It's too funny!" Only a few dozen women lived among the thousands of civilian and military men.[42]

Women certainly are an oddity here! Everyone coming in is supposed to register—but _where_ for me? I'm staying at Mr. Clark's "residence." His wife was flown in about 2 mos. ago and is the only woman here other than local girls working in laundry, nurses, a scattered secretary or two and 4 Red X girls on the Am. side; she's definitely the only older one. (Letter: May 25, 1944)

Barbara went to the hospital to see the woman she would be replacing; Celesta Gerber Acreman was about to give birth to her first child. She was an American nurse who had come to St. Anthony in 1940 to work for the Mission, serving in several nursing stations and the St. Anthony hospital, before marrying Gordon Acreman, whom she met when she worked at St. Mary's River on the Labrador south coast. He was a carpenter at the base, while she was the Industrial assistant in North West River.[43] She likely told Barbara about the duties awaiting her: dispensing sewing materials from the shop, receiving the sewn and embroidered items made by local women, and determining their quality in order to figure out payment. Barbara had some familiarity with crafts from the north but she wasn't an expert needlewoman. Her closest exposure would have been when she and Harriet had tended tables full of wares at sales in New York.

The airmen and officers on the base were the Industrial Shop's best customers, men earning regular wages with no place else to spend their money. When the ice cleared, they would arrive by boat to visit the shop and purchase souvenirs for their families. An outing to North West River, the largest settlement in the bay, was a distraction to the airmen stationed there, to "buy things in a store, and to see a female for the first time in months."[44] The Canadians and Americans had done the Mission many favours, not the least of which was flying Barbara north, and then feeding and accommodating her, but she was finding out that the thousands of men, their mighty bulldozers, and noisy airplanes had caused quite a social disturbance in the middle of Labrador.

The base has not done this part of the world much good I fear—too much drink and other vices of "Civilization"—it is really a pity. As Mrs. K [Keddie] says one used to be able to go anyplace alone at any time, but not now near any of these places—you even have to lock the door—an unheard of thing to do! Many of the men have been here too long a stretch without going out, and it's not doing them or the local people any good. (Letter: June 2, 1944)

The war had caused a lot of changes in attitudes toward charity and the Mission. In one of her columns, Bette Hamilton wrote that she had heard people say it was hard to get interested in Labrador "because the people there were neither heathen nor black."[45] Before the war, breadlines wound their way around city blocks in New York and thousands of unemployed people stood in line for a handout of food. Now anyone could get work in a factory or join the military, and the problems of the people on the coast seemed less urgent. They were not being terrorized or bombed, like people in Europe, and if they needed a job, plenty were on offer at the new military base in Goose Bay. With the great difficulty the Mission was having in recruiting volunteers, Barbara figured she would be welcomed with open arms when she finally arrived in North West River.

Chapter Eight

DOWNALONG AND UPALONG

Still, people do write letters in this day and there are some who possess the divinely flexible gift for a fresh turn of phrase and delightful keenness of observation.

—Emily Post, *Etiquette*

As soon as she got settled in North West River, Barbara began documenting her experiences and observations. She had a typewriter at the Industrial Shop and wrote long, descriptive letters to "Everybody," using carbon paper so multiple copies could be sent to friends and family. She wrote abbreviated notes in a tiny diary, mainly as a memory aid for when she composed the detailed letters about her work and life in the community. She left little out, starting with being fetched from Goose Bay.

The Mission boat managed to make it through the patchy ice to collect her. The trip took over three hours, leaving Goose Bay at Otter Creek, heading northeast into Lake Melville, also called a bay, as it opened through Hamilton Inlet to the ocean. Navigating it was a nightmare for boat skippers unfamiliar with the shifting, sandy bottom of Terrington Basin, at the mouth of the Grand River, but merely routine for the Grenfell Mission's general foreman from North West River, Jack Watts, and his crew.

Jack Watts came for me—how he had aged—his hair is almost white—I never would have known him from pictures I'd seen. 5 local men came too—Sid Blake one of them—he was the one in "Northern Nurse" persuaded to get married and he brought his girl up to N.W. Incidentally,

Olive Michelin of the dysentery family in Traverspine—remember her? is our maid here at the hosp. It is fun seeing in the flesh so many I heard about for so long. (Letter: June 2, 1944)

Barbara had not set foot ashore at North West River and already she was meeting characters from *Northern Nurse.* Jack Watts, the indispensable Newfoundlander who had lived there for years, served the Mission in many capacities, in charge of keeping all buildings, boats, gardens, and grounds in good order. He was married to Annie Baikie, the North West River woman who had worked with Harriet at Indian Harbour. The "dysentery family" story about the Michelins was one of the most dramatic in Merrick's book. Kate Austen went on an emergency call to trapper Robert Michelin's home at Traverspine River, 22 miles by dog team, and stayed three weeks nursing his wife, Matilda, and their five children, all desperately sick, while Robert was on his trapline, unaware of what was happening. Now here was Olive Michelin, alive and well and working at the hospital. Barbara had read and heard so much about the people that they already felt familiar to her.

North West River is in the middle of Labrador, about 100 miles from the coast, on a wide, ridged peninsula washed by Lake Melville on one side, Little Lake on the other. The earliest inhabitants were Innu; there was evidence of ancient camps on both sides of the river. A fur trading post was built by French traders in the mid-eighteenth century, then taken over by the HBC in 1836, the location chosen for its proximity to the major rivers used by trappers to venture into the interior—Naskapi, Grand, Kenemish, and Kenamu. The trading post grew into a community when the Mission built a hospital and school. Families gradually moved from their winter houses on the rivers leading to the trapping grounds and settled there.

After a hundred years, there was still no sign of modern development—no cars, hardly any roads, and no electrical wires overhead. A long wharf extended into deep water from a gravel and sand beach, near the hospital and the HBC store. The squat white clapboard and red-roofed store was the hub of the village, women inside shopping, men gathered on the steps and around the front of the building exchanging jokes and news, children playing on the wharf and beach.

Whenever a boat arrived, everyone turned out to help carry cargo, some with wheelbarrows, but much of the freight was hefted to the store on men's shoulders.

Along the shore were huge stands of logs, drying in teepee formation until they would be cut for the hospital furnace. The Mission had large gardens, surrounded by white picket fences, and kept chickens and a small dairy herd to provide fresh eggs and milk for the staff, hospital patients, and dormitory children. A white clapboard church was tucked back in the trees, its spire visible from the wharf. Yale School, named for the American college students who donated money to build it, had between 60 and 80 pupils most years. Two buildings, called cottages, were dormitories for about 30 boarding-school children, some were orphans and the rest came from families in settlements all around Lake Melville. The children from Rigolet hadn't seen their families since August of the year before and wouldn't get home until the bay ice disappeared.

Neat houses, built from round logs or whitewashed sawn lumber, some displaying bright red and pink geraniums in their front windows, were distributed along the shore on either side of the store and the Mission buildings. Directions were simple—you either lived "downalong" toward the Point or "upalong" the shore of Little Lake. Near the door of every house was a worn tree-stump chopping block, top softened to a fuzz after thousands of cuts, the ground around thickly covered with fresh fragrant chips. Tidy piles of split wood were lined up, ready for the kitchen stove. Picket fences enclosed kitchen gardens planted with potato, carrot, beet, turnip, lettuce, and cabbage. Impressively robust rhubarb plants had burst through the ground, promising early fruit. Some people had henhouses, every house had numerous sheds, and privy outhouses were placed discreetly in the tall trees nearby. Ten-foot-long wooden komatik sleds leaned on end against the walls of woodsheds, stored out of the way until winter. Skinny clothesline poles bounced lines of laundry in the breeze. Galvanized washtubs and scrubbing boards worn white were drying in the sun. Well-trod mossy footpaths intersected in the shade through the trees to each house, exposed roots polished bare by walkers. An agreeable smell of spruce and fir forest and smoke was in the air. The homes were heated with wood, and bread was baked on even the hottest summer days. Sled dogs were tethered on the shoreline, huskies with upcurled tails and black-rimmed eyes, just like those depicted on the Mission's trademark hooked mats. Canoes were ashore, stored bottom up on sawhorses, and painted wooden rowboats bobbed at anchor. The sounds of axes splitting logs and voices of children playing could be heard. After the airplane and machine noise and strong smells of the airport and base at Goose Bay, it was wonderfully peaceful and pretty.

Around "The Point" that extended into Lake Melville, out of sight of the main community, a long, curving, sandy beach, "The Bight," was washed by brackish water. The rounded tops of the Mealy Mountains, some still snow-capped, were clearly visible on the south shore of the bay. Nestled below the mountains and too far away to see were the McLean family community at Kenemich, and Mud Lake (formerly Grand Village), populated by Bests, Blakes, Hopes, Whites, and McLeans. People also lived in several places on the north shore, the largest were Mulligan—Baikies, Campbells, and Blakes were most numerous there—and Sebaskachu, all Michelins. Closer to North West River was Butter and Snow; Barbara heard that it got its name because one spring the people had nothing left to eat but butter and snow. A few more Baikies lived at North West Islands. The sparse settlements were miles apart and though there was no way to travel but by foot, dog team, or boat, someone was always coming to North West River to the store or hospital or to visit. Word of births, deaths, illness, good luck, misfortune, and newly arriving mission volunteers travelled rapidly in a place where most everyone was connected by blood or marriage.

Barbara was brought to the staff quarters at the hospital, a prominent two-story white clapboard building set on a fenced lawn, and welcomed to her new home.

I have the corner room on the ground floor, three windows facing south and west. I think it is the best room of all for many reasons. The disadvantages are really not such at all—they are no heat, but I have a little Franklin stove, and am quite cozy—in fact tonight I lighted it shortly after dinner and now at midnight it is almost too hot, altho' the fire is out; I have the advantage of being alone when I want to be, the john is upstairs but that's good for the figure! and until a year ago there was no john in the house—so I can consider myself lucky—the base, by the way is responsible for that modern convenience. I am awakened early by the girls setting the table, but then I can lie in bed and listen to the fire crackle and that somehow warms me up—was I glad to get here and have my little pillow to keep my back warm!!! (Letter: June 2, 1944)

She was indeed lucky to be living in the Mission's quarters, awakening to the sound of the girls setting the table in the morning, in that way no different from Thousand Nine. Mission staff became accustomed to a certain standard for their accommodations and food. Millicent Blake Loder from Rigolet worked there as a servant girl in 1929 when she was 14, several years before she went away to nursing school. Every morning, she would bring a jug of warm water to each room and, while the staff members dressed, she prepared their breakfast. The table was set "just so," and when the coals in the stove were ready for toast, a bell summoned staff to the table. After breakfast, the girls would clean the rooms, make beds, and empty slop pails. The evening meal was a more formal affair. Millicent recalled making patterned butterballs, and for meal service she wore "a black dress with a frilly apron and a little white headdress." Doctors, nurses, and teachers had specially cooked foods: "they were not used to our kind of cooking."[1] Some of those practices were abandoned in wartime, but girls still set the tables and cleaned the rooms.

American nurse Ruth P. Byerly spent an enjoyable summer in North West River in 1945 and had no complaints about Mission accommodations or working conditions. Nurse Byerly was impressed with the glass-enclosed entrance to the hospital, which lead to a "charming" living room that left her "spellbound," a wall of windows filled with blooming begonias, abundant records for the record player, a crackling fire in the recessed fireplace, and a tea table set with colourful cups.[2] Her observations were for publication and quite a contrast to Barbara's more critical view in a letter to family after only a month in residence.

N.W. could certainly do with a few of the comforts of St. A.—and do the staff have thoughts on the subject!! But honestly, I agree too—the school is practically falling down, the wharf is a menace, and the hospital is full of death traps! Laundry, etc. is hung in the attic, and every time you go up you crack your back on a beam—it is almost impossible to stand straight in it—it was the Clothing Store for ages—imagine. The cellar is worse (at the moment it is flooded, pipes someplace have not thawed yet). If you want a bath you start the heater several hours in advance, and care for it most tenderly and at frequent intervals—the water gets nice and hot if you are lucky enough to have kept the fire burning—you can hardly turn your back for a moment. The other night Mrs. P [Paddon] and I got a tank full of water and with much anticipation went up to run the first bath—no pressure and not a drop of water!! There sat our tank of water and no earthly way to get any of it, and it would happen at the time the water pump was on the blink—they worked for several days on it, and finally connected it up with the light plant—(We are getting a new pump on the CLUETT). (Letter: June 29, 1944)

The hospital had its quirks and faults, and also some unusual artwork. Barbara's bedroom on the first floor was once a classroom and had "a fresco painted free hand by the Paddon boys' tutor who once occupied the room—shows the evolution of shipping from a Viking ship to the *Queen Mary* or her equivalent—very interesting and well done." Barbara said when she woke early, she would "lie abed and gaze upon it."[3] The painting was by Cyril Redhead, who had been a fighter pilot in the First World War and came to Labrador because he "was bored with England and looking for adventure."[4] The Paddon boys were the four sons of a doctor and nurse who were longtime Mission staff. Dr. Harry Paddon came from England to Labrador in 1912; he met Canadian nurse Mina Gilchrist when they both worked at the hospital in Indian Harbour. They married in 1913, spent a winter in Mud Lake and summer in Indian Harbour, and, in 1915, established a cottage hospital in North West River. He worked in Labrador until his death in 1939 and was a revered figure, perhaps even more than Grenfell, for Paddon lived and worked there all year long.[5] He knew every family and probably also their dogs, according to how often he borrowed them to make up a team. Paddon visited outlying settlements by boat in summer and had his regular winter routine, travelling by dog team to bring medical care, often leaving food and clothing behind. After his death, Mina Paddon continued on in charge of the hospital, with no resident doctor during the war years. Only one of the Paddon boys was in Labrador in 1944.

Harry Jr. and his English wife lived at Saltwater Pond near North West River. John was in boarding school in the United States. Richard (Dick) and Anthony (Tony) were both in the Royal Canadian Navy.

As a Mission staff member, Barbara, along with the teachers, nurses, and doctors had special status in the community.[6] It always took a while for "outsiders," whether they were English, Canadian, American, or Newfoundlander, to be accepted by the local people, and in some cases, they never were. Staff worked and lived together and, for the most part, socialized together. While no policy prohibited fraternizing with the locals, it was not encouraged. Every volunteer was given a copy of the pamphlet *Instructions and Information for Staff Members*, a code of conduct and rules that they had to sign. It provided guidance on relations with local people, pointing out some of the cultural similarities and differences, and also suggestions for clothing needed, travel arrangements, and personal funds. They were advised: "remember that the people among whom you will work are white, of British extraction and English-speaking" with different customs and speech, "but they are of the same stock as ourselves," although very conservative due to "living in isolated places far from the changing fashions of the world." Wops were warned not to talk about the people: "they are very sensitive to comment or criticism." Female staff were advised not to smoke or drink alcoholic liquors, and to go to church.[7]

The instructions may have been some help for the majority of volunteers who were assigned to stations in Newfoundland, or the south coast of Labrador, where the fishermen and their families were English, French, and Irish descendants. It did not accurately describe the people of central Labrador; the settler families descended from Scottish, French, and English men and Inuit women. Barbara hadn't figured out exactly how everyone was related, but she was on the right track when she noticed how mixed up it was: "all these people look so much alike and are so related—I can't tell them apart. Almost all have a mixture of every kind of blood and I'll be darned if I can tell who is Eskimo, Indian, or a portion of one or both. Wish me well, please."[8]

One person on staff would become Barbara's close friend: "Florence Goudie is a local girl and the nurse here now. She is fat and jolly and related to almost the whole town."[9] Barbara came to know everyone in Florence's large extended family. Florence was one of the younger of 13 children and had been partly raised by the Mission, as both her parents had died by the time she was nine. From then on, she lived in the dormitory when school was in session and "was put out to someone else for the summer." Dr. Paddon arranged for her to go to St. Anthony for high school and he and Mina Paddon helped her apply to nursing school and raised the money to pay for it. She worked as a ward aide in the North West River hospital while waiting to be accepted, assisting the doctor with operations and helping to deliver babies. Working with Dr. Paddon, Florence received a good deal of practical nursing instruction and experience before she went for formal training in St. Catherine's, Ontario. It was agreed that she would work for the Mission for two years in exchange for its paying for her training. She came home to North West River after graduation in 1943, when Mina Paddon wrote to say she needed nurses. Florence earned $300 a year for "duty all the time, around the clock."[10]

With Florence and Florence's friends and family, Barbara would go everywhere and meet everyone, including the intriguing people who lived in canvas tents across the river. In summer, the Innu people camped at North West River, but on the riverbank opposite the community. They came for the store, to trade furs, and to meet the Roman Catholic priest who came from Newfoundland to minister to them. All winter they moved through the country in family groups, following the caribou herds. She had seen them around the Hudson's Bay store and met some who came into the Industrial Shop, and was eager to make a visit to their side of the river, a short distance away but tricky to get across.

Last night Florence (nurse) and I went over to see the Indians—gosh are they filthy! In their tents where men, women, children, food, dogs, & everything else sleep & eat on top of each other—they had such modern things as alarm clocks & sewing machines. Just looking at them made you itch! In time I hope to navigate the river, the current is very strong in the center & you have to row way up and then cut across while drifting and hope to hit the other side at the point you wish! Quite a job! (Letter: June 11, 1944)

Barbara was somewhat daunted by what was expected of her in the shop and had received her first inkling of the poor relations between the Industrial Department and the rest of the IGA. Katherine (Kitty) Keddie, the Industrial's manager for Labrador, was in North West River from her base in Cartwright to meet Barbara and acquaint her with her new responsibilities.

I'm glad Mrs. K has been here for there's so much to learn about records, workers, books, etc. but in a way it will be easier when she's gone— some aspects of being alone terrify me—how to talk to Indians & buy from them, etc. but Annie [Wolfrey], the girl who helps, knows far more about most of it than I will <u>ever</u> know. Mrs. K knows it all so cold and <u>is</u> a "business woman" and has more energy than 10 others! I couldn't go at her pace & I thot I had energy. I certainly haven't since I arrived! (Letter: June 11, 1944)

Mrs. Keddie, as she was usually called, was a widow of 57 whose husband had died in an influenza epidemic six months after they married. She had grown up in the north, the daughter of James A. Wilson, HBC Chief Factor, and had been with the Mission since 1930.[11] Steeped in the Mission's internal politics, she warned Barbara to be alert to any encroachment of the Industrial Department's territory, which she fully expected to happen.

Gosh—the petty difficulties that exist between the Indust. and the rest of the Mission—I am told this is my affair—I am not to ask or take advice from anyone—no matter who! If I want anything I am to write K, and <u>no one</u> is to put their finger in my pie—that can [be] helpful—but also has a bad side to it—or could at times. The whole job—as a matter of fact—appalls me. It is certainly a FULL time one, and the selling end is a small matter and doesn't bother me for I've had plenty of experience with that. But the rest—cutting, designing, choosing colors, amounts of material to give out, passing on goods that come in, paying for skins (how do I know how much they are worth?), trying to understand the Indians and make them understand me—and their children are almost as bad for they are so shy and mumble into their coats. At moments I feel positively dull-witted, and wonder how on earth I will ever do it. Then everything that goes out must be entered here, there and everywhere, everything coming *in also, marked, cost prices to figure out, selling prices, etc. etc. I suppose in time I will get it, but I sure have my doubts—And when half a dozen things happen at once I feel like a Grade A Moron. Fortunately—oh, how fortunately, I have a grand little girl as assistant—a local girl who sews well and knows most of the ropes, so I can call for help when needed.* (Letter: June 2, 1944)

Kitty Keddie guided Barbara around, taking in the scenic points, and no doubt giving her the lowdown on the community, the Mission, and the Industrial Shop.

Yesterday Mrs. K and I walked up Sunday Hill and saw the sunset— what a view looking up Little Lake to the Rapids and beyond to Grand Lake with the Mts. behind, and then in the other direction over the Bay and to the Mealies. Grand Lake was still packed solid with ice and there was a fine mist hanging low over it. And Jo—I wish you were here to tell me what all the lichens, mosses, etc. were. Lots of Reindeer, and British soldiers, and fairy cups, plus others I don't know. It's heaven to walk on, just like a feather bed. I doubt if there will be much time to walk on it tho' for somehow or other we have got to keep the store filled and apparently almost every boatload wipes us out!! That means much preparation of work to be given out. (Letter: June 2, 1944)

The boatloads of shoppers would have been airmen and officers from the base at Goose Bay. The "work to be given out" that required preparation by Barbara and the other store staff referred to sealskin and duffle cloth they would cut according to patterns and distribute to the sewers to finish. She and her helper sewed some Grenfell cloth items that women would take home to embroider.[12]

Yesterday I cut sealskin all day—the day before duffle—the day before I made eight bridge table covers—made of Grenfell cloth bound in contrasting color and with embroidered corners—the corners are done by local girls & we make up the covers. The sewing machine is a hand driven one & guiding with one hand is not as hard as I feared 'twould be! (Letter: June 11, 1944)

The handicrafts produced in Labrador were different from those she had seen at the shop in St. Anthony. Her old acquaintance from her summer in St. Anthony, artist and designer Rhoda Dawson, pinpointed the specific types of crafts by materials used and geographic origin in an article for the *Among the Deep-Sea Fishers*:

> We find knitting and mats confined to the north of Newfoundland, and the Labrador from the Battle Harbour district to the extreme west in Canada [Harrington Harbour, Quebec]; and wooden toys, boats, etc., and birch brooms belong to these districts. Tanned skin boots come from the Newfoundland side of the Straits of Belle Isle only. Embroidered deer-skin work, tanned or white, mitts, moccasins, and bags, and grass baskets come from Cartwright and Hamilton Inlet; and painted deer-skin from beyond Nain. Sealskin work, carved ivory (Eskimo), soapstone and birchwood, black skin boots, Eskimo models, and more baskets are sent from Rigolet northwards.[13]

North West River was one place where all three traditions merged. The women made boots for their families from sealskin and moose hide. They used deerskin (caribou) to make moccasins and mitts. Warm duffle, the woven wool fabric as heavy as blankets, was made into slippers, mitts, and lining for parkas and skin boots.

The work produced here is fun to work on—colorful and daintier than some—no weaving or knitting—mostly duffle and Grenfell cloth work with embroidery—also skin work. Later we will have Indian basketry from the North and the regular knitted goods, weaving and ivory work from St. A. and Cartwright. Thank heaven most of our customers are men—they come in such droves, and paw enough as it is not knowing what to buy— but can you imagine a bunch of females trying to make up their minds— Mrs. Keddie says it's hell when the few women who are around come in!! (Letter: June 2, 1944)

While she admired the sewn items made by the North West River women, Barbara was not impressed with the quality of some needlework sent to the shop, and neither was her assistant: "Annie's remark was that Mrs. K must have sent us some of the things she couldn't sell." They couldn't keep knitting bags in stock. The bags were made of Grenfell cloth, with an embroidered design and the word "LABRADOR" stitched across the side. Barbara found them "so touristy" with "Labrador splashed all over." She had a request from one of the men at the base for six and she was tempted to refuse the order: "told him I could not fill that number, then the atrocities came in from C. [Cartwright] and I was tempted to pawn off the worst on him—but my conscience got the best of me, and I remembered that he had presented me with a tin of lobster and I couldn't do it."[14]

The shop was busy and some of the best customers for sewing materials and supplies were the Innu women from across the river. They were great sewers, who made much of the clothing for their families; they carried their precious, heavy sewing machines everywhere with them, loaded into canoes with the rest of their possessions when they would head out into the country in the fall.

The Indians and I are getting along fine—in fact, I am getting quite pally with one or two and we have a wonderful time outfitting the families— the one I like best seems to set the style, what she buys the others all do in due time. First we had a run on hideous cretonne, which I have seen since as: shirts, pillow covers, trunk covers and bags. Then bandannas, then baby clothes—one young couple was in yesterday getting prepared for their first and between us all with many suggestions from others—all jabbering Indian at a great rate—we got a very cute outfit together. (Letter: June 29, 1944)

When the ice cleared from the bay, Barbara had an opportunity to visit another settlement. In a letter to her family, she described a trip to Kenemich, on the opposite shore of Lake Melville. She was also invited to go canoeing with Florence and her "devoted beau," Cyril Michelin, and to check seal nets with Florence's brother, Harvey Goudie.

This past week I've been very lucky as far as boat rides are concerned. One Sunday I was asked to go down the Bay as far as Green Is.—for those of you who know where that is, and last Sunday the Henry Blakes took several of us to Kenemish—that is where old Malcolm MacLean [McLean] settled and at present his widow and her four sons (his second family) have houses there. All the children have bright blue eyes—something not seen here—and they all looked healthy and intelligent. The houses were clean and scrubbed. *There are only the four houses in the place; and old Mrs. MacL. insisted we have tea in spite of the fact they had had* <u>nothing but tea and bread for days</u>, *she even had to borrow a bit of butter. Even the fishing had been nil, and other supplies were used up. Henry Blake is one of Sid's brothers. (As I think I have told you everyone eyes my "spy-glasses" with a covetous eye, and want to know if I'd sell them—Sid said he'd make me a seal coat if I would!!) Florence (nurse, and a local gal) has a most devoted beau—Cyril Michelin—who is extremely nice, and one of the better ones around here—an excellent trapper, hard worker and even working at the base doesn't seem to have hurt him yet. He has wangled all these boat rides so far, and Florence has always asked me to go along—very nice for me! Cyril also took three of us canoeing one evening up Little Lake—it was a beautiful night—clear, cool, and calm—frogs chirping, thrushes singing and a brilliant sunset. Cyril has gone back to the base now, BUT he has loaned us his canoe for the summer; that delights my soul for I can think of nothing nicer than spending the evenings in a canoe and there are lots of little brooks to explore.* (Letter: June 29, 1944)

Cyril Michelin, a quietly competent man who included her in many outings, would become an important person in Barbara's life in North West River. He was born at Traverspine River and lived there until his family moved to North West River when he was young. He went trapping for the first time with an uncle, Philemon (called Pleman) Blake, at 14. He had worked for the HBC, delivering mail and supplies by dog team, and also for the Mission before becoming a full-time trapper and salmon fisherman. He was devoted to Florence. They didn't see each other for three years while she was at nursing school and would have exchanged letters only a few times a year.[15]

Some important visitors were coming later in the summer, so the Industrial Shop got a coat of paint outside—"we look quite handsome"—while inside Barbara and assistant Annie Wolfrey "had a regular housecleaning," then spent an evening painting a chair and a chest. Barbara found an old pair of caribou antlers and hung them on the wall, "hoping that some silly person will buy them and go home saying he shot the caribou they belonged to."[16] She enjoyed the way Annie "comes out with the most wonderful expressions and ways of describing things."[17]

Barbara said Annie worked very hard, despite having been ill and in hospital most of the previous winter with tuberculosis. Hardly a family in the bay had been untouched by the disease.

Peggy [Knight] Paddon was a central character in Barbara's letters that summer. She was staying at the hospital, "infanticipating" the birth of her first child. Peggy and Harry lived down the bay, and Peggy would stay in North West River only until the baby came.

I'm going to miss Peggy P when she leaves—she is really grand fun and even about to have a baby any minute doesn't cramp her style much. She was a housemother here for four years before she married Harry, and did all the things I enjoy doing and am looking forward to doing. Not stuffy like the Nfld. teachers none of whom have been to a dance or gone sealing or hunting or anything with anybody in all the years they have been here. Gosh—that is half the fun, methinks. Unfortunately, the duck hunting was over only a few days after I came so I missed out on that for no one had discovered that I would have liked to have gone. Peggy did all those things and says you get anywhere you like if you show an interest and take plenty of "grub"; hospital staff are particularly popular because of the quality of said grub—one thing in my favor! (Letter: June 29, 1944)

Barbara had been advised by Peggy to take advantage of whatever chances she had for outings, and by Kitty Keddie to make a friend of Jack Watts.

I just typed the seed order for the next year for Jack—in my next life— if I live to have one—I am not going to know anything about anything—or if I do I'm not going to let anyone know it. When I arrived Mrs. K said if Jack is on your side all will be well—so far he is. Gosh—it is amusing—how the rest of the staff hate the Industrial and all that goes with it—Jack says it pays "our salaries" so he is for it. I hear both ends of it—first one side and then the other. (Letter: June 29, 1944)

The D-Day Allied invasion of France happened on June 6 but not much news sifted down to North West River. Barbara thanked her mother for newspapers she had sent about the invasion and mentioned that the Mission's radio "doesn't work most of the time—so we know hardly anything of what is going on." While the war was the only story in the outside world, the biggest event in the whole bay would have been the annual spring fair to raise money for the Mission. People gathered from all the other communities for a chance to see everyone after a hard winter. It had to be held on a perfect day, as activities would be outdoors.

The day of the Fair dawned dull and drear, so it was put off for the day—all preparations had been made so we had nothing to do but gripe. At the end of the day, I put on my rubber boots, slicker and so'wester and trugged down the portage to the Paddon's house to get some apricot brandy to cheer us up in the evening—it did. The next day was better and we radioed up to the base that we would have it. Several boats had gone up to get people and the others came down too—100 people in all from there. Many local people—all in fact—and others from around the bay. The women all dolled up, the children clean and the men so scrubbed and shaven you could hardly recognize some of them. There was shooting, bean bags, the sale itself—everyone standing about an hour before the sale was opened with their hands clutching the things they wanted! Many things were auctioned off, from komatiks, sweaters, snowshoes, Steve Hamilton's pictures,[18] etc. Lots of other things sold on tickets—in all we cleared about $1700—and most of this from local people—the I.D. [Industrial Department] did a sale afterwards of about $200. We had a half-holiday, but I opened up for a short time before supper.

Money was certainly spent wildly that day—have you ever heard of a basket supper? I hadn't before, and when suggested I have a basket too I said sure—made a hit with Florence and Bella [McLean], another local girl who is one of the housemothers now, because [Miriam] Hiscock, the single teacher and the others [who worked there] before they were married never would have baskets or go to dances, etc. and the local people rather felt it. Anyway, the idea is this: the single girls make baskets—with crepe paper, etc. and supper is in them—unless you [are] on the staff and then we provide it. Said baskets are auctioned off to the highest bidder, and he gets the girl and supper. The average price paid was $15—that is what mine went for—but some went as high as $20. Afterwards those who had baskets helped wash the dishes, and there were plenty as we fed about 200 people in all. The Canadian Army provided the bread—about 40 loaves, the McNamara Co. three Roasts, the RCAF 1000 cones and the Americans 20 gallons of ice cream. After supper the men "kicked" football and then *the dance. I'll continue tomorrow, as it is now almost eleven, and I guess I better go home and switch off the lights.* (Letter: June 29, 1944)

The donated ice cream caused a sensation. Twenty gallons gone "in no time." They saved enough cones to have one each, although "some of the children bought two at a time, gobbled them as fast as possible and were back for more." She and Peggy were doing the scooping and their backs and wrists were aching from the effort. As always, after the day's events, the adults danced until early morning.

It was one of the best dances for a long time they said for so many of the older men were there—Jack turned up in the hall, and Annie asked if someone were ill! He even danced—the first time since his wedding—and had a marvelous time—he practically swung me off my feet every time we passed each other. When the rest of the staff heard he was there they were furious they had not gone just to see the show! He says it will take another good Fair to get him there—we think he went to stay awake as he was taking the local boys back to the base at 3 A.M. (Letter: June 29, 1944)

Barbara wrote long letters to her mother and sister, full of lively and humorous descriptions of new experiences and friends. Her typed letters to "Everybody," her best wop pals, usually had the same stories, but sometimes with personal notes handwritten at the end. In the June epistle, there was one reference to how she thought her mother might react to her new life and language.

Tonight we are going down to the tilt for supper, and the proud canoe owners I believe will paddle with the "grub"—I can hear Mother shudder at that word!!!! (Letter: June 29, 1944)

Barbara couldn't resist relating anecdotes of Mission life but knew she should be careful when mentioning staff. On July 15, she included a caution, after making a reference to Maria Stryker, the Director of Needlework Guild Juniors, who since 1925 had been amassing legions of toy dolls and animals donated by American children for the girls and boys in Labrador, "who had never seen dolls, except the little wooden faces carved by their fathers and wrapped in a bit of blanket." Miss Stryker asked that the dolls be made of "rag" material to "endure in the extreme climate of the North."[19]

First of all, the weather has been horribly hot these past few weeks, and the grass is burned brown—the first time he has ever seen it so, says Jack. Can just hear Stryker and her tales of the Kiddies of the Great Frozen North!—but it sounds good and so I won't disillusion her—might hurt the doll business. Incidentally, you gals who are reading my letters to others— for heaven sakes use your bean and censor when necessary—don't forget the underground in the IGA is pretty good and some comments of mine might not go over so well should they find their way back!! (Letter: July 15, 1944)

Some households in the community had a shortage of food. Not much salmon was being caught yet and everyone was anxiously awaiting the arrival of the *Kyle* from Newfoundland, the first supply ship of the year. No such food shortages existed on the base and amongst Barbara's military contacts. She celebrated turning 34 on July 1 with "an excellent birthday supper on board the crash boat" and a dance on the Canadian side of the air base. She could not say it in letters, but in her diary she noted that the place was "underground packed with men and planes," de Havilland Mosquitos used for reconnaissance and bombing, Douglas A-20 light bombers, Martin B-26 Marauder medium bombers, North American B-25 Mitchell medium bombers, and Canadian-made Norseman bush planes. The constant overhead drone of planes was heard not only at the base but all over Lake Melville.

A juicy bit of Mission news was the arrival of another wop, 19-year-old Priscilla Randolph (Randy) Toland from Pennsylvania. Randy's arrival caused a stir in Goose Bay. Randy remembered an airman saying "Jesus Christ!" as she climbed down a ladder to the tarmac because he was surprised and happy to see a woman.[20]

Randy is 19, very pretty in a way, does and says the most unexpected things, and is apt to be found anywhere—on top of the windcharger one day. Her language at times is appalling—even to me, and I don't think I'm easily shocked. She is really quite fun and certainly livens this spot up. She is also fine for business—all I have to do is tell her that some really lovely thing has come in and she buys it immediately—never saw a girl spend money so freely—we had a beautiful pair of deerskin mitts that I would have loved to have had, but I thot they were a bit too high—she never asked the price and she had already spent an awful lot. (Letter: July 15, 1944)

Randy Toland had grown up on a 550-acre farm in Westchester, Pennsylvania. She was from a well-to-do family and had "come out" in society, but far from being a prim debutante she was a tomboy who was used to horseplay and she loved to dance. One of her brothers had been a Grenfell wop before her. She brought life to the Mission group that summer and worked in the gardens, the clothing store, and the hospital. Barbara got a great kick out of her younger friend.

The first night Randy went to a dance here the stove collapsed among other amusing things—and she will never live that down. She is the most energetic thing—Mrs. P says before long she expects the men to ask for overtime pay for dancing with her! (Letter: July 29, 1944)

The Industrial Shop had a reliable stream of customers in the crew and friends of the United States Army Air Force and RCAF "crash" boats, the high-speed rescue vessels stationed at Goose Bay.[21] They could make a trip from their base at Otter Creek to North West River in a little over an hour and frequently found some reason for doing so. If a routine patrol took the crew out in the bay, it was no trouble to stop by the community for a quick visit, which usually meant they would come to the shop. Barbara was glad to sell them things but she was trying to save a unique carving from St. Anthony for some very important visitors coming later in the summer. Getting to know the crash-boat crews had advantages, even if the men were demanding and disruptive, bursting in at inconvenient moments. A word to one of their crash-boat friends brought a special delivery, ignoring Mission instructions on alcoholic beverages, a big surprise to Bob Gillard, the HBC factor.[22]

The crash left us some beer and I wish you could have seen Bob Gillard's eyes pop when we offered it to him in the evening—I think it was the first that has crossed the threshold of the hospital—all because Harry & I decided we wanted some and dropped a gently put hint to the right person!! (Letter: July 19, 1944)

Being friendly with the military men had further benefits, as she found out one day in July. The new Commanding Officer for the RCAF, Group Captain Albert Hanchet-Taylor, flew in on a Norseman and made an offer that couldn't be refused. Would she and Mrs. Paddon like to fly over Grand Falls in about 30 minutes? She fled the store, leaving Jack

Watts in charge, and jumped aboard the Norseman. Sadly, the weather turned to rain and the flight as far as the falls was cancelled, but Barbara had a turn at the controls on the way home.

Barbara hoped she would have another chance to fly over the famous Grand Falls. Flights to the base and, she hoped, even farther afield, were an unexpected perquisite of her work in the Industrial Shop and her good relations with military customers, one of whom came up with a nickname for her.

Next time I write I hope to be able to describe the Falls—but maybe I will have to have a little more patience. If I see that plane coming nothing on heaven or earth will prevent my getting off in it—even if I just walk out and close the door in the face of ninety prospective customers—the "mercenary" (named by the staff because they LOVE the industrial so) "missionary" (named by a tight COL. who thot he needed to be Christianized)—will just forget the fact that we are about to make a record in sales for this month. (Letter: July 15, 1944)

Barbara and the other single women working for the Mission became good friends that summer with two American pilots, whose first aerial survey of North West River caused quite a fuss. It all began when she was out for a walk "down the Bight" and "almost had [her] head chopped off by a tiny plane which buzzed [her] for almost a half hour"; the pilot dropped notes telling them to "Keep kids off runway," meaning the beach. The note thrower, always called "Swede," was never fully identified, and Barbara complained several times about his difficult surname.[23] It may have been because she knew it would be censored, but she didn't explain what assignment Swede and his friend George (Brownie) Brown had at the base in Goose Bay, or how they had constant access to an airplane, but they became frequent visitors to North West River after the small plane finally "pitched" the first time. Nearly every day, Swede and Brownie would buzz over the community and every other evening they would land, sometimes bringing the women to Goose Bay for a party, since it was possible to "beetle up in 15 mins. to the dance."[24] Just a few years earlier, like everyone else in the world, Barbara was in awe of the men and women who were the first to fly across oceans, saving clippings from newspapers about their exploits.

Now she was hitching rides with her pilot pals on a moment's notice.

Barbara was canoeing frequently, reading Merrick's *True North*, and comparing the book to stories from trappers like Sid Blake.

Sid made me wild telling of the trip up the River in the fall when they go trapping—says I should get John Michelin to bring me down by canoe from the Falls—gosh, how I would love to. John is about the best guide here—was the one who took Austy and Bud I think. (Letter: July 19, 1944)

One evening she went for a walk on the beach and found a crowd of men engaged in a big job moving a house, helped along by Jack Watts leading them in a Newfoundland song, always sung when anything heavy had to be hauled.

The men are moving a house tonight—lots of fun to watch—even the Indians came over for the fun—Jack singing "and it's to my Johnny Poker" at the top of his lungs—Once the rope broke and they all went in a heap. I wonder if there is anything in the world these men can't do or haven't tried to do! (Letter: July 19, 1944)

Barbara's letters often mentioned hauling and carrying things, a constant occupation when all goods for the Industrial Shop, hospital, and store arrived at the wharf, but plenty of willing help was available when needed.

After this load of raw materials I think I should have a recommendation as a stevedore—when things got too heavy I'd stick my head out the door and hordes of little boys came bustling to help—that is one thing about this place: I never lack children to help do ANYTHING no matter what. It is wonderful and in the evenings when we want our canoe hauled up or taken down Bella calls "Hey boys, come carry our canoe" and whoever is about comes along—quite a system. (Letter: July 19, 1944)

The Innu were a constant presence in the summer months and one old woman was known to all. Peenamin (also spelled Pename, Penamie, and Penamee) McKenzie braved North West River, wrapped in her shawl and smoking her pipe, going into the hospital and homes to ask for things she wanted, expected to be given, and usually received. She had success in most places, but not on this day with Barbara.

Penamie—the old Indian beggar who is called by other names not fit to print—has just been in again—this time asking for scissors and pointing to her crooked finger—what connection there is I do not know—I finally asked her if she wanted to cut it off, which caused her to laugh so heartily she almost lost her one remaining tooth! She also wants clothes to impress the priest with, but there is no use giving her anything for she will only give it to someone else and return the next day in worse rags. (Letter: July 29, 1944)

Peenamin McKenzie would return in worse rags because she distributed whatever she was given to people who needed things on her side of the river. Harry Paddon Jr. recalled Peenamin had developed an understanding with his mother, Mina, often dropping in for tea, a snack, and a session of either trading or begging. Once she arrived with a small bearskin and left with a bundle including dishes, cutlery, and clothing. Paddon figured Peenamin performed a useful function to her people, who shared what they had, and believed "those who had plenty should need only a gentle reminder that now would be an appropriate time to share that plenty with a less fortunate neighbour."[25]

The *Kyle* finally arrived on July 29. Barbara was invited to have tea on board with Captain Thomas Connors,[26] "which of course was supper, and [she] almost fainted when given a choice of steak or cold roast beef."[27] It was a treat to dine with the captain of the *Kyle*, as food in the store was "too expensive for most to buy." The menu at the hospital was limited as gardens had been planted only a month earlier and, still, not many salmon had shown up.

The shop had been cleaned and painted and a few special ivory pieces set aside for the eagerly anticipated visit of some extremely important people, not a mere commanding officer this time, but royalty. The distinguished guests arrived a day late, and unannounced, on the RCAF crash boat on Thursday, August 3. Everyone was eating lunch when "just before dessert Canso began flying over—[they] went out, Jack racing down path—[they] all leapt to change," and then they were at the wharf welcoming Canada's Governor General, his wife, and their party of attendants and military escorts.[28]

They were the Governor General of Canada and his wife, Princess Alice [granddaughter of Queen Victoria]. The G.G. is the Earl of Athlone, bro to Queen Mary [uncle of King George VI]. They came down just after lunch and stayed to tea. We certainly enjoyed their visit and we hope they did too. They seemed to anyway. And Mrs. P said she enjoyed showing them around more than most people for they showed a real interest and asked intelligent questions. HRH bought quite a few things—we had saved our best for her—and the thing that pleased me most was that she bought a dickie I had designed especially for Annie—flowers done in silk right on the hood. Annie did not like it as well as she thot—I had it done in various shades of bleu (don't mind the French) and green-sprays of forgetmenots— and she wanted red to brighten it up—so I did another for her and we put this out for sale. It really was a lovely thing. (Letter: August 9, 1944)

Another important event that day was the birth of Harry and Peggy Paddon's daughter, Margaret, who arrived in time to be introduced to the royal guests; "at less than 12 hours old she was dressed up in a cunning little dress to receive her visitors."[29]

Barbara's work in the shop was going extremely well, thanks partly to the royal visit. "Princess A. bought $71.35 worth including Annie's dickie, deerskin mitts & jacket to which we must match a hood!" Barbara would later exchange letters with Vera Grenfell, coincidentally a cousin of Sir Wilfred's, lady-in-waiting to Princess Alice, requesting payment for the matching hood. Miss Grenfell replied that the hood arrived in Ottawa safely but the bill must have been mislaid: "Her Royal Highness also does not remember having it." Barbara sent the bill again and a cheque for $3 was sent in April 1945 from Her Royal Highness. Barbara's abilities in account keeping were coming in handy after all. She bragged that July sales in the shop were "the best yet for any month— over $2000" but stressed this was "NOT TO BE REPEATED."[30]

Barbara probably expected her life would be very peaceful, and usually it was, but even when it was quiet, it was never boring. It was all quite to her liking—satisfying work, good companions, and pleasant surroundings—and in the autumn she decided to stay longer. She sent her passport to be extended: "have decided to stay 'till February. Hope I'm right in doing so—wish I knew what comes next."[31] The respite from New York may have started as an escape plan but after just a few months she was comfortable, always busy, and involved in the small community.

Her decision followed some sobering events that quarantined North West River from late August until September 17. A young boy,

Pat Rich, was admitted to hospital with diphtheria. Barbara's diary entry noted that she relieved Florence on Friday night, sat with the boy, and it was "very sad. He was so sweet. MD came at midnight & Pat died at 6:45. Diphtheria—nice mess!"[32] The next day they started inoculating everyone and no boats or planes were allowed to land from the base. They were fully occupied with the effort to control the spread of disease.

Sat: Over 100 given toxoid, those thoroughly exposed got anti-toxin too. Randy, Bella & I went up Grand Lake berry picking while men got "sticks" for slip for Loon *[IGA motorboat].*

Sun: I was asked to make cover of flowers for coffin—Randy helped— looked nice & Mary was pleased. Funeral simple & lovely—little boys brought flowers, Annie's wreath of pansies, dog sitting by grave. New baby baptized. Clayton Montague came in with lighter case [of diphtheria]. Did laundry.

Mon A.M.: Decided no work should come or go as we are completely isolated—no boats in or out—should see them run! Took names as about 70 children got anti-toxin, including myself. I got it in small doses. A case at Mud Lake landed in hospital much to their disgust. Brought all anti-toxin at base from all sides, ran out here—have sent for 5 million more units!!! (Diary: August 26-28, 1944)

Fortunately, no more serious cases occurred and no more deaths, but for over two weeks North West River was cut off from Goose Bay. On September 2, Barbara wrote in her diary that they were "all a bit edgy," although they got their mail and other goodies, including beer, when Jack Watts went to the base with the Mission boat and then had "all crew of the crash boat running errands." Their crash-boat friends must have felt sorry for the quarantined Mission workers. Barbara wrote, "Really amusing—what a haul—anything they had they sent."[33] She was outdoors as much as possible, picking berries and mushrooms, and canoeing. On September 11, she "canoed to Bottle Pt. with Flo, Bella, & Randy for fine picnic on beach—wonderful fire, paddled home by northern lights. Best fun since [she'd] been here."[34]

The women were excited about a trip they planned to make two days later. Barbara, Randy, and Bella, who was housemother in the dormitory, took a few days off work to accompany the Grand River and

"Height of Land" trappers as far as Muskrat Falls, the first big portage of the journey up the Grand River. It was a major expedition, starting out in a motorboat loaded full and towing some canoes, and "men quite gay on foul smelling home brew." They had good weather and "the best group of men" to go with.[35]

We started off about 9 A.M.—the three of us, six rivermen, six canoes, five dogs and all supplies for their four month's stay in the country. There were: Harvey and Victor Goudie (F's brothers), Ira Best, Francis Thevenet, Fred Goudie and his son Ernest. It was blowing some, so the Loon took some of the stuff as far as Rabbit Is. where we all transferred to the Squid—a small open boat. Everything was piled on top of everything else; three canoes on board, three being towed. We left the wharf with guns being fired by everyone—on the boat, and on the shore. One of the HBC clerks [Noel Groves] knocked himself right over as his gun went off. The firing continued until we were beyond the point, and then every boat we passed it started again, and always there was a reply. Just like the book "True North"; Bud was accurate in that one.

We did not know it when we started but it turned into quite a "cruise." First we stopped at Mud Lake for some traps and boots for Ern; then Traverspine for a sled for Francis. There we went ashore and visited with Rob [Michelin] and "Aunt Mathilda" (who gave up swearing for a while because it was "no damn good"). Then across to Henry's Pt. to pick up candles for another—by that time it was too late for us to get to the Falls that night so we camped about 4 miles or so beyond that.

Camping in "the wilds of Labrador" was what you might expect if you kept from looking in one direction where you could see range lights. The tents were up in no time—we had one of the men's for until they get to their own ground and separate they double up at night to save putting up so many tents, so there were three extra. In about five minutes—or so it seemed—the brush was down (balsam) the camp stove lighted and the kettle on—as cozy as could be. We had a fire on the beach and a boiled dinner then sat around for a bit hearing tales of ghosts, etc. that the men encountered and their troubles with the Indians—Uncle Fred had had times with them when they tried to starve him out. It was fascinating listening to them. (Letter: October 8, 1944)

The next morning, after beating out a fire on the edge of Randy's borrowed sleeping bag, it was on to Muskrat Falls. The entire expedition was still being towed by the motorboat and arrived below the falls at about 10 a.m. This portage wasn't the worst on the river, but they had a lot of provisions to carry up and over. In 1935, Dr. Harry Paddon watched trappers do the same portage and said the "usual load carried over at one time is three forty-nine-pound bags of flour or a corresponding load of other equipment." It was, no doubt, gruelling labour: "Some would-be champions even crack on a fourth bag of flour."[36] Barbara was impressed and carried a few loads herself.

It was not tough as they go—but being their first it was not so good for it takes time each year to get in condition. This one is straight up hill for about a half mile and then a level space and straight down again. I never in my life saw men work so hard carrying all their stuff up. They would get it all at the top and then start the trip down. Each one had four or six trips and then the canoe. Each time the load was heavy—nothing to take two bags of flour, a knapsack, gun, and any other heavy thing or two they could discover. We all helped—my heaviest load was: 22 pounds of pork and a few odd cooking gear on my back, a gun and snowshoes in one hand, and a grub bag in the other—that was quite enough for me and about 1 tenth of what they would fling on to themselves and dash off with. It was not a hot day, but they were dripping as they reached the top.

It was very interesting to see it all—Bella said she wished in a way she had not gone for she thought it was awful for any man to work so hard; but I said I thought they loved it so it wasn't so bad. They do love it and all prefer it to any work the base could offer. It certainly is a wonderful kind of life if one is physically able to take it. These were the ones who go over the Big Hill—that means they all trap above Grand Falls—350 to 400 miles up. It takes them about a month to get to their trapping grounds and they are there—each man alone on his own ground—for about two months and then they meet again as they come out—on foot! (Letter: October 8, 1944)

The three women and the motorboat crew left the trappers on September 15 to return to North West River, and on September 24 they learned that Fred Goudie had drowned and his son Ernest had returned home. It was shocking that this had happened to an experienced riverman, the most senior of the group, and one of North West River's most beloved and respected trappers. Barbara wrote her friends about the last time she saw him.

That night [Sept. 14] we camped again with them on top of the hill where Indians had been only a few days before. Bella and I went in berrypicking in the afternoon—it reminded me of Maine—very sandy, desert-like in spots like the Desert of Maine. I went with Uncle Fred while he set his rabbit snares and then another evening of stories and cards and fun.

About six the next morning they were off again and we bid them farewell. Uncle Fred was the first to go and I wanted very much to go down and get his picture with his loaded canoe and beautiful huskie, but two of the men had to put us aboard our boat, as we had not had room to take along a small boat and I was afraid of holding things up too long, as we were to have been back the day before and the rivermen had a long day ahead of them. I am doubly sorry now—I had said I'd get his picture as he returned, but Uncle Fred will never return. He was drowned a week later in the Mininipi Rapid. That is one reason why I haven't written this letter before—it was such a tragic ending to such a good time—I hated to write about it. It was doubly sad for this was to have been his last year, and his family had tried to persuade him not to go. No one can understand it for he had been going up the river for 42 years ever since he was 16 and he was so very much more experienced and older than any of the others. Once years ago when he had been dumped in the same place he had turned around and shaken his fist at the river when he was hauled out and said, "You may have gotten me this time, but I'll be back and get the best of you yet."

When it happened Ern was alone with him—behind—and the others were around the point making camp. Ern had a new, heavy canoe and Fred had stayed behind to help him. They were tracking their canoes thru' the roughest water when Fred's stern shot out and apparently his tracking line caught him around the leg—in a flash he was in the middle of the river and that was the last Ern saw of him. His body has not been found— they are waiting for the last men to go up in hopes of having a service, but they have been gone a week now and no one has come back. Three others have been lost in the same place and none ever found. Uncle F's *canoe was swamped and of course, Ern lost his too. Two of the men went back with him until they found his canoe—and most of his stuff in it—at the foot of the rapid and then he came back alone—was weather bound and it was two nights before he reached the base and could send word down—fortunately Jack was up there and brought him home. He found his Father's canoe below and brought it back as far as the Falls. It has been a sad summer for NWR—Pat [Rich], the sweetest child almost here, and then Uncle Fred—as Harry said "there wasn't a finer man in the whole bay." I think the really hard time for his family will be when the others come back and he isn't with them—now it just seems unbelievable.* (Letter: October 8, 1944)*

Even with the sad outcome, Barbara wrote: "a wonderful trip and I felt just like the Merricks—I wanted to go on and see what is in that so little known land. It must be fascinating."

With the quarantine over, people were allowed to come and go again: "The teachers finally came and with them the new [Newfoundland] Ranger, wife and small baby—they had no furniture or anything, so we took them in until they could get their stuff up the bay."[37] Trappers continued to leave. The first Nascopie river trappers departed September 24 with "no fanfare at all," and another group left September 29.

Two crowds of men have gone off since the first—one load went minus one man [Murdock McLean] who was waiting for lard and ammunition—he intended to paddle after the others and catch up—they having started a day ahead and gone 70 miles by motor boat! (Letter: October 8, 1944)

Fewer letters were saved from the later months of 1944, perhaps because fewer were written. North West River was quiet, most of the men were away, and the frozen waterways prevented float-plane and crash-boat visitors. Randy Toland's duties had dwindled and she went back to Pennsylvania on October 28. Royal Air Force Lieutenant Lee White surprised everyone with his arrival home on leave after being gone for years. Everyone was delighted to see him and to hear about his adventures.

Lee White's trapper father died when he was young, leaving his mother to care for the family. His older brother, Gerald, went trapping at age 15 and the Mission helped by taking Lee into the dormitory. As a teenager, Lee had worked summers as a deckhand and second engineer on the Mission vessel *Maraval*. Jack Watts showed him how to operate the radio set, a "one-tube transmitter and receiver between North West River and St. Anthony," and taught him Morse code. In 1940, at 19, he went to St. John's to enlist in the RAF and was sent to Signals School in Montreal, receiving a Commission at the end of his training. Lieutenant White had served in northern Africa, Malta, and South Africa, "teaching the theory of aerial sighting." After four years without being home, he was granted leave, and arrived at Goose Bay only to be told there were no boats in the water and no way to get to North West River. On his second day, the RCAF crash boat was launched especially for him, and he had a "wonderful homecoming."[38]

Barbara's diary entries in late October mention a "spring-like day, snow gone," then the snow came again and it seemed that real winter struck with a blizzard lasting two days. Halloween was a good excuse for a party and dance, "good fun, music & step-dancing."[39] By mid-November, there had been several days of blizzards, dumping so much snow that it was drifted up over doors. People were telling her it was unusual: "Granny Blake says it's the most snow for this time she's seen in her 65 yrs."[40]

As one old man who's been here for years says: "I think the world is coming to an end—I've never seen the likes before." We have more snow now than is usual in winter—it's unprecedented and am I glad it's happening the winter I'm here! The smartest thing I ever did was buy those Indian snowshoes ($11) for it's impossible to get anywhere without them. I've found some skis in the attic & they'll do fine 'till I hear from Steve, but I think there'll be too much snow for much skiing. The river is full of slob ice & huge breakers in the bay blowing it in. We walk over fences & dig down to get in buildings—I shoveled our door out this A.M. with a dust-pan & started about 4" from the top! What fun if I fall off my snowshoes (I was blown over once) I sink in as far as I can go & don't hit bottom then. (Letter: November 12, 1944)

Barbara hunted for partridges and fished through the ice for trout. She spent a night with Harry and Peggy Paddon, eating "delish" porcupine and enjoying her first dog team ride. Lee White stayed at the hospital, and Barbara's diary often mentioned him and how they played bridge, skated, and danced. When he left by dog team on November 22 to return to duty, she wrote: "We'll miss him—he added much to hospital group—good fun and very nice to me. Hope we'll meet again."[41]

A broken dental inlay called for a trip to the base dentist. Barbara went with Ralph Blake and a team of five dogs: "took us 6 hrs, straight, no boil-up. Went thru' portage & across Bay. Met Bert Blake partway. Got there about 4, saw RAF girls—pleasant evening." They returned three days later, leaving Goose Bay at 4 a.m., arriving back in North West River at noon: "Loved the trip & want another soon."[42]

With Christmas coming, Barbara went off, "ax in hand & with snowshoes," searching for a suitable tree for the shop. On December 15 she hosted a tea party, the shop "fixed up very attractively" with "candles & nuts, candies from home," which was attended by "staff, girls, Mrs. Chaulk & Aunt Jessie."[43] She made an effort to celebrate the season but she knew Christmas would not be the happy occasion it ought to be. They were too busy in the hospital with women having babies and others seriously ill. One patient, Jane Groves, was slowly perishing.

Friday night the 15th Jane Groves seemed better than she had been in a long time, cheerful and talkative. We were sitting in front of the fire when Evelyn Michelin, the ward aide, came running down and we knew something awful had happened. Florence and Mrs. P went right up to find that Jane had suddenly woken with a most terrible hemorrhage—much too unpleasant to describe. For some strange reason she lived thru' it and lingered on, completely conscious most of the time until the following Thurs. The first and second nights F and Mrs. P stayed with her, after that we others took turns, I going on between 2:30 and 3 A.M. until 8. There was nothing we could do for her really, except make her as comfy as possible and hope she would die quickly without another bad time ... (Letter: December 31, 1944)

Barbara was sitting up with Jane on the night she died, Thursday, December 21, the darkest day of the year. She began a letter to her mother at 3:30 that morning. She explained how Florence had worn herself out working long days all week, three women were having babies—one a difficult birth with premature twins—Barbara was doing night shifts in the ward, and that night was her third. Dulcie Broomfield, the hospital cook, was sick and coughing, but it was Jane who worried them the most. Barbara was chilled to the bone, as Jane wanted the window kept open.

Guess it's your turn tonight—if my hands don't freeze! It's 20 below outside & almost that here in the dispensary for the windows are open in Jane's room. She is still here, far quieter tonight—I guess just from weakness—I wish she'd go—we can't give her morphine or anything as it excites her rather than putting her out. (You won't believe it but I can see my breath!) (Letter: December 21, 1944)

From *Northern Nurse*, Barbara knew that (Sarah) Jane (Oliver) Groves had first come to North West River as a young woman, after a summer working for the Mission at Indian Harbour. Jane arrived at the nursing station with her mother and two brothers from their home 12 miles away at Bluff Head, her mother bringing exquisite needlework to sell.[44] She cooked at Indian Harbour all summer and then accepted a job at the hospital in North West River. Jane was a main character in the book, singing to herself as she worked, getting up early to light the stove and prepare breakfast for nurse Kate Austen before she left on a winter's journey by dog team. Austen said Jane and another staff member, Pearlie, "were so good to [her] it made [her] almost embarrassed."[45] Austen had dubbed Jane "the Unattainable Female" for turning down three marriage proposals before finally accepting one from Russell Groves. Barbara knew her as one of the best sewers to bring her work to the shop.

Jane is slowly going into unconsciousness, I think—what a relief, and I've just fixed D [Dulcie] up & she's asleep & quiet. Florence is sleeping in my bed hoping to get out of sound as there's a baby in & a baby out due any moment! What a life. (Letter: December 21, 1944)

Jane died that afternoon, "a great blessing," said Barbara in her diary. Tuberculosis had claimed her and the year before her young daughter Betty (Elizabeth Martha Groves) had died of tuberculosis meningitis. The terrible news was sent to her husband, Russell, at the base in Goose Bay. He came to North West River as soon as he could to comfort their daughter, Phyllis, only five years old, staying with her grandparents while her mother was in hospital and her father worked.

She was buried the aft. of the school concert and no one had either the time or the energy to have the staff party and dance the next night—nor did it seem quite right to have it so soon when Jane had been part of the hospital for so long. (Letter: December 31, 1944)

Tuberculosis was a common, dreaded disease in Newfoundland and Labrador and the Mission doctors were used to it striking patients old and young. Until his death in 1939, Dr. Harry Paddon made fighting it a crusade, preaching about the hazards that spread the sickness. He hoped to prevent infection caused by the simplest of things: "deficient ventilation, the common water dipper passed from hand to hand and mouth to mouth, as well as other eating and drinking utensils recklessly shared by diseased and healthy alike—all these, added in many cases to poverty and defective diet and clothing, were enabling tuberculosis to reap a ghastly toll."[46] Paddon declared war on tuberculosis, and believed he had made some progress. In 1935 he said "there was not a known active case of TB within fifty miles of North West River."[47] Unfortunately, that would not be true for long. Perhaps things changed because of the moving and mingling of people when the base was under construction, fuelled by the primitive and crowded living conditions in the camps. Tuberculosis was a scourge in Labrador and Newfoundland until the mid to late 1940s, when treatment improved dramatically after the discovery of streptomycin, the first antibiotic effective against the disease.[48]

At least the births were happy news, but over the community there was a widespread atmosphere of mourning. It wasn't just the death of Jane Groves. Word came from Goose Bay that 15-year-old Tommy Blake had died, and then there was the discovery that Ewart Michelin had drowned. The circumstances of these deaths would have been difficult for New Yorkers to understand or even imagine.

Tommy Blake died of Tb. Meningitis—at the base—several weeks ago—and his family are just beginning to get over the colds they got taking him up and going up again. They left one night after getting an urgent call and it took them 'till nine the next morning, going all around the shore, among the willows, thru' open water—had to build a raft at one point. They had another terrible trip back and sent Lucky up for Tommy—he too had hard going. Ewart Michelin was drowned a few weeks ago and that has been frightfully hard for Harry and Peggy. It happened two weeks before anyone knew it, they at home thinking he was at Mulligan and they thinking he was home. He thot Harry was in his tent one beautiful moonlight night and he said to some one he was going to skate up with an extra pair of skates for Harry—he went thru' bad ice about a mile before he reached H's—actually Harry did not expect him and he wasn't there, he says he couldn't have heard him even if he had been there. After they became worried Harry went out to look for him and found his gun, snowshoes, etc. by one of his tilts and finally discovered the hole in the ice ... (Letter: December 31, 1944)

The three deaths and the funerals dampened Christmas spirits, worsened when the minister and his wife, "feeling half sick," did not have energy enough to decorate the church. Barbara took over training the children's choir and Florence played the organ. For their Christmas breakfast, Nellie the hen obliged, laying "just the correct number of eggs which [they] had been hoarding for that day, so [they] each had one." Barbara was pleased with presents of two pairs of deerskin slippers, one with old Innu beaded tongues.

A year earlier, Barbara had been on the verge of announcing her engagement, dressing for the opera, and shopping in Macy's for Christmas gifts. Now having an egg for breakfast or walking alone on snowshoes in a quiet forest were special treats. She assured her correspondents that she was where she ought to be. She cared about the people and the place, sharing in their sorrows and small pleasures. Life in New York—life in general—was taking on a different perspective.

Certainly the winter here far surpasses the summer in every way— and I am ever thankful I am here and not at St. A. for the people and the life here are far more interesting than there. I am very lucky in knowing the people here better—thanks to the job and Florence—I like them tremendously and I hope—and think—they like me.

Goodnight and Happy New Year to all—let's hope it is a happier one than '44 turned out to be. (Letter: December 31, 1944)

Chapter Nine

A REAL LIFE ... WITH JOY

*I wish the boys in our family could have a year up here—
they'd learn to be real men.*

—Letter to Mother, April 8, 1945

Barbara's first seven months in North West River ended on a bleak note. Three families were devastated by the loss of their loved ones, young people killed by disease or misfortune. Now it was bitter cold, snow was piled high over houses, and there was a shortage of kerosene. She might have been forgiven if she had expressed any reservations about being there, but she had none, and everyone's spirits were raised when the first trappers—those who trapped around Nascopie River—began arriving home.

The trappers are beginning to come home now and it is fun to look out at dusk and see three figures with sleds off in the distance and try to figure out who they can be. The Blake boys, the Montagues, Murdock [McLean] and his sons are back—also several others. Trapping has not been too good this year. I've been hunting a couple of times and am going tomorrow with Edward Blake. Had to go to the base once and loved the trip up by dogs even if it was hard going. We had to walk or run a good part of the way, but it was fun. The portage was beautiful—huge banks of snow. Mrs. Mackenzie's house is COMPLETELY covered today—Ike had to dig her out and you go down a good ten feet at least to reach her door—I'm going to get a picture of smoke coming out of a snowdrift someday. (Letter: December 31, 1944)

After weeks of caring for others in the hospital, the staff was left exhausted or ill, including Barbara, who spent a week in bed. She took advantage of the time to write one of her lengthy letters to Everybody.

About 5 feet of snow have fallen this year on the level, so you can imagine what the drifts are like. Everyone says there has been more snow than they ever remember and more gales—storm warnings on the coast every night. Some houses have had the tar paper all torn off, one house is completely buried in drifts. I love it but it makes trapping very difficult and it's hard to get anywhere. At the same time the Bay is still open in spots and one has to be very careful of bad ice. It's been a queer winter. I can't believe it is already half over, but there is a considerable difference in the length of the days, already they are getting longer. I've not seen many northern lights, but the evening skies are beautiful now, and it is heavenly these frosty mornings below zero to see the pink and white smoke coming out of all the houses, and the vapor rising from the river, which is open again. I HOPE to get off on a trip this week if all goes well—but first I must get rid of the "graveyard" cough I have. (Letter: January 20, 1945)

Barbara did not dread winter or wish it to be over. She learned to walk on snowshoes, yearned to travel by dog team to one of the nearby settlements, and admired the beauty in the snowy landscape. She passed along a household hint: "to those who housekeep—snow sprinkled on carpet is a very good way to clean carpet—has the same effect I suppose as damp sawdust on subway stairs!" From her sick bed, with the little Franklin stove warming the room, she could keep an eye on outside activities and also hear what was happening inside.

Well this is Sat. and since Monday I have lain in bed watching the snow banks get higher and higher—the warehouse is covered, little boys are sliding off the roof of the old Industrial and there is a bank across the middle of the living room window. I'm up now but not out for I simply cannot breathe thru' my nose. Oh well—I hope to get out with my snowshoes someday.

Honestly, the snow is wonderful—I have never seen anything like it— nor, it seems, has anyone else. I forgot to mention one of the nicest things about the return of the trappers—they all blossom forth in their new and fancy deerskins and leggings—men here can be gay in their clothing—in fact, this is very much of a man's country—you have to be tough to make a living, but they have such a wonderful time together whether it is trapping, sealing or deer hunting. I'm sure they work harder than anywhere else, but I am equally sure they have a lot more fun out of life. (Letter: January 20, 1945)

Barbara thanked her mother for her Christmas gifts, although she expressed disappointment that the things she had given "the girls," probably Annie Wolfrey and Doris Goudie, hadn't been seen since.

I liked your knives very much as I did everything—what makes me mad is those pretty flower hair dos have <u>not</u> been worn yet! The girls are too "shamed" to wear them 'cause they're different; same with that lovely green necklace I gave Bella [McLean]. She hasn't worn it or the very pretty earrings Randy sent her. It's discouraging! (Letter: undated January 1945)

Barbara understood the reason why hair ornaments or jewelry had not been worn. Even though the men were "gay in their clothing," and the women sewed mitts and jackets decorated with beautiful embroidery to sell, anything new or flashy might draw a comment. The girls would never want it suggested they were *big feelin'*—thinking too much of themselves. Few women in North West River were ever a target for such a remark, dressed as they were for their daily, dirty work of caring for babies, chopping wood, washing clothes, setting rabbit snares, or ice fishing.

Women did all their housework and then hunted and fished, doing whatever they could to bring fresh food to the table while their husbands were on the trapline. Even young children were expected to contribute to the household. Barbara told her mother about a boy of 11 who went off alone one day and came back with 14 partridges and 40 smelts. She wrote that she wished her nephew Peter "could have had a life like this," but probably did not mean she wished he could quit school to go on a trapline by himself at age 12 or 13. One competent young hunter, 15-year-old Edward Blake, took her out for a day and she managed to get enough partridges to send a few to New York, a special treat for her mother, who was living with wartime rationing.

I went hunting!! and I hope by now my poor starving family have had a good meal thanks to my prowess as a huntress! Edward Blake (Sid's oldest boy) and I started off as the sun was beginning to rise (about 9:30

A.M.) and frost was still falling. I usually have great trouble with my glasses steaming up—this time it was freezing. I couldn't see so finally took them off and then had fits for fear I would slip and break them. It was hard enough to stand up for under the snow was slippery ice. Fortunately I had borrowed F's logans, for seal boots would have been terrible. We went up this side of the lake and were beginning to despair of seeing anything when I spied a company of 5 white partridges. Edw.'s gun, alas, was frozen and when I took a shot it frightened them off, so they were lost to us. When we got to the Rapids we had seen no more, so thot we would try our luck at fishing—soon gave that up as we got no bites, and standing still at 20 below zero was rather chill. So we continued on and it was then that I got my first one—I shot three times, twice missing completely. Edw.'s got away. We boiled up and it is still rather miraculous to me how one can be so cozy at such a temperature. In about twenty minutes the kettle was boiling, brush was down and there we sat, temp. below zero, sitting on snow as warm as could be. Between us we had a good mug-up, even deer meat! (Letter: January 20, 1945)*

By mid-afternoon, they still only had one partridge and Barbara was afraid of being labelled the "bad luck critter," as Edward had a record of never coming home empty-handed. Their luck changed when a company of 10 birds was spotted. At the end of the day, Edward had four and Barbara two. She packed the frozen birds in ice and salt and, through her contacts on the base, the partridges were delivered to New York "in record time," the entire transaction described in a letter with gaps instead of names and aircraft identification, so the censor would not strike the details. Fresh partridges sent from Labrador to New York, with the free assistance of the United States Air Force, were a gourmet treat. All this effort yielded only a comment from her mother that freezing the birds must have made them tough. Barbara discussed it with her friends and the consensus was that it was the cooking, not the freezing, that was the problem. No doubt there was also silent agreement about the old bird residing 10 floors above Park Avenue.

In January, the event most keenly anticipated was the return of the Height of Land trappers. They walked back on snowshoes, some using a dog and others hauling their sleds themselves, over the frozen snow-covered river. They hoped for good ice and weather conditions to allow a quick trip down without the heavy grub they had carried into the country in the fall, hauling a load of fur instead. They would kill porcupines and partridges along the way and had food caches on the trail nearer home. Barbara had been out with her camera and managed to get some pictures of men with their dog teams and sleds.

The men are mostly home now and I have been very fortunate by being allowed to see the skins of two of them; they don't often show them to others than their families, and of course, I don't even say I have seen them. Some have had good hunts, others not so good. I did see one beautiful silver fox that a few years ago would have brought 400 to 500 dollars— now it is practically nothing thanks to fox farms. How I would love to own a marten or two, but there is a closed season on them here. Mink are lovely too, they and cats (lynx) bring the best price now. Most of the men give their children the squirrels to sell and it is too cute to see four year olds trotting up to the company [HBC] with their fur bags over their shoulders. Often there is a trap for each child and they are allowed to have the money of anything caught in it, some fare rather well. (Letter: January 20, 1945)

She saw Cyril Michelin's furs and noted exactly what he brought back from all the effort of three months trapping.

5 cats (lynx), 12 fox (11 red, 1+), squirrels, weasels (ermine), 2 beavers, 1 otter, minks (10?), 2 muskrats. Also saw a marten—lovely. $1000 perhaps for all, good year. (Diary: January 10, 1945)

Barbara couldn't help but make comparisons between a trapper's annual income and that of a New York stockbroker, like her father or brother, or even what her mother received in alimony.

Trapping was not too good this year for any—Harvey, one of F's brothers, I think did the best of all and that best—the usual income for the year—is what some people would make in a couple of days in certain professions I could mention! (Letter: January 31, 1945)

Newfoundland Ranger Clayton Gilbert had the task in 1945 of gathering information for the official census and counted about 200 people in North West River. Trappers' incomes ranged from $400 to $1,700. A truck driver on the base made $2,400, a clerk made $1,500, and an aircraft maintenance worker earned $1,000.[1] It was easy to understand the attraction of a guaranteed wage at the base, a warm bunk in the barrack block, and all you could eat at the mess hall. Every year, fewer men went trapping and instead found work at Goose Bay, but even if they worked on the base, they would still go hunting to keep their families supplied with fresh meat.

Deer [caribou] hunting on the other hand has been wonderful, more deer than in many a year—perhaps because the fires this summer have driven them into the mountains around here. Yesterday there were 15 teams over in the mountains and it is lots of fun to see them come back and wonder how many deer they have got—some have had to make two trips to haul them all home. (Letter: January 31, 1945)

It was "pretty hard" to be at Fred Goudie's house that winter when the trappers returned, for the first time in over 40 years Uncle Fred not amongst them. His widow, Lilla, son, Ernest, and daughters, Doris and Sona, were still mourning their loss. To make matters worse, Ernest had not been well since returning home in October with the devastating news of his father's drowning.

A more cheerful occasion for Barbara, if not for the boys involved, was helping with the induction ceremony of a new group of Boy Scouts, followed by a dinner, which she knew would sound like a royal banquet to her American friends.

Last night we inducted the first group of scouts—eight boys had to come before the "court of honor" and prove they knew all the proper things. Mrs. P, Miriam [Hiscock], Jack [Watts], the "Rev" [Burry] and I were the ogres. I have never felt so sorry for any youngsters in my life—it was pure agony for them and I was terrified one was going to burst into tears. I was particularly hard on four, for Jack's two sons and F's two nephews were among them, and Annie and F were in the room too. They got thru' it beautifully tho'. All the staff came for dinner, and we did not know what to feed them—a choice of fresh pork, roast beef, deer meat, rabbit, partridge and something else—I forget what! I suppose it is mean to mention such things—I assure you it does not happen often! (Letter: January 20, 1945)

Barbara announced to her mother her wish to stay longer in Labrador, expressing some irritation that Eleanor Cushman, the secretary in the IGA office in New York, had asked Mrs. Mundy about

Barbara's plans, instead of asking her directly.

Just recently Mrs. Keddie wired to ask if I'd "stay longer" & I wired "yes." What longer means I don't know—to me it means thru' the Spring. Actually, if asked I'd like to say I'd stay another year. I feel it took so long to get on to my job and to know the local people that if I left now, I'd be leaving just as I was getting to the point where I'd begin to really get something out of my stay—and some pleasure out of it. I felt so rotten when I first came & it's taken a long time to break the ice. But now I know my job, I know the people & I would begin to enjoy myself a bit & except for the moment, I'm feeling better. (Letter: January 30, 1945)

It was the first but it wouldn't be the only time Barbara would explain to her mother why she wanted to stay longer. She was over her anxieties about her job in the shop and was often involved when needed in the hospital, as was clear in her description of the arrival of a new baby, born prematurely to a mother living in a tent across the river.

Great excitement yesterday when we thot we were going to have an Indian baby born in the hospital. Swasheen came over and said one was on its way and F said to bring the Mother over—we all peered out to see the goings on. (The tent is just in sight across the river.) Much to do outside the tent then everyone, including dogs and children disappeared inside and we decided that the baby was probably born. About 4 P.M. we see Matthew walking down from Goose (he was the father); shortly thereafter he, a 14 yr. old boy and a girl come down the bank with a bundle and get into a canoe. F said "Guess here comes the mother with the baby" such a thing being perfectly possible with Indians. Matthew, beaming, comes in and gives F the bundle and says "Squish" (girl) and asks if she will keep it. She undoes layers and layers and finally finds lashed in the cutest down nest you ever saw a minute little girl VERY Indian looking. I wish I could describe the cradle she was in. It was a down affair, with a nice little scooped out place in the centre, in that was placed the baby dressed in the cutest little clothes, then various blankets and the last a tartan one with deerskin loops all the way around—this was placed under the baby and then a pink ribbon was lashed thru' these loops back and forth on top. All was stuffed into a pillow case. When they came in the baby was COMPLETELY covered with blankets etc. not even the nose showing. They say they are carried this way and when they are pitching their tents they just stick them up in the ground like a stick until all preparations are made. When weighed this wee thing came to 2¾ lbs. F says she doesn't think they come that small often and that probably they were scared to keep it and since Matthew had recently been in here he figured it might not be a bad place to park her. (Letter: January 31, 1945)

Two weeks later, the baby, named Mary Madeleine, "is doing very well, and is very bright, looks around and takes all in and has a huge appetite."[2]

Barbara hadn't felt well since late December and finally it was decided she should see a doctor at the base hospital. That meant making a trip to Goose Bay by dog team, safely tucked in the box on a komatik sled.

For most of January I was either in bed or up feeling half dead—no gumption to do anything. I was all stuffed up and got quite deaf. The weather was awful, so I couldn't go up to base, and after about a week of treatment by radio, I was bundled into a komatik box (like a coffin without the lid!) and off to the hospital I went with Sid Blake. I felt like a fool and by that time was feeling much better. But it had gone on so long and I was still deaf and had ear ache, so all thot it best that I go. Sid was a very nice person to go with—he has that reputation—and saw to it that pillows, blankets, etc. were comfy and that I was warm enough. Even with Mrs. P's fur-lined dickie it was none too warm. Before we left the portage to go out onto the Bay he tucked me all in so I could hardly move! As we went along we saw a long line of Indians on their way to NW. Got up to Goose in a little more than 3 hours and I was stuck into a room miles down an empty wing—most dismal, for even the windows were so banked in snow that about 6" of sky were visible—honestly I didn't know if it were night or day, fair or gray. (Letter: February 17, 1945)

The arrangements to get Barbara home again took several days, with messages crossed and radio communication problems. Finally, word came that Alvin Michelin was on his way to retrieve her. The trip turned into quite an excursion, with the added bonus of the unexpected and very welcome company of Lee White, who had not returned to active duty after all. Since leaving North West River he had spent two months in hospital with pneumonia and had been given leave to return to Labrador. Lee hitched a ride with Barbara and company, stopping at Groves Point along the way to visit John, Charlie, and their families. Barbara had heard that Charlie's house was "lots of fun" and John's was "more staid."

When we got to John's who should we find but Burry and his wife— the last people on earth I wanted to see! (He is the minister here and you have probably gathered from previous letters how most of us feel.) Well, here I was looking forward to my first night in a local home, and then to find them established there too—fortunately Mrs. said something about my having their room, and I quickly said by no means, and asked Lee to see if it were OK to go to Charlie's. I supped with the Johns—but that too was maddening for the Bs and I ate alone, and all the others were having a far better time in the other room. Lee and Alvin came over soon after and we went on to the other house.

They are wonderful fun—Mr. has the most amazing eyebrows that point up and make him look as if he were perpetually smiling. Russell (Jane's husband) was there too, and their little girl is sweet and not a bit "shamed"—guess she is very used to people now. Had a very good time there, and a very comfortable night. The next day was a "pet" day—simply beautiful and we started for home about 9:30; Russell came down too. (Letter: February 17, 1945)

Reverend Lester Leeland Burry was a United Church minister from Newfoundland who had been in Labrador with his wife, Marie, for 14 years. He first visited North West River in the summer of 1925, at the invitation of Dr. Grenfell. When the United Church asked Burry to accept a posting there in 1930, he quickly agreed. He commissioned a vessel, *Glad Tidings II*, and supervised its construction at Little Bay Islands, Newfoundland. For 20 summers he travelled Hamilton Inlet and parts of the Labrador coast.[3] Every winter, the Burrys would go as far as Cartwright, in Sandwich Bay, by dog team. After he came to North West River, the church and parsonage were built.

Burry was a radio innovator. In 1937, he learned all he could about setting up an amateur station with the help of Allan Lunan, a radio operator based in North West River by the Labrador Mining and

Exploration Company. By autumn 1937, he had supplied four trappers with small receivers and three sets successfully made it up the river. Burry asked them to be listening on the night of November 20 and didn't know if his first transmission had been received until they returned home in January. Using old parts supplied by business friends, Burry outfitted other trappers with receivers.[4]

Barbara wasn't fond of Lester Burry and her letters never explain exactly why. Perhaps she inherited from other staff a proprietary attitude about the Mission, which as far as they were concerned, in Labrador was only Grenfell. When Barbara met Burry, he and his wife were well established in a mission of their own. There was at least one period of tension and ill will between him and the Mission in the early 1940s. Grenfell Mission Superintendent Dr. Charles Curtis wrote about it in 1942 in a letter to Dr. Tony Paddon, who enlisted that year in the Royal Canadian Navy, but hoped to work at home when the war was over: "The Mission wants to run Northwest River and if you have a minister who is willing to cowtow, then all is well, but if you have a minister who is not then there is friction between two organizations that are trying to benefit the people."[5]

Curtis was probably correct in his observation, but Tony Paddon knew Curtis was not a well-informed source on the community politics of North West River. Curtis had not visited Labrador at all between 1915 and 1934.[6] He came to North West River in 1940 to attend the funeral service for Dr. Harry Paddon and did not visit the northern Labrador stations until 1950.[7] Any information Curtis had about Mission and United Church rivalry in central Labrador was second-hand.

Barbara would have been on the Grenfell side in any issue with Burry, and she also knew from her friends that Burry was a social damper at times, like when men made homebrew to drink at weddings or dances.[8] Her dismay at seeing the Burrys was more than made up by her delight in meeting Lee White again. His second visit to North West River in a few months was a pleasant diversion, her earlier complaints about having no gumption long forgotten. She was "feeling grand," dancing with Lee at Florence's birthday party and "sitting up till all hours chatting." She had liked Lee from their first meeting, telling her mother "he certainly is a credit to NWR."[9]

As the weather got milder, Barbara spent even more time outdoors. She had been to Butter and Snow with Doris Goudie. Ernest "came down & picked us up with 5 dogs—a beautiful ride home in moonlight best going yet 'good slipping.'" On the evening of Sunday, March 25, "about to mug-up on deers meat & onions," she wrote a note to her mother on American Red Cross stationery she had purloined from the hospital on the base. She was eagerly anticipating a trip to Mulligan. Barbara wanted to see some of the women who did needlework for the shop and Florence had nursing business.

F is going on a medical trip and we'll meet in Mulligan where there's more than one house to put us all up. She'll make her stops on the way down, I'll make mine coming back & I'll help her with the inoculations in Mulligan. Her bro is driving her & Selby (Cyril's bro) me—I hope we have good weather. (Letter: March 25, 1945)

Barbara was glad to accompany Florence, as she wasn't used to "just walking in to a house of someone [she] did not know and spending the night." She got new sealskin boots in time for the trip, "hairy legs" with fur on the outside, and was wearing them when she set off with Selby Michelin and a motley team of dogs he had managed to assemble.

We had a frightful time getting dogs—several we had counted on we could not get and at ten P.M. the night before we were both canvassing the town. I went up to Burry's and asked for his, as he was about to come and ask for the few I had. He announced he was off at the crack of dawn to find some, so I tore back to Selby's and told him to be up betimes and beat him to it. Wed. came and at 10 A.M. we had only 3 and needed 2 more. Selby said he would try one more person, so he went across the river and twenty anxious minutes passed before I saw him walking back with two. We were ready and off in no time. These were pups—only in harness once before— and the trip was enlivened (??) by puppy trouble most of the way. (Letter: June 19, 1945)

Barbara slept on the kitchen floor by the stove at the home of Percy and Esther Chaulk. She enjoyed visiting Mulligan, where the people were "extremely nice, and more untouched by the base." They stopped in to visit a couple of the Baikie families at the islands and had dinner with Peggy and Harry Paddon at Saltwater Pond, on the way back to North West River. All in all, it was a wonderful excursion, riding on a sled pulled by dogs. Selby, the driver, was "thotful and fun to go with" and very skilled in his handling of the unpracticed team.

Driving dogs amazes me—the men speak so quietly—except for one or two who blaze away—and they chatter away, pulling all sorts of tricks to get the beast to "step on it." I was amused once or twice to hear Selby say: "all together b'ys, house ahead b'ys, supper soon b'ys" etc. and the dogs actually perked up their ears and went to it until they discovered he was only fooling! (Letter: June 10-July 5, 1945)

At Easter, teacher Grace Layman came for a visit, a welcome addition, with fresh gossip and stories. It was Barbara's first Labrador spring and she saw something else she had never seen before, people probing the deep snowbanks for whatever was underneath.

Grace Layman—the teacher at Cartwright, came up by dogs for her Easter holidays and she was quite fun. Her tales of their trip were amusing—at one point the only houses were crammed with Eskimos and not too clean, so she and her driver decided to pitch their tent some distance away, hoping to get away from the grubbiness—not at all—they all moved in too for most of the time! They had one night in a tent, one in a house, and one in a tilt, took them 3 days each way. She loved it as I know I would. The snow began to melt about then, got sinky to the waist and beyond—the children began playing seal in holes and tunnels in the ice and spring began to arrive. People began to dig for boats and had a terrible time to find them. Jack had 3 digs before locating his and was asking everyone if they remembered where it might be! Once we looked out and saw only the top of Harvey's head in a hole still poling around trying to locate it. Stores and small houses began to appear as did other things that I had forgotten even existed. (Letter: June 10-July 5, 1945)

After 10 months in North West River, at last Barbara was officially asked to stay another year. Barbara told her mother she had received a letter from Kitty Keddie: "she 'hears' I am doing a fine job and feels I am the solution to the big problem NWR always has been. Just what she knows or doesn't know is a mystery to me." Barbara was getting her own reports about Mrs. Keddie from "everyone who has seen her": she "has aged frightfully—she has arthritis or something in one knee & can hardly wobble around and her disposition is worse than usual! They say she is 'impossible' now! If she turns up here for any length of time the chances are I'll resign!"[10] Barbara really wasn't thinking of resigning. In her diary for the same date, her decision to stay rated as many words as her project to knit a smelt fishing net: "have decided to stay another yr. & have started smelt net under Stewart, Aunt Jessie's & Warren's tutelage."

She knew her "Dearest Ma" would be disappointed with the decision to stay longer, so it had to be properly explained and justified again.

When I came up here I had qualms, but on the whole, it's been a wonderful experience. The time has sped and there are many things I want to do that I've not had the opportunity to or I've not known how to go about it. I hope I'm not going to ruin my first year by staying another, but I figure it this way. I know my job better, I know the people better and I ought to have an even better time. Florence is undecided after next Dec. but will be in NWR anyway, there will be two new teachers and here's hoping they'll be more spirited. Mrs. P expects to live in her house this summer so that will make a change and she might go out next winter for a while perhaps— she's said nothing about that tho'. It's a gamble but all things are and I can't get much real information about future jobs with ARC [American Red Cross] or anything else up here. This job is very interesting in ways, dull in others. The staff is certainly not what it was at St. A.—too few and too dull for words—but the people are swell—they are honest-to-goodness people and live a life that fascinates me. (Letter: April 8, 1945)

Barbara's mother must have raised the possibility of moving from Thousand Nine, especially if her daughter did not return to New York. The prospect of losing her longtime home aroused a somewhat worried response, even though going back to live with her mother again was not what she wanted.

In answer to your last letter, as you know, what I want more than anything in the world, is my own home—someplace, no matter how small, that will always be there to come home to whether I'm away a day or a year. The uncertainty & constant wondering I don't like—I was never meant to be an apt-city-bred girl, I'm afraid. I wish we'd been born in the days when homes stayed in one family & were always there—if I can't have it as I always hoped to have it, I guess I'll have to have it alone if I can have a job (God knows what) and can afford it. It is not that I don't value or enjoy the only home I've known—I certainly have both valued it & enjoyed it—the years we've been at 1009 have meant more than any other years to me and the thot of not having that home to come home to makes me feel rather queer inside. It's that I want my own home—even if I don't know how to manage it or run it. I certainly know far more than lots of girls. I haven't the foggiest notion what lies ahead of me on my return—I don't like to think of it. To return to NY with no place to stay, all I possess in storage, etc. is not a cheering picture. I wish I knew just one person who had experienced that to find out just what one does. It's lonely here sometimes but it's a loneliness that can be stood, quite unlike the loneliness I've felt at home—and there in NY there's no escape to beautiful country as there is here. Loneliness when surrounded by people is far worse than loneliness alone. I wish I could put into words what I feel about the life here—not the life of the Mission staff—but that of the people. It's hard, it's tragic, it's poor but with all that it's a real life—with joy and fun along with all the rest—no petty worries etc. that one runs into in "civilization." (Letter: April 8, 1945)

Mrs. Mundy never did move from the tenth-floor apartment on Park Avenue. Perhaps she was using the possibility of moving as a lever to influence her daughter, but Barbara made it plain she would not be returning to New York for at least another year. The community of trappers and their families, so near to one of the biggest military air bases in the world, was an interesting place to live as a single American woman working with the Mission. And the best part, she was beyond her mother's purview and control.

In Goose Bay that spring, there were more Americans and Canadians in residence than there were people in all the rest of Labrador. Now that the base was built and running smoothly, everyone comfortably housed and supplied, the war in Europe was winding down. The Allies were on the offensive, the Nazis in disarray. Word came that President Franklin D. Roosevelt had died in the United States on April 12 and his vice-president, Harry S. Truman, was sworn in. Dick Paddon arrived home on April 21 from his military service, "sobered & saddened," as Barbara

Barbara in "hairy legs"—boots with seal fur legs, 1945(?).

North West River Industrial Shop ready for Christmas, 1944.

The first time Russell took Barbara duck hunting, June 8, 1945.

Russell presented this fox fur to Barbara in January 1946.

Russell arrives home from the caribou hunt, spring 1946.

Barbara, Nora Groves, and John Blake at one of their camps on Grand River, August 1946.

John Blake and Russell at the foot of Gull Island Rapid, August 1946.

Russell guiding a canoe through Mininipi Rapids, August 1946.

Russell, Barbara, and Flop at Grand (Churchill) Falls, August 31, 1946.

Trappers' camp on Grand River, 1947.

Barbara carrying a load on a portage, October 1947.

Russell boiling the kettle on the north trapping path, 1947/48.

Barbara outside the main "house" at Fig River, 1947/48.

Spot relaxing by the tent on the south trapping path, 1947/48.

Russell pauses for a smoke while hauling canoes down Grand River, 1948.

Russell in the foreground, Sandy Island Lake, Grand River, September 1948.

Russell and Harold Baikie at Grizzell's (Grizzle) Rapid, September 1948.

Harold Baikie, Russell, Francis Thevenet, and Warren (Baikie or Morris) at the foot of Mininipi Rapid, September 1948.

Russell, Barbara, and their daughter, Marjorie, North West River, 1951.

Russell and Barbara's house in The Bight, North West River, 1951.

observed.

In early May, a diary entry about a peaceful camping trip she had taken with friends occupied more space than the news of VE Day.

Mon. May 7: the war with Germany is over—what now? It's wonderful but the joy is certainly tinged with sadness for those whose men will not come back. On Fri., F, Cyril, Miriam [Hiscock] & I went up to the Rapids for wkend—we camped on a high spot with a glorious view up Grand Lake—sunset, reflections, peace & beauty. A cozy warm & comfy tent— complete in every detail. Fished, walked, & just drank it all in. A perfect change, & wonderful fun. Deersmeat stew, stovecake—the whole thing seems like a dream—over much too soon.

On May 8, the community celebration was held. That week was memorable for another reason: the loss of the Mission's firewood, stored close to shore.

To celebrate VE day we decided to have the dinner for the employees that we were supposed to have at Christmas. There were about 24 here after which we had a huge bonfire and dance in the Social Room. On May 12th we had a couple more feet of snow to cheer us up! The ice from Grand Lake never came down this year which was a disappointment to me for I missed it last year—it came in the night then. A part of Little Lake came all at once and it was fascinating both to see and hear. The ice from G.L. tho' was blown up to the head of the Lake by terrific gales and it just rotted and sank there. The water got so high and strong that a lot of the wood cut and piled waiting for open water to be hauled home was lost. About 2,000 rounds went down the river and the rest was scattered all over the place, amongst the willows, etc. Some is gone for good. The river was a real rapid for a while, white water. (Letter: June 10-July 5, 1945)

It was that dangerous time, between ice and water, like a year earlier when she arrived in North West River, when travel was risky and even experienced people could be suddenly stranded. That spring, though, the wind and rushing water also brought something valuable to the hospital.

When the river was white here—the Indians were afraid to cross and portaged their canoes up to the lake and over that way. I can't get used to the fact that these Indians at least are very much afraid of water, and the thot of drowning terrifies them—they believe a person drowned can never rest, his soul can't that is. The [hospital] basement flooded and we were without any means of having hot water for days—there was about a foot or more of water—everything floating every which way, and to top it all one night I went down and stepped into the well! It was towards the end of this time that some of the men, including the HBC manager, went out to Sandy Point for a day's hunting. The ice shifted and they were stuck almost a week—Cyril was on the other side of the Run and went on up to Goose when he found he couldn't get home. On his return paddle he stopped with food for the marooned ones, and found them smoking cigarettes made of paper bags and dried grass! They were a sorry looking bunch on their return, but they had had a very good time despite it—there were about 8 of them.

The same wind brought several hundred little bottles ashore, all neatly sealed and containing a scrap of powdered crystals—and what a smell when water was added. At first we thot it might be concentrated plasma— Tony [Paddon] came the next day (grown quite fat) and immediately recognized it as penicillin—our stock at this time is worth over a thousand dollars as each little bottle is worth about $8. It must have come from one of the crashes this winter. Wasn't it fortunate that it chose this shore to come up on, and other shores where friends and neighbors who quickly heard that it was of value lived. (Letter: June 10-July 5, 1945)

People in the community were pleased when Dr. Tony Paddon arrived home safe from the war, having served three years in the Royal Canadian Navy, including time spent as medical officer on a minesweeper during the Normandy invasion. Barbara was among those who assumed the Mission would let him stay, as the hospital had not had a doctor in residence since his father died six years earlier.

Tony is here now—if only he could stay—for he certainly has the welfare of this place at heart and there will be no quibbling once he is in control—a man is badly needed here and I think he will be the right one. People like him, have confidence in him and he is wonderful with the children. You'll see a great difference in management when he takes over. (Letter: June 10-July 5, 1945)

In June, Barbara began writing a lengthy letter to Everybody, a letter with a wonderful story about duck hunting. At first, it may have seemed just another Labrador experience to document in *True North* style, as she had written about partridge hunting or dog driving, but as the weeks went by and she added to this diary-type letter, it was plainly more important than that. Her duck-hunting companion was widower Russell Groves, and she delighted in his company. Barbara cautioned her correspondents to keep these stories to themselves.

JUST A WARNING—THIS IS A PERSONAL LETTER AND NO PART OF IT IS TO APPEAR IN PRINT—THE DEEP SEA FISHERS IS NOT TO HAVE ANY OF IT UNDER ANY CIRCUMSTANCES.
Sunday, June the 10th 1945

Well, to start telling you of the main things of interest—on Friday last one of my greatest desires came true—if I were more "brazen" and less "shamed" I would get more of them, but alas I don't like asking people to take me places etc. unless I know them pretty well, and they (both men and girls) wouldn't ask me for fear I might not like being asked or some such dumb thing. For quite a while Cyril and others had been telling me that Russell Groves was going to ask me to go duck hunting—but it took him weeks to get around to asking me himself. (Russell, by the way, is Charlie's son and Jane's husband, or was, she died as you remember before Xmas.)

Why I am not sleepy at this point I do not know—last Tues. I didn't sleep and read 'till 3 A.M., Wed. I danced 'till 3 A.M. and Thurs I never went to bed at all! Thurs. R asked if I could go the next A.M.—he was to wake me a bit before three. Well, I went walking and got side-tracked chatting with Tony as he burned rubbish on the beach, then went in and sat with them all fascinated by T and Dick swapping tales of their sea adventures, mugged-up, went home, found F and Cyril still up so talked to them 'till 12:30, remarking at that point how it was hardly worthwhile to go to bed for 2 hrs. F took me up on that and said how about keeping an eye on the new patients and letting me get the sleep! (four dying TBC. Indians had been admitted that aft.) So I made a fine fire, did odd jobs, listened and looked at the pts. 'till Russell arrived a bit before 3.

Barbara was well bundled up but shivering with cold in the bottom of the canoe, "a beautiful morning star over the Mealies," and not a bird in sight before dawn. The sun rose at five and they went ashore at John

Bull Island to make a fire and have breakfast.

After breakfast we went on—it grew lovelier every minute, we had now come to pan and floating ice. We had to go far out around a pan which was covered with seals—hundreds of them sunning themselves in the laziest manner. Ice in all shapes and sizes went by. Then we went in among the islands and pan ice everywhere—the wind had gone down, the ice was indescribable, yellow, blue, grey, white, snowy, "candles," in shapes of birds—that and drifting sticks fooled us many times. I now no longer lay in the bottom but "spied" and then when R kneeled, and took the little paddle and we went along without a sound I sat up and looked thru' the tiny peekhole in the fly, only the tip of my motionless head above and that did not matter as I too had on the white outfit—mine being a snitched operating cap and white jacket. It was fascinating to get closer and closer and then bang and they were ours.

R is an excellent hunter and he hardly ever misses. He wanted me to have a shot but I wouldn't at first for there were few birds and I did not want to miss. After we had six he insisted and as he turned for me to shoot the darn bird dived and we never saw him again. We think he was a crippled one for he was so "cute" in hiding. Then we saw a young seal and went after him—got him too. Dinner on another island, grassy and soft, this one. The water was still, the reflection of the trees and the ice pans were unbelievable—I almost had to pinch myself to realize I was actually there—I just couldn't believe it—it was so tranquil and beautiful. R was in no hurry to get back and I could have stayed forever. (Letter: June 10-July 5, 1945)

On the way home, they saw men setting seal nets in the evening light. At suppertime, they spotted Cyril on an island getting ready to boil up, so they lingered and ate trout with him. They made it home by 9:30 that evening, still not dark, "the sun was setting amid fluffy pastel clouds." Barbara said Russell was fun to go with, thoughtful, interesting, and helpful, going out of his way to explain things to her. After the very successful day of duck hunting, Russell Groves quickly became Russell, and then just R in her diary, a rapid promotion putting him at the same level as F and C, Florence and Cyril, her closest friends. He was included in many evening paddles, was one of her canoeing instructors. Russell and Cyril were dubbed her "guardian angels."

R & C are teaching me to paddle and when we got out of sight of people I took over—both men say it looks too lazy when they recline and I paddle—but how else will I learn? As a matter of fact, I find that is not too efficient, for they are always there to grab a paddle and save us when necessary—lately I have taken one canoe and they have gone in the other. Just recently, I simply go alone! That evening I paddled half way up the Rapid itself—how I do not know for I ached all over when R took over. I was very proud of myself and he was quite amazed that I managed it all as I did. (Letter: June 19, 1945)

She was enjoying herself tremendously but there was talk generated in some quarters about the unmarried Mission wop and the recently widowed trapper. North West River was no different from anyplace else; there were those who felt they were the moral arbiters, entitled to pass comment on what was proper behaviour for a man widowed six months earlier and a single woman. Barbara and Russell were aware of the gossip, but it didn't stop them seeing each other. Their friends, Cyril and Florence, were likely pleased to see them happy.

This town is the worst for rumors and stories—all most absurd and most untrue—they bring moments of surprise, anger and hilarious laughter. Some of the staff are worse than the local people—one at this moment who dared to say in some of our presences what she has said in others would be much surprised by the response she would get. Florence and Cyril are laying in wait for her, and we all hope before she leaves that she lays herself open for a withering blast; she is too clever for that I fear! (Letter: June 10-July 5, 1945)

Being the subject of gossip made Barbara angry but it did not spoil her enjoyment when her guardian angels came up with a couple of surprises. Cyril offered her his small canoe for the summer and, although she was "dumbfounded and scared to death [she] would wreck it," she took him up on it.

One night shortly after that Russell came up and wanted to know what I would like to do—I bluntly said—you go get your canoe, I'll go get mine and I'll have another lesson thank you, and by the way, bring your .22 along and I'll practice shooting which I find good fun. Off we went—

on our return R handed me the gun and said I could have it to practice with—and that he wasn't going to take it into the country with him, so I could have it until next Spring! It's a pump shot .22 and he only bought it this winter, because he "took a fancy to it" and he really doesn't need it. I was telling C about it with great glee and he said he had known for several weeks I was going to get it—only he said nothing "in case Russell changed his mind." So—a gun and a canoe—I might almost say what more could I want. The canoe will give me lots of pleasure during open water, and the gun will mean lots of hours hunting and perhaps a bit of meat for us next fall and winter. I'm really lucky don't you think? (Letter: June 10-July 5, 1945)

If only it could be known what Barbara's friends in New York and Boston said about her delight at having her own canoe and gun, and a man to take her hunting. Her wop pals, Bette, Jo, and Randy, would probably have thought it was marvellous, but if Mrs. Mundy shuddered at the mere mention of the word "grub," it is easy to speculate how unimpressed she was with her daughter's improving frontier skills, increasing comfort with Labrador life, and hours spent with a recently widowed fur trapper. One person in the Mission circle back home—Bud Merrick—would have appreciated her paddling and shooting abilities, especially if he knew how she spent her 35th birthday, on July 1.

Last Sunday I went out to the seal nets with Harry—in fact I had quite a nice birthday—out with him from about 11 to three, then I paddled myself across the river, came back as C was about to go to his trout—no, salmon—net so went along with him. I was out all day, so much so that I even turned down another invite to paddle in the evening. (Letter: June 10-July 5, 1945)

Canoeing, and even gardening, could be done long into the evening in summertime Labrador. Barbara planted delphinium seeds in front of the shop "with the idea that in a few years time the little white building will look quite nice with towering blue flowers against it." The sandy soil required a lot of manure and she had help from Cyril and Harry, working in the late fading daylight "a couple of nights 'till after ten."

The spring fair was held and deemed a success, raising $1,600 for the Mission. As usual, families came from every community in the bay, and boatloads arrived from the base. It was a long exhausting day for the volunteers, who fed about 500 people, hauling water for cooking and dishwashing, as their water pump was broken. As tired as they were, they had to rally their energy for the dance that lasted nearly the whole night.

The majority of the visitors from the base returned there at midnight, and then we all went up to the dance, before that you couldn't even find a seat. As in most dances, it got better and better as time went on. Everyone was keen on dancing and the music never ceased—the men had to stand up for places for the next dance before the present one was over. Our boats were taking the local men who were working at the base back at four A.M. The dance was over about a quarter to 4 and I came home, expecting to work at the books for about an hour and then to bed. I found about six people sprawled in the living room and Frances trying to get them a mug-up and trying to make up her mind whether to go to Goose for the ride or not. I told her to go, took over the mug-up and woke two more dead bodies in the Social Room. Saw them all off AND LEFT THE DISHES WHERE THEY WERE. (Letter: June 10-July 5, 1945)

Business in the Industrial Shop was not as frantic as the year before. Fewer airmen were at the base since VE Day; airplanes and crash boats full of customers would not be arriving on a frequent basis. Barbara decided running the shop should not spoil her summer.

This year, I am not going to be a fool and be here to open on Sundays— I'm off every chance I get and if I don't sell to Goose, we'll ship it out. We are not to open Sundays anyway, and I have been weak minded and done so if asked. They seem to expect it now, despite the sign—but they will soon learn differently. I've wasted too much time doing none of the things I want to do—for several reasons, not feeling well enough to do it, not knowing how to go about doing it and not having the implements of warfare to do it alone, not being experienced enough to go off safely without freezing, drowning or getting lost. Them there days are gone forever, I hope in every respect. I know more what I want to do, how to go about doing it and I feel fine and energetic. So—here's to it! (Letter: June 10-July 5, 1945)

At the hospital, the staff were dealing with new and difficult tuberculosis cases. In June, four Innu patients with advanced disease were admitted. Tony Paddon had been home only a few weeks and his hands were more than full. It was difficult to imagine how they had managed all those years with no doctor, just Mina Paddon and Florence Goudie doing everything, and perhaps a visiting nurse in the summer to help. Barbara noted in her diary early in July: "Penami & others singing to Indians in ward & praying for them."[11]

She hadn't written her mother in a while and dashed off a short handwritten note in late July telling about a motorboat cruise with a North West River family.

Last weekend I had a grand time—Emmy Baikie & Wilfred asked me to go off on a "cruise" with them and I accepted with glee! They, their children, boy 4 [Treadway] and twins—girls—18 mos. [Katherine and Lucretia] and Blanche [Anderson], about 12 yrs. old, a cottage girl staying with them for the summer. It started off at 1 P.M. Sat. for the "Valley"—a local cluster of houses near the base. We had a very rough trip, got soaking as all we had was an open motor boat. We spent Sat. & Sunday nights there. Sunday were up at the base for Emmy & Blanche to see—the evenings visited around with local people (the trip was profitable industrially also). Monday we went to Traverspine & on to Mud Lake— which is a beautiful spot. Houses on mainland and island & canoes must be used (like Venice!). (Letter: July 29, 1945)

Her mother hadn't been told the whole story about the interlude at Mud Lake. Barbara's precious binoculars were tipped overboard when she was paddling with John Blake. Two days were spent dragging a hook over the bottom, trying to find them. Her diary entry was a wish: "can't believe it yet, a week later. Please may they be found." The search would occupy many in the weeks to come.

The cruise with the Baikie family was typical of what she wrote in her diary and letters that summer. She described an active social life revolving around Florence, Cyril, Russell, and people she had met through them. There were stories about midnight picnics, almost daily canoeing, and shooting practice with her borrowed gun. Often mentioned in letters was the disapproving Mina Paddon, who, after years of being the Mission's sole administrator for the hospital and school, was accustomed to being obeyed. Fortunately, Mrs. Paddon was not in charge of the Industrial Department and Barbara was not a teenage wop, fresh from the debutante ball.

Florence is trying to get out for a month or so and I shall miss her dreadfully for she and her friends are the saving grace. On her return we have a plan which we hope and pray will materialize. Here one doesn't speak of such things or they're spoiled before they begin. If I can manage my own affairs here and keep sane and moderately happy I will indeed have accomplished something. All I can say is, "Thank God for the local people!" This all sounds dismal but it's not quite as bad as it sounds I guess. The few marvelous times I've had have really more than made up for it, I think. (Letter: July 29, 1945)

If Mina Paddon rubbed Barbara the wrong way at the breakfast table, it was the least of her worries. After her husband Dr. Harry Paddon's death in 1939, she was saddled with running the hospital, certainly more responsibility than she wanted at that stage of her life, and she assumed the role of advocate for keeping the hospital open. The war years were difficult ones, with staff in even shorter supply, and then there was Mission Superintendent Dr. Charles Curtis in St. Anthony, not making her job any easier. For years he had been trying to convince the IGA Board to have the hospital in North West River demoted to a nursing station. Curtis thought anyone needing a doctor should be taken to the hospital at the military base in Goose Bay. As soon as peace was declared in Europe, the heavy guns came out in the battle between St. Anthony and North West River.

Dr. Tony Paddon had hung up his Navy uniform and immediately stepped into his late father's shoes. He wrote the Board warning that tuberculosis was assuming "frightening proportions," military medical services were being withdrawn from Goose Bay, and "a doctor is urgently needed."[12] Curtis sent a nasty letter to Cecil Ashdown at head office in New York about expenses at the North West River hospital, predicting they would go even higher if Tony Paddon stayed there.[13] A few months later, Mina Paddon angrily implored Ashdown "not to produce that stupid saying that this country, 600 miles of coast, riddled with disease and with practically no medical or educational facilities, is not sufficient work for a young active doctor."[14] The Board finally decided in 1947 to station Tony Paddon at North West River hospital and the battle went underground again.[15]

Only a few Mission insiders would have known how close the North West River hospital came to being reduced to a clinic and what role Mina Paddon played in making sure the hospital was safe. Overburdened, underappreciated, and tired of it all, she had successfully held the line until her son returned home from the war and took up the cause. Her contribution was recognized when she was made an Officer of the Order of the British Empire on January 1, 1949, for her work in North West River since 1915 and especially during the Second World War.

In Barbara's world, tactics to avoid antagonizing Mina Paddon seemed to be the most sensible ones to adopt, and, anyway, she had more pressing concerns; she had to figure out a subtle means of bringing up a sensitive topic with her mother. In a letter written in late summer, Barbara began by asking about her sister, who must have had a disappointment in her love life.

How is H? She seems to be very busy & enjoying life—very gay in fact! I'm afraid I didn't write her as I should have—I didn't know what to say and what can anyone say—none of it helps—it didn't help me much in similar circumstances and there's no use saying all will be fine & being a Pollyanna encouraging person. That all sounds well but there's not much truth in it. I can stand being lonely in a place like this where I can get out & be out but in a city, where there's no place to go, surrounded by thousands who are enjoying life, it's just unbearable. H & I ought to be more understanding—for she now has discovered, I guess, how I have felt at times. (Letter: August 25, 1945)

The real purpose of the late August letter was to introduce Russell Groves properly, explain how they met, and attempt to derail any concerns her mother might have about impropriety, while carefully laying out reasons for extending her time in Labrador. Would Mrs. Mundy believe that having a canoe has changed it all?

Two years isn't as long as it seems—it isn't long enough to do all I'd like to do. I'd like more free time to do all I've always wanted to do. Can't you imagine how grand it is to be able to go out in a canoe, walk where you please, etc. etc. etc. and there is comparatively little opportunity when there's a full time+ job besides! I dreaded the summer if it were to be like

last—but having a canoe has changed it all. And besides F & Cyril, who have been <u>grand</u>, Russell Groves has also been swell—and we've all had wonderful paddles, picnics etc.—done things I couldn't have done alone. R's wife, Jane, died before Xmas & as you know I stayed with her two nights. She apparently, was most grateful & told someone who in time passed it on to R. For some reason he seems frightfully appreciative of that & told Cyril he couldn't do enuf for me in return. Besides that he seems to like being out as I do and it keeps him from being terribly lonely. The problems I've had had resulted from my having had a few good times with him. Here, if one <u>speaks</u> to anyone, or if they are courteous enough to see you home from a dance, you're practically married. The little courtesies we from the outside expect & take for granted, here mean that a person is nuts about you. It's absurd and too silly to even think about—but one person says "Oh he took Miss Mundy duck hunting" and before you know it you hear you went with him <u>all</u> spring when actually you went <u>one</u> day!
(Letter: August 25, 1945)

Once again, community happenings outweighed momentous world events in her diary and letters. The war with Japan ended in mid-August and community attention was paid to Randy Toland, back that summer as a volunteer, who had two brothers in active service in the Pacific. On the night of the Japanese surrender, as Randy came down the hospital steps, people were lined up on both sides of the walk, not saying a word, just waiting to shake her hand or embrace her.[16] Barbara's diary entry was typically brief: "War over on Aug. 14th. What of future?" She told her mother the base was winding down from wartime operations.

Going to the base doesn't mean much social life really, and if I did go I'd be "chasing men"!! (what Mrs. P would doubtless say). Actually, I'm really happier here. The times I've had to go to the base I've not enjoyed it much. The first week there, of course, was thrilling. I'd never seen anything like it before. But my subsequent visits have been dull—days long, no place to go, everyone busy—evenings a movie or a dance (<u>lots</u> of fun) but too much drinking & too much of other things—I've been very thankful I've had no one I cared about there—it's rather disillusioning—or has been to me. And as you know, I'm not very good socially—again, I'd rather be alone here than there. The base is beginning to fold up—when, no one *knows, we constantly hear rumors of all kinds, but these are often false too!* (Letter: August 25, 1945)

The summer before, Barbara and the other single women had been hopping on the Norseman and flying to Goose Bay for parties and dances several times a week. Although the private air taxi service was no longer offered, the base and its social activities held little interest for Barbara, who would sooner go canoeing with Florence and Cyril or, even better, with Russell. At the end of her second summer, she had good friends, knew her job, did it well, and was beginning to think perhaps her future could be in Labrador—although not with the Mission.

Chapter Ten

THIS COULD BE MY HOME

Life at North West River is not without its merry moments.

—Sgt. Melvin D. McLean, "North West River"

B arbara's letters in the fall of 1945 had a settled, more confident tone. Most of the news was about her activities with friends and whatever was developing with Russell, and less about her work at the shop. She mentioned in October that Annie Wolfrey's tuberculosis had recurred; she would lose Annie as shop assistant: "Annie is out of the picture for at least a year and probably for good." It was too late to send Annie to the hospital in St. Anthony, where she could be treated, so she would spend the winter in the North West River hospital. Barbara and Doris Goudie would manage the shop together.

Barbara told her mother it had been a "confused summer—for [her] personally," but on the whole, wonderful. As for the shop, she had finally discovered that "working hard and over-time gets no more recognition than if [a person] don't work at all." She was "spending every available minute in [her] canoe, or walking or doing something": "People think me a bit daft anyway because I love to be out so much—so I just was out and loved every minute of it. This summer passed far too quickly."[1]

The tale of losing her prized binoculars grew longer due to repeated unsuccessful attempts to retrieve them. No longer shamed to ask a man to do something for her, she brazenly recruited Russell, who must have been preparing to go up Grand River for the winter. He took her across Lake Melville to Mud Lake, a physically trying 36-hour excursion that started on August 31.

Well, having decided I must go I had to find a boat and a man to take me. Russell offered and we got Warren's boat. We left right after work on Sat. and got to M.L. a little after midnight. R had not been to M.L. for about ten years in a boat, that and the fact that many of the shoals had changed made it rather difficult. The channel into M.L. is hard to find at best in daylight, but not many would attempt it after dark even if they knew it—but we went ahead and bounced from shoal to shoal and finally made it! As Harry remarked at his first night trip to Goose Bay this Spring—"I made a new channel"—well, that is what we did for M.L.

We spent the night at the Blakes and of course it had to rain all night, muddying up the water that we had counted on to be clear. We spent the entire day jigging—John with us in the aft.—but it was no use. I even turned blue and numb again—Russell tried to go in with me but it was too cold for him—I just waited till I got numb and couldn't feel it and then started to walk around!! We stayed till dark—went back to the B's and they had saved some meat for us—my first "nanceries" (yellow legs),[2] which were delicious. They wanted us to spend the night, but I wanted to get home for work the next morning as it was blowing hard and promised to blow harder. They thot us crazy, saying we could never get out to the mouth of the River in the darkness, but I said we had got in and could get out. R was not too keen, but said he would go to the mouth and if it were blowing too hard we could get back from there.

So we started off about 11—all went well, we only hit a couple of shoals on the way out! We got as far as Rabbit Is. and the gale began—you should have heard it. R said we would have to anchor in the lun for a bit to see what was going to happen for he would not take the Run at night in that wind; if it got worse we could get back to M.L. from there and if it got better we could go on. So we anchored for a couple of hours, and it did die and by the time we got home (at 5:30 A.M.) it was clear and heavenly—the morning star and a newish moon in the east. R was about frozen, but I had been asleep all snug in a sleeping bag on the bottom of the boat out of the wind, so I was fine. By noon the wind was up again & it blew for three days. (Letter: October 13, 1945)

Florence returned from her vacation, "flying back to be ready to go on [their] trip." Barbara and Cyril were in charge of preparations for the three of them to go camping, but there were a few snags. They had hoped to have another man along but it turned out that John Blake was unable to go, so the three left on the evening of September 8. Warren Baikie brought them, their canoe, and gear in his motorboat to a spot on the shore of Grand Lake, where they pitched a tent. Two Innu men coming down the lake stopped and had dinner with them. The next day they proceeded on to Nascopie River and camped near the river mouth.

We stayed there two nights as it rained all the next day. However, we tried fishing and I explored a very rocky, bubbling brook, and tried to hunt but never even saw a partridge. To date we had had one trout (we put a net out each night), one rabbit (snares too each night), and 3 nanceries; oh, and a duck we had picked up in perfect condition to eat—had been attacked by some bird and C found it on the shore while tracking. I tried tracking too for a bit, but the walking was ghastly—sinking into the mud to the knees. We usually went on 'till almost dark and by the time we were camped and had had dinner it would be about ten—F and I usually went into a dead sleep—much to our disgust—and to C's too, I'm sure—and then we would wake up for a bit before really getting ready for bed. F had a mouth organ—she'd play and C and I would sing. One night I went out for a walk and you have no idea how cozy a tent looks lighted up and how cheery it sounds to hear someone playing inside. (Letter: October 13, 1945)

They tramped and tracked, paddled and poled their way, conquered by a 3-mile-long rapid, which Barbara hiked around to satisfy her curiosity. At the Red River portage, they met the Innu men they had seen earlier that week.

At the Red River portage we met the Indians again—they had come up and were about to go into the portage. To my great surprise one of the ones we had seen on his way to NW came out when we stopped to chat with them and handed me a letter! Well, I have had letters find me in strange places—on cross-country trains in the middle of the desert, in ports where the boat I was on would stop for a night, but I never thot that an Indian would meet me in the middle of Labrador—about 70 miles from NW with one. It seems Indians are very good postmen! (Letter: October 13, 1945)

Windy weather forced them to stay at Black Point, a place where there once had been houses and where they thought they might find more berries. Barbara mentioned the tombstones of "three little Michelins." It was the grandest spot; "the wind raged and almost blew the tent down, but it made it wonderful for walking as there were no black flies." They wandered the burnt woods, enjoying themselves, cooking rabbit over the campfire. It all had to come to an end as Cyril was beginning to be anxious about the work awaiting him in North West River, and he had run out of tobacco. Their last day was "a perfect ending to a perfect trip." Cyril told her she looked 10 years younger, that her eyes were sparkling. She managed to write diary entries while travelling in the canoe on the way home: "the end of a very grand 10 days. I'll never forget them. I was 'suffering comfort!' all the time—rain or shine!"[3]

After 10 days apart, with Russell about to go away for the winter, he and Barbara had an important conversation. On September 22, they took an evening walk and the next day she wrote: "this could be my home if I so chose." They hiked "into the marshes and ponds back of Birchy Hill—a place [she] had wanted to go all summer," had supper and then turned around to come back.[4] This was a time when she really appreciated having Russell with her, especially after dark.

There was no moon, no stars, no northern lights, no nothing but the butt of R's cig. If he got more than four or five paces ahead of me I could not see him. Well, we went STRAIGHT alright—awful going, windfalls all over the place, I simply picked up my feet and put them down, trusting they would land on something. I could see nothing at all. Every once in awhile R would peer down thru' the trees and see something—I never found out what, for if I peered I'd only see more trees, more dark sky etc. We could have been going in circles for all I knew, and finally he would tease me and say "We may make it by 3 A.M." I had to admit I was a bit weary—but I had asked for it. I have always wanted to just go cross-country like that, never could safely alone, and F, with whom most of my walks had been taken, has a great aversion to going off the beaten path—and my aversion for staying on it is about as great. So tired or not, I was having the time of my life. (Letter: October 13, 1945)

On September 27, Russell left for his trapline, planning to be back in January. Barbara kept herself busy, sometimes with solitary boil-ups, canoeing and hiking with friends, much more fun than writing the monthly sales report. In early October, she took every opportunity to go paddling before the weather got too rough.

Another night I went off for supper—F and C were to join me if he could get his work done—I had one heck of a time getting the fire going as it was dark when I got there. About eight I had finished supper and was writing a letter and then decided I would just lie back and enjoy life. About 10:30 I figured F & C would not be along so let the fire die out. The next thing I knew I saw a light, heard voices and the sound of another canoe being beached and there they were—11:45. I had dozed off. We had a mug-up and started home about 2 A.M. I drifted down the river, wondering and hoping it would NOT be my last paddle at that hour and at that spot! The following Monday C and his crowd went off—the last to go. Life will be rather dull from now until they begin coming home in Jan. (5-6 weeks and 400-500 miles to walk—round trip—they have to go back again for their canoes!)

F & C are being married when he comes home, and F has asked me to be a "bridesgirl." The boat that took them up to the Falls brought F back some deersmeat C had sent her—it was delicious—the fall meat is better than the spring. The nights are cold now and the frost is like diamonds on the ground—then white all over in the A.M. It tries to snow a bit—and in another week or two it will begin to freeze in the Bay, and another winter will have begun. (Letter: October 13, 1945)

Barbara adored dogs and was really pleased when a member of the hospital staff adopted a husky pup. She had gotten used to the company of Russell's dog during the hours they had spent together; now he was "gone up the river with his master! That is a thing I would love to do—and how!"[5] Russell had been away a month by then.

In a note written to her mother days later, she raised the possibility of living in Labrador permanently. Her example was her friend Peggy Paddon, another former Grenfell volunteer, now a mother and wife.

I think I could be happy in almost every way—If only there were <u>someone with the same background</u> etc. who loved it here as I do. But few outsiders could make a living here—Peggy certainly got the perfect *combination—for Harry has the education etc. for her but he lives as the men here do. It's a _hard_ life, but worth it. Everything "outside" seems so petty & stupid compared to here. Can you understand that? I don't see how I can live in a city or a place where it is always _don't_ walk on the grass, trespass on my ground, or where it isn't safe for a girl to wander alone at any time. I only hope I won't spoil the few remaining months by thinking about how hard it will be to say good-bye to it all. My first full year here was so spoiled by worry & feeling so punk. I worked so much & worried so much about _what_ to do. This summer was happy—I did so much that I enjoyed and for a short time I forgot the past & the future and just _lived_— really lived—and now I'm beginning to stew again. Darn!* (Letter: October 21, 1945)

The Mundys were bird watchers, and after receiving frozen partridges in New York, reading about Cyril trying to shoot an owl, her daughter enjoying a tasty meal of shore birds called yellow legs, and participating in duck hunts where dozens were killed, Mrs. Mundy must have commented on the slaughter of wild birds for food. Barbara, the former Audubon camper, had adopted the Labrador way of thinking.

Mr. Audubon would not be shocked as you think, I believe—for here one shoots to eat and never in that disgusting way we do at home—that time we went duck hunting with Pa in Pa. [Pennsylvania] has left a bad taste in my mouth which is still there—that wasn't necessity or even decent sport. We do get hungry for fresh meat, you know, and the local people don't even have canned meat half the time. (Letter: October 26, 1945)

Barbara's letters had no stories about killing for sport. She hunted all the time and began setting a few traps that fall. In her diary on October 13 she reported seeing an owl but it was "too dark to take a shot." On October 19, "no rabbits—gorgeous moon." On November 5: "got 1 white partridge & found my way up hill!! Hunting every morning—set 2 fox traps with Doris & snare, 2nd. partridge too. A good way to live! Fox in trap on Burnt Woods." She was fishing for trout on November 13.

A detailed Christmas list was compiled and sent to her mother. With a willing shopper in New York and airmail service to the military base, things could easily be shipped to Goose Bay. She wanted to get something special for Florence and Cyril for their wedding gift, and some useful nice things for them for Christmas too, as they had both been so good to her. She enlisted her mother to fill a few other requests for some "thrillers"—cheap paperback books the men could take up the river and a harmonica for her.

Barbara was planning to make as many gifts as she could for her New York family. Among the lovely things in the Industrial Shop were smoked deerskin (caribou) mitts for women, trimmed around the cuff with fox fur. Colourful floral designs were usually embroidered in the soft leather and they were lined with warm duffle cloth. She thought her sister might like a pair, but not her mother, who disliked the smell of smoked deerskin. Barbara loved it. If anyone gave her a pair of deerskin mitts, she told her mother, she would be "thrilled to death."[6]

The late October letter ended with a story about a gale of wind nearly taking the boats away, and high water causing damage.

Sat. we had quite a time—it was <u>rough</u>—and I just had to be out so I shut up shop early and helped the men pull in all the boats and try to save the lumber they had gotten from the base for the new school. The sea was rougher and higher than I have ever seen—only once before in the memory of the most aged has the tide been so high and then there was no gale with it—this time we had a gale and a blizzard to boot. There are few men around now, and the teachers, F & I helped. We lost a lot of lumber, matched and otherwise, the new warehouse is tilted, and the new wharf sunk at this end, and rather rolling. Several men lost their wood—it has been a bad year for that. (Letter: October 26, 1945)

By mid-November, the ice was thick enough to go skating with Bella McLean. "Huge red moon out of water, frost like diamonds on trees. Frost like feathers in A.M."[7] Unlike the year before, Barbara wasn't writing in her diary daily, or even weekly, and her letters were shorter. Many of her experiences were repeats of the previous year, but not when she became the hospital cook. Her home economics training finally came in handy.

You and Ebba [Mrs. Mundy's cook] can have a good laugh! for I am now cooking for 18! have been since Sat. We have a whole family in here delousing them—6 children from 5 to 17 and Mother—all but one crawling! & two starved babies—one 4 mos., other 4 years (this one abnormal to boot). Mrs. P is not here, Florence has had to take a patient she thinks is about to produce twins or triplets to Goose so all jobs are switched. I'm in charge of hospital and am cooking as the cook is in charge of patients' department at the moment. One teacher in bed with bad boils—hope F doesn't get storm-bound for if she does I have to inspect house before those well enough to return can return. Honestly, the poor kids—hardly a thing to wear—that mostly holes and a great deal of it had to be burned. Have just given that green and white striped dress to the oldest girl. (Letter: December 3, 1945)

Mina Paddon had gone to the United States for a while, relieving the tension in staff quarters. "It's been wonderful while Mrs. P has been gone—everyone so pleasant and cheerful and congenial," although it was hard on Florence, who had to shoulder all responsibility. Barbara didn't miss Mrs. Paddon at mealtimes: "No sitting around listening to the same old stories & gossip over & over again. And perfectly free to go hunting early every morning, try deerskin emb. [embroidery] etc. etc. without some dirty crack from her." Barbara, left in charge of the clothing store, put it "in order."[8]

In the hospital, things were routine; unlike the previous Christmas and New Year, no serious illnesses or deaths occurred. A new nurse was on the way to take over from Florence, who had served more than the two years required and would not work for the Mission after she married. It was the quiet time at North West River, everyone waiting for the men to return from trapping. Children who hadn't seen their fathers in over three months were alert to the sounds of sleds scraping over ice. Mothers were telling children to "look out for Pa," silently praying their man was among those hurrying home. It would be enough that he was safe and even better if he had a heavy load of fur. That year, Barbara was awaiting the trappers' return as anxiously as anyone in the community.

After Christmas 1945, the letters Barbara received from her mother must have told about a difficult time of adjustment in post-war New York City. Unionized workers, under wage controls for years, were on the march demanding increases. Tugboat crews, dockworkers, truckers, garment workers, elevator operators, and doormen were calling strikes. At times, the city was nearly paralyzed, no freight moving, fuel shortages, no groceries on store shelves, and hundreds of thousands of people who worked or lived in high-rise buildings stranded on the ground. Mrs. Mundy would not do well during an elevator strike, with her health problems. To Barbara, it was remote but worrying.

Gosh, the situation at home with servants, strikes, etc. etc. seems awful—I wish it did not get me so muddled up just even thinking about it—it makes me boil! I just can't bear the thot of going back to all that confusion, unrest and turmoil. People shouldn't live that way. (Letter: January 30, 1946)

Her mother sent thanks for the Christmas gifts, saying Harriet liked the smoked deerskin mitts. Barbara gave instructions for their care, asking her mother to tell Harriet, "she had better use them, even if they do get soiled," after all "smoked deerskin can be washed" if done carefully. Barbara was proud that she had made all the things she sent home, her embroidery was improving, and she wanted everyone to appreciate how much time it took to do the intricate work.

I did all of the deerskin mitts—embroidered and made—the first mitts I ever made of any kind! And the deerskin was the worst possible kind to start that kind of work on to—thin and very stretchy—but I could not help that as it was one I had bought for myself—I thot the color smoking was about the loveliest I had ever seen. If you thot my embroidery was nice you should see some done by experts! (Letter: January 30, 1946)

Weeks passed without a single diary entry; there was nothing from November 20 to January 10. Barbara broke her diary silence with a note that her traps were buried under snow, foxes were running over them, and Christmas had been busy. "Men coming home—most seem to have done well." Russell wasn't among the first to arrive, but Cyril was back, and wedding preparations were under way. Dresses were made and flowers improvised for the wedding day on January 24. After the event, she wrote, "F & C married—Janet [Best], Olive [Michelin], self, Victor [Goudie], Selby [Michelin], John Blake. F looked lovely & it was a very nice wedding & party. Dance 'till 5 A.M." She described the dresses and hats in a letter to her mother, but not the all-night dance.

I am enclosing the picture of the dress and samples of material— they were very pretty—Randy got the patterns and material for F. The

"Bridesgirls" were F's sister, C's sister and myself—the "bridesboys" a bro of each and John Blake from Mud Lake. The dresses were grey skirts and rose bodices—mine had stiffening and a facing of rose. Mrs. P made it all, except I had to put the zippers in—I told her it was time she learned how (!!) but she did not see it that way. She was very nice and made it all— what has gotten into her I wonder what is up! It's lovely while it lasts—let's hope it lasts! We all had our hair waved—Bella, who does the best job was not here but Hazel [Hoyles][9] made it look quite well—you know just the ends curled softly and then we made halos braided the two colors together and then a few little half bows of the material and a few white partridge feathers. It was very pretty—later on I am going to take pictures. F wore her graduation dress—a soft pink, my pearl clip for luck and her veil was a bit longer than shoulder length and caught at the side with begonias. I even had to put it on—gosh, the things I have done up here—it's a liberal education, I tell you. I could get no flowers so we cut all the begonias and made a little old fashioned bouquet with one of the lacy doilies you sent me for background. Candles in the church and little tiny boutonnieres for the men—they had once been attached to nut dishes from Denisons! (Letter: March 4, 1946)

Russell missed the wedding by three days. Barbara had been keeping watch but "just missed seeing him actually come." She was especially delighted by a gift he had for her.

Wed. Jan. 30: R gave me a lovely silver fox caught about 3 mi. above his house on Fig River (left side!). I can't quite believe it—in a way 'twas mine before it was ever caught. Gosh, what a lovely thing to own, especially knowing the land & the man it came from. Teachers & I down to see his fur; I get a thrill every time I see someone's fur. (Diary: January 30, 1946)

If she told her mother about the silver fox fur she was given by Russell, it was not in the two pages that were kept from the single-spaced letter typed on January 30, full of Christmas chatter about family and friends, but nothing about her private life. Barbara's diary entries for February and early March were written mainly on weekends, when she had a day off work, and Russell was frequently mentioned. That winter he did not go back up the river for a second hunt, but stayed at home. They went for day and night walks, fishing trips, boil-ups over a fire in the woods. They had suppers alone or with friends at "the Bight," her code for his house located away from most of the houses in North West River, on the curving beach facing across the bay to the mountains. The gossips were back in business.

Mrs. Mundy and Harriet were pressing her to decide what she would do when her contract with the Mission was finished. On March 4, she announced her intention to stay longer, even without a contract.

You asked me once if I thot I could ever be happy in N.Y. again—the answer I am pretty sure is NO. I never have been really happy there, or contented—I like the freedom here—the whole world is yours and there is no one to say "keep off"—if you get blue you can go off and be surrounded by so much that you sort of have to forget it. And you need so little to be happy here. The things that seem to matter so much outside make no difference really here—and outside if you don't have them you are miserable—but here no one had them so what is the difference? You feel rushed and upset inside, even if your outward surroundings are more or less placid—but here you even get peaceful inside—I certainly don't want to be an industrial worker all my life—far from it, I want more than that—it is the same old story I want what I have always wanted and what I will always continue to want. But I do think I could be very happy here or in a place of this sort—away from all the turmoil and unhappiness that seems to go with life outside—at least for us it has seemed to be that way. If only I could look ahead ten years or more and see how I would feel then. I realize only too well that the end of my contract is at hand—and whether or not I will be asked to renew it I don't know—nor do I know if I would if asked. I feel sort of sick when I think of leaving here forever—I just can't think about it. When I first came up I felt so badly, both physically and otherwise that there were times when I just didn't think I could go another day. I tried to work it off, but it only made me more tired and ill. It was desperately lonely, until I got to know the local people and they began to accept me. I may be wrong but outwardly they apparently like me—at least they do not dislike me as far as I know. The really good times I have had have been with them—not with the staff. I'm around the hospital very little now—Miss B [nurse Ethel Brown] retires to her room and I go out to F and C. I have far more fun than I did the first year and I think my job has improved rather than been hurt by it. I don't take it so darned seriously but I think I do it just as well if not better. I frankly don't want to leave—and I can't tell you now when I will. If I am not asked or do not want to renew I think I would like to stay here a bit—completely free to try to do some of the many things I would like to. You and H make your plans regardless of me, and if I do come out I will have [to] make mine accordingly. (Letter: March 4, 1946)

Before she clarified her reasons for not returning to New York in the spring, she began the letter with some very sad news about Ernest Goudie, last mentioned in June 1945, when he was taken to Goose Bay on a stretcher. The news came by radio message to Jack Watts, from the hospital in St. Anthony, where Ernest was being treated for tuberculosis.

I had to take bad news to D [his sister Doris] about Ernest on Sat. and of course they are pretty well shot by it—he had flu and there is little hope—just as they were beginning to get on their feet after Uncle Fred's death. It is a rotten shame and will leave them without a man, which is no joke in this country. Her Mother will make things very hard as she has always and it is pretty tough on D. (Letter: March 4, 1946)

While in the midst of writing the letter, Barbara heard from Jack Watts that another radio message had come to say that Ernest had died.[10] He asked her to break the news to the family. First Uncle Fred and now Ernest—it was a lot to bear in a little over a year. Barbara knew it would be a struggle for a family of women, the small salary Doris earned in the shop their only income, but at least they had that. In Labrador, keeping warm, and clothing and feeding yourself and your children was full time work for a couple. At least the Goudie women had many relatives who would share fish and meat and help with firewood.

The new head nurse was on duty and "seems quite nice and jolly—and I think capable of holding her own."[11] Canadian Ethel Brown was an experienced Mission nurse who transferred from the station at Mutton Bay, north of Harrington on the Quebec north shore.[12] Barbara was very glad that Miss Brown enjoyed the outdoors and was always keen for a walk on snowshoes or some ice fishing.

This morning there was light snow on everything and we just <u>had</u> to go out. Miss B is quite good fun and we both love this land—we came back *thinking and saying in one breath—"how could anyone be unhappy for long with so much beauty to look at all the time." Perhaps tho' for those who live here it is so much hard work that they don't have time to look at it and enjoy it as we do—maybe that is why they don't seem to realize how lucky they are.* (Letter: March 4, 1946)

Barbara and Ethel Brown both knew the view from the hospital dining room, with table set for breakfast, was very different from that in a trapper's home with hungry children clamouring for food, or in Lilla Goudie's home, with no man to provide for the family. That contrast was much on Barbara's mind, as shown in her letters home.

I know if I stayed here without a job life would be very different—I wish I could picture more clearly just what it would be like; without the job, without the comparative luxury we have at the hospital and without the contacts we do have occasionally—I think I could be awfully happy, but I wonder really how I would make out—would I be able to work as hard as I would have to, would I be terribly cut off, would I eventually miss the things I don't seem to now? Could I make a go of it? It is awfully easy to feel I want to risk it, and yet I know, in fairness to myself and everyone, I must not decide until I have been out again. We have so few contacts outside, and so little chance to make new ones—and I'm tired of trying to—it seems like an endless search for something that can't be found. Perhaps it would be better to give up the struggle, and just stay right here. I don't know! Our life is so limited at home—at least here, everyday you see someone to speak to, and there is so much else so close at hand and so inexpensive—it is the freedom of the place I guess that gets those of us from outside. When I am not all upset trying to decide what to do, I have been happier and more content, I think, than ever before in my life. I know there is a lot to consider, but everything is a gamble, and if you are constantly afraid to take a chance, where do you get? Whatever I decided on might prove to be wrong, and I have decided it is best to take your happiness where you find it, if you are sure of it, even if it lasts for only a short time. I feel darn lucky to have it. Do you see now why I don't want to go yet? (Letter: March 9-18, 1946)

Barbara felt she would rather be in Labrador than New York but thought she should not make up her mind about her future until she had been back to New York. She still hadn't told her mother or her sister very much about her feelings for Russell and must have been struggling with how to break the news. If her mother had thought Leland Burt unsuitable, how in the world would she ever accept a Labrador fur trapper for a son-in-law? On March 18, Barbara was more forthcoming in a letter to Harriet. Perhaps she hoped her sister would plead her case to her mother. She told Harriet that she hated the thought of leaving North West River: "I feel more a part of it here than I've ever felt anywhere. I feel more at ease or something."

I go to F's and have lovely times there with them and Russell. Every Sun. R and I go out for supper someplace—have a lovely fire and often fried deer meat. F and C join us sometimes. It tastes so good outdoors particularly after a good long walk—My, I've had good times with them all. How I love just walking <u>anyplace</u> and with them I can—no fear of getting lost. My boots are tapped and double tapped, my snowshoes getting worn out, my pants so shiny they look like silk, but it's worth it all and much more. I've <u>never</u> been so happy and it must not end yet, <u>not yet</u>. Perhaps it need never end, but if it must I want a few more months. (Letter: March 18, 1946)

The deer meat she mentioned was the bounty from a 10-day hunting trip Russell and Cyril had made across the bay. They brought back as much meat as they could, but had to leave some cached, hoping to go back for it later. Whenever hunters had success, they readily shared the meat around the community: "R brought me horns & gave me a fore quarter—luscious steaks."[13] When he got back from hunting, Russell then went up Grand River to his trapping grounds, a "quick trip for striking up & canoe—only 17 days."[14]

While Russell was gone, Barbara walked down to Saltwater Pond on a stormy day. All the walks she had done with him, Florence, and Cyril had given her the confidence to head out on her own and she proudly related the whole adventure. She hadn't planned on walking—it was a business trip to see the women who did needlework for the shop and normally she would have had a sled and driver—but the combination of dogs "dying off at a great rate" and a missing driver contrived to keep her in North West River. She went to the dog-team driver's house and found him still in bed—he thought conditions were "too blowy" so he "give it up." She took off by herself and all went well: "rather glad I had a chance to do it & to 'boil' under my own power. 4½ hours walking." She spent the night with Harry and Peggy and baby Margaret.[15]

On Tuesday I took Margaret out for a stroll in her komatic box, and ended up at the Islands—came back by team. (Harry's, by the way, is about 15 miles from here—the Islands another 5.) Did not get to Mulligan as there were so few dogs, and no one was sure where they were, there, over the mtns. or hauling wood, and then we had had such glorious weather for so long everyone expected a mild and a bad one, and had I walked I might have been badly stuck. The only part of me that was tired was my shoulder where the game bag had rubbed. It was not a proper one with cross straps but one that rested just on one shoulder and it had a buckle in just the wrong spot—and my snowshoes behaved like sails in the wind, and the walking was really not bad enough to wear them!

Well, I got back with a wonderful sail with Harry on Thurs. Sailed all the way, at times the dogs had a bad time keeping ahead—they never once tho' tightened their traces. It was the best ride I have had all spring. If I had to miss any of my workers it was best to miss the Mulligan ones, for they are hard workers and continuous ones. (Letter: April 26, 1946)

A church fair and a wedding meant two consecutive nights of "dancing until daylight" with no complaints from Barbara, who was "very chipper and awake." The Mission staff were pleased for Dulcie, their cook, who would also be married that week, but "what we will eat after she has gone no one knows."[16] Barbara planned another working trip and Russell rounded up enough dogs to take her, so they drove to Happy Valley, Mud Lake, and Traverspine. She loved going to Mud Lake, staying with the Joseph Blakes, a "friendly & happy couple."[17]

With Russell at home in North West River, Barbara had many more opportunities for hunting trips and winter boil-ups. She loved it all, but especially riding on a komatik behind a team of dogs. In early May, she went with him across the bay to retrieve the deer meat he had stored on scaffolds. Cyril couldn't make the trip, "marvelous luck," so Russell asked Barbara if she wanted to go. It was a dodgy time to travel. There had been some rainy weather, making the ice soft and open in places, but he was determined to get the meat before warm weather ruined it. They left early on the morning of May 3, after a mighty struggle with a rambunctious team of dogs, in which Russell, "worn to a frazzle," had his glasses broken.

We lit out straight across the Bay [to Gillard's Bight] and the ice cracked almost all the way over! Stopped at the Whites for breakfast—the place was in a mess, only an old man and boy having been there for a week almost alone, and I shivered at the thought of having to stay the night there—said to R I was sleeping in his sleeping bag no matter how many offers of beds I had and he was to back me up—never thinking of course that would put him just where I did not want to be! but I guess he could have managed another bag or something.

Well, we tried to go across from point to point but we went thru a couple of times—really went thru' so had to beat it for shore and go the long way around by the cracks. Even going thru' I found rather fascinating—and wasn't the least bit scared. We got down to the deer—on scaffold—about 11:30 and had them lashed on and started back by 12:10. From the Bay was a high bank and then about 3 miles of marsh to the foot of the mts. It was lovely to be so near them. Then it began to blow and snow squalls came and it got thick, and the going was bad, and all in all we thot we could not make it after all.

When we got back to the Whites we were going in to see if there was a crack lower down we could follow back, have a warm and set right off again. We arrived, it was thick and too bad to go immediately, we got inside and found the rest of the family home from Dulcie's wedding and the place was spotless—you could have eaten off the floor! It was warm, and tea tasted so good with several newly baked things to add to it and we stayed until it cleared. Then altho' it was cold and the wind in our faces we thot we would try it.

We could not cross where we had in the A.M. with a load, so had to go farther down. As it was we hit bad going and kept breaking thru'. At first R would not let me get off the komatic for he was afraid I would get wet—go above my boots. But everytime we went thru' we would go that much farther with my 150 lbs., after a few times I paid no attention to him and jumped as fast as I could when we started to go thru'. We struggled on,

*and R thought for awhile that we might have to leave the deer on the Bay
'till morning, for he would not take them on after dark—could not see well
enough and the dogs would be "beat out." However, we just made this side
by dark and came along the cracks.* (Letter: May 13, 1946)

The description of the trip across the bay was written 10 days
after it happened and included a complaint about Mina Paddon being
"grumpy" on her return. Immediately after the trip she rhapsodized in
a diary entry: "I had a <u>wonderful</u>, wonderful, wonderful time—about
35 mis. each way. 'Not the first time we've boiled together, eh girl?' Bless
him!"[18] With the ice loosening up in the bay, her time would best be
spent bundled up in a canoe looking for ducks overhead. She told her
mother she planned to hunt with Russell every day, if weather allowed.

*This A.M. another try—got 4. I stayed the morning in hopes of a goose
but none coming by noon came in for work this aft. It is cloudy again, and
beginning to rain. The early morning hours are too lovely for anything—
the moon is almost full, and as it sets and dawn starts the colors on the
water, the ice and the clouds are indescribable—mauves, pinks, deep grey
blues and then the reflections of the trees, the ice and the canoes—all white
with white flys and the occupants dressed in white. It is really thrilling—I
love every minute of it in spite of the cold. It is so quiet and not a sound
as the canoe glides along—not even a drip from the paddle—for it doesn't
come out of the water. And you hear the birds call as they fly in—I wish I
could get it across to you—what it is really like. And then it is interesting to
see how real hunters really hunt—and the people here are real hunters—it
is their life not just a hobby for sport. I made no mistake in staying a
second year—I have done things I will never forget as long as I live—I have
really LIVED this year.* (Letter: May 13, 1946)

Just as the Mission staff expected, the hospital kitchen was suffering
the loss of Dulcie Broomfield, with "no cook at the moment and only a
very young and inexperienced second girl." Barbara was managing to
find appetizing things to eat outside the staff dining room.

*Had a taste of really good black duck yesterday. The only other time
I had it, it was cooked too much and all dried out. R baked the 2 we got
Sat. and we were going to have them on Sun. night. But it turned out to be
a very wet, damp day, no kind to go out for supper, and then his brother*

Hayward turned up for dinner and one duck was consumed. Then Phyllis met us as we were going down to F's and said "Daddy, I want to go to the house for supper," so he took her down and the other duck went—but he saved a leg and wing for me and brought it up this evening and I munched it as we paddled up the River. My it was wonderful! R is off to Sandy Pt. tomorrow for a hunt and I hope he repeats a day he had one year—between 30 and 40 ducks and 9 geese in one day. He'll be gone a week and so I hope he gets a lot! I might get a taste or two—who knows! Pig, pig, pig, aren't I? (Letter: May 13, 1946)

In a postscript at the end of the typed letter, she described her full ensemble for a day of duck hunting, the list taking a whole page. Russell told her she was in danger of getting stuck in the canoe.

Feet 2 pr. stockings, 2 pr. sox, 2 pr. duffle vamps—deerskins

Legs long woolies, yr. skating panties

Legs cont'd H's G.C. [Grenfell cloth] pants, Ski pants lined with old slacks, Red X scarves wound around knees

Body Wooly shirt, Sweater, Vest, Flannel shirt, Sweater F gave me, Green cable stitch one, R's eiderdown jacket, My dickie, duck hunting coat

Hands 2 pr. wool mitts, 1 pr. duffles, 1 pr. leather mitts with fur

Head Estonian beret, Duck hunting cap

Getting up at 2:30 a.m. to go out with Russell on a cold, blustery bay full of ice: "wonderful fun—I love everything connected with it."[19] Insulated in her multi-layered outfit and buried under a quilt and blanket, Barbara was comfortable enough to snooze in the canoe, while Russell paddled the icy water.

Thurs A.M.—R woke me with a k.—calm as could be full moon—lovely—2 teal (gr. wing) and I shot nanceri! Gosh I'm happy (& sleepy!) Birds calling, pitching, goose against moon & R honking. Utter silence so wonderful.

May 17: left at midnight—no birds to see or hear. R got 1 piebird—picked, cleaned, cooked, and ate my nanceri. Pussywillows—long, grey ones on reddish stems. Morning, evening hunts & paddles.

Mon. 20: R off to Sandy Pt. Left home 2 yrs. ago tomorrow—how I hope the next 4 mos. will be happy & that I'll be here all that time. (Diary: May 16-20, 1946)

On the day he woke her with a kiss, she wrote a very important letter to her mother, confiding that she and Russell had talked of getting married. Either Mrs. Mundy or Harriet had heard of Barbara's deepening involvement with Russell from other sources, perhaps staff in the New York IGA office or a former Mission wop. As Barbara warned her friends two years earlier, "the underground in the IGA is pretty good." She defended herself and Russell, addressing her mother's concerns about their conduct and the talk it caused.

You have probably gathered from my letters that there is one man here who has been perfectly wonderful to me, and with whom I have had many, many very good times—some of them the best times I have ever had in my life. But when I decided to stay the second year I knew only his name and hardly his face, for I had spoken to him perhaps twice. I talked about staying on this summer last summer, before our good times began at all. It is not because of him I stayed; it is because of him tho' that I will not want to leave next fall.

As for trips—I would love nothing better than to take the one Austy did—on a small scale that is what F, C and I would have done. Cyril does not go that distance. But even before that was definitely off, I knew I would rather go differently. Don't worry if I ever do take a trip of that sort I will be married before because I want to be, not because I have to be.

There are exactly three people here who know how I feel about it all— and none of them are on the staff—there are however any number who think they are quite qualified to know all about it—but anything they say is not true. They know I do things with Russell, for we can't very well do things without it being known, and I am sure I don't care if they do know it but beyond that they know nothing at all. People jump to conclusions here in about one second—a man can't be polite and walk home with you once from a dance, before the tongues begin to wag. I loved the place and I loved the life before R ever came along—but he has made me love it more than ever.

If I do decide to come back for good we would not live here at NWR— neither of us want to. We would live away someplace alone but within reach of someone else if I needed anyone while he was away. He would be away a lot—and that is one thing that bothers me—I wouldn't be afraid but I'd be lonely—not that awful loneliness I have felt sometimes, but just lonely because he wasn't there with me. In all I'd only have him a few months really—he'd be gone from late Sept. to Jan., again in Feb. until March sometime, and then even there are lots of things to take him away, deer hunting, sealing, wood-cutting, duck hunting, and probably even more. I would be much occupied tho' with just living as one does here—there is not much to make housekeeping easy—and in the last two years I have learned to do lots of things I never could before. I could sew a good deal, and I could also learn to hunt a little perhaps—and have a few snares to get me out and around. I don't think I would be sitting twiddling my thumbs much.

We are very different I know in many ways; education, background, etc.—but I am so much happier and content here than I have ever been before. The lack on his part of the advantages I have had I don't think would make much difference here and here we would stay, for he is a trapper and a hunter and would be perfectly miserable as anything else, and I would be miserable having him anything else. As I do more with him I am getting to know him better and also getting a bit clearer picture of what it would really be like. That is another reason <u>now</u> why I want to be here this summer—to see if we wear well and to know more definitely what lies ahead of us if I do come back. I think it would be a wonderful life if I could learn to do the many things I would have to learn—I think I could with R's help—and he would give me help I feel sure. He has had to do so much for himself that he knows how and I think he'd be patient in teaching me. I hope I could make him happy—I think I could; and I know he could make me extremely happy if he continued to want to as he does now.

I have written no one about this, nor do I intend to—and I hope you will keep it to yourself—I'm only telling you because I know his name has crept into my letters to you pretty frequently and you have probably already guessed that we liked each other. But it is no one else's business and you can tell them so when they start prying. I don't believe I have written as I have talked to you in my mind—it's harder to write than talk. If you knew how truly kind R has been to me I am sure you would like him. (Letter: May 16, 1946)

She had committed herself to a plan. She would marry Russell and live in Labrador, but before they married she would return to New York to spend the winter with her mother while he was trapping. She wanted one more summer and fall, and a chance to take a canoe trip up the Grand River, maybe all the way to the falls, before she left for the winter. Although she would be working through summer, she would take time off for trips, the first one to the islands in Lake Melville, for a week of hunting, "when the ice breaks up." Barbara was getting all her shop work done: "working hard and sleeping hard so I can hunt again when R comes home."[20]

Sun. [May 26] 3 P.M. Have much to do—so much I'm considering doing none of it for tomorrow A.M. at 3 we plan to go. Russell got home at noon yesterday with 53 ducks—his best hunt for one trip and F & C couldn't go yesterday because of wind, so if the wind goes down we'll all go together. What fun. I spent last night baking cookies. Today R is baking 4 or 5 ducks and he having no bread for stuffing I've just been to F's to make it. We'll be gone a week I think and hope—suits me fine if wind, ice or snow keep us longer! At least 'till we run out of grub. P.S. Did you ever think I'd be going off duck hunting for a week! (Letter: May 21, 1946)

Ducks were roasted and cookies baked in preparation for a trip up the bay to "the Islands"—she mentioned Dry, Ambrose, Upper, and Pork—where many North West River residents had cabins and other people lived all year. They hunted seals, which were "all over the place," killed ducks and partridges, and pitched their tents in a different place every night. They started for home on June 3.

Mon. [June 3] calmer & we were able to paddle home. Dinner (all of us) at Upper Is. & supper (R & me) at Pork Island—ate partridges. Shot with shotgun. The wk. passed like a minute & was a very happy one. I forgot everything & everybody at NWR—a <u>real</u> vacation. I learned a lot too, practical Lab. jobs, plus things about myself & R. (Diary: May 27-June 3, 1946)

Her diary skipped over the rest of June and most of July, noting only "picnics & plans for trip up Grand River."[21] There were no eight-page typed diary-style letters to Everybody and fewer letters to Mother. She was busy with a working visit from Kitty Keddie and preparing to hand over responsibility for the Industrial Shop. She complained it was too windy to go out on the water alone, making it difficult to tend her trout net. The spring fair came and went—for the sale she donated a smelt net she had been knitting all winter. She wrote her mother a brief letter on the day after her 36th birthday without mentioning Russell. In a longer letter she began on July 23, she said Russell was working for the HBC that summer: "[He] has much to do in the evenings and by the time I see him it is often too late to do much." Barbara complained about the latest batch of "unbearable" summer wops, disturbing her by grinding coffee at midnight. The new Industrial worker, Margaret Beckett, had arrived to take her place and Barbara was helping her settle in.

Barbara was getting impatient to be clear of her Mission duties and was fully absorbed in preparations for a canoe trip up the Grand River. It would be the same trip taken by Elliott and Kate Merrick and described by him in *True North*, except Barbara and her party wouldn't be travelling in the autumn and staying the winter. Some considerable discussion took place about who, and how many, should go.

The original idea was for three of us to go—Russell, myself and another girl. Then Miss Brown suggested if there were to be only three it would be wiser to have myself and two men, in case something happened and with one man we would be stranded—I did not want that, and thot the idea of anything happening rather ridiculous—as did Russell—he was rather put out I think, having successfully travelled the River for 23 years. I got scared tho', and figured with my rotten luck it would have to be this time and this trip that something would happen—and usually if you are afraid it is the sure time it will happen, then everyone would say—I told you so—and I would feel I could have taken the precaution. So I got another man—it will make it easier for R, but more expensive for me. However, it is something I have long wanted to do and that same money could quickly be spent on stupid passing things and I would have nothing to remember—but a trip like this will never be forgotten. I am here, I have most everything I need for such a trip—and what a fool I would be to give it up. I would not hesitate a second to go alone with Russell—for if anything happened to us we'd be dead and it would not matter—but if anything like that happened and one poor girl was left alone it would be hard on her.

So there will be four of us: the other two are Nora Groves, Russell's half sister, and John Blake—a great friend of Cyril's who was to have been the fourth on the trip last summer. If I can possibly wangle a trip to Indian Habr., I will go there too if I can. But there is much work, and much play I want to do right here in NWR, and my days will be fully occupied. I am planning to leave in late Sept.—still don't know whether by boat or plane. So you can expect me home late Sept. or early Oct. (Letter: July 23, 1946)

Barbara's obligations and responsibilities at the shop were done. She was "leaving the hospital and glad to go." Her belongings were packed and moved to Florence and Cyril's house. Now all she had to do was get organized for the trip up Grand River, with luck, all the way to the legendary falls.

Chapter Eleven

THE SILVER HIGHWAY

Barbara wanted to go to the Falls, 'cause she was an American girl and she wanted to see it and we took Russell Groves for a guide. I was never up there meself, not before that.

—John Blake, "Trapper and Guide"

HBC trader John McLean felt the rock shake under his feet from the force of water surging over a "stupendous fall" in August 1839. McLean was the first to write about the Grand Falls; in his account he called them the Great Falls of Hamilton River. His expedition began in June that year at the mouth of George River in northern Quebec. He was stationed at Fort Chimo, Ungava Bay, and was instructed by his superiors to attempt to establish an overland trade route to Fort Smith, now North West River, as a way to keep the northern posts supplied when ice blocked Atlantic coastal navigation. His report of "one of the grandest spectacles of the world" intrigued and encouraged others who hoped to make a name for themselves by measuring or photographing the falls. McLean strongly discouraged the notion of the overland trading path due to the obstacle presented by the falls and the impracticability of the rivers.[1] Canadian geologist A.P. Low calculated the volume of water spilling over the falls as 50,000 cubic feet per second when he saw them 55 years later, on May 14, 1894.[2]

The remarkable waterfall originated from the outflow of the hundreds of lakes, rivers, and streams carved out by glaciers on the Labrador plateau during the last ice age. The weight and action of the moving ice created a plain in the interior of Labrador, which is "not quite level but is lower at the centre than at its rim, like a saucer."[3] The drainage basin is 92,500 square kilometres. Rivers contained within the basin combined and found a channel to the sea through a weak spot; the flowing waters were known to the Innu as Mishta-Shipu and to the trappers as Grand River. The Newfoundland government called it Hamilton River, after Governor Sir Charles Hamilton, and renamed it Churchill River in 1965, following the death of Sir Winston Churchill.[4] From its headwaters in western Labrador near the Quebec border, to Lake Melville, the river is 856 kilometres long.[5]

The difficult journey to Grand Falls had been well documented by the time Barbara was planning her trip; numerous scientific or adventure groups over 100 years had made maps and measurements, naming rivers, hills, and canyons they assumed were unnamed. And yet, few people had seen the falls, except for Height of Land trappers and the nomadic Innu who had occupied the country for millennia. After 1891, some who made it to the falls left their names on pieces of paper sealed inside a small glass jar left by two members of the Bowdoin College Scientific Expedition. Of the 44 names left in the bottle before August 1946, there was one woman—Kate Austen was there in 1930 with Elliott Merrick and John Michelin.[6]

In *True North*, Merrick had written that he and Kate made trapper John Michelin promise he would take them to see the falls before they left the trapline to return to North West River. Michelin wasn't as keen; the falls were 6 miles in the wrong direction, he had seen them before, and he wanted to get home. Despite Michelin's reservations, on Christmas Day they went there. Merrick did not romanticize the sight of the waterfall, although his description of stretching out on their stomachs on a mound of ice, taking turns "holding each other's feet to peer into the witches' cauldron a long way down" is stomach-churning:

It is a breath-taking sight, the boundless power of the frantic rapid, crowded between narrow walls, thundering down a steep slope to leap far out from the brink and plunge into the maelstrom below. But a dish of apricots we had for supper in honor of Christmas was also very good. It is unfortunate, when things have been talked about so much that one feels compelled to like them. For me the Grand Falls is an interesting incident of the trip, no more appealing than the fact that a tilt can be built without a nail or the knowledge that you get cracked heels if you don't wash your feet. As always, it is the travelling and the people met on the way, not the getting there. The people around North West River insisted that we were going up the river to see the Grand Falls. So be it. We have seen them.[7]

John Michelin first put his name in the bottle in 1923 when he and another North West River trapper, Judson Blake, stopped there on December 10. They had come from Fred Goudie's tilt on a fine day: "No vapor flying. It's a fine sight."[8] Michelin and Blake were there again in 1925, as guides for Varick Frissell. The Labrador men didn't bother putting their names in the bottle that time.[9]

Aerial surveyors had photographed Grand River and falls in 1931 and 1932, judging it an extremely safe flying region, with plenty of landing places for float planes on the river. The surveyors had finished their work on the north Labrador coast in August 1931 when Alexander Forbes allowed the crew to take the plane in to Grand Falls. They flew their large Fairchild seaplane from North West River into the interior, landed on a lake near the falls, camped and spent several days photographing the falls and gorges. Their names went in the bottle.

On August 23, 1932, pilot Harold G. Crowley and three others again flew a Fairchild seaplane from North West River to the Grand Falls. On their return to North West River, they noticed a plume of smoke, investigated, and found a broken-down plane and three prospectors, "subsisting on hard tack and blueberries" on the north side of Jacobie Lake. The Forbes team made a Good Samaritan flight bringing food to the stranded men, charging a nominal fee to the three Mission staff they had brought along for the ride.[10] When the mission of mercy was completed, they flew over the falls, snapped a few pictures, and were home in four hours, declaring that trip to be the first tourist flight to the Grand Falls.[11] Perhaps it was also the first air search and rescue in

Labrador. It certainly proved the interior of Labrador was being staked out by hopeful prospectors.

Crowley had flown up the river three times: "It is impossible to get lost—simply fly over the river coming and going, and you are following a silver highway which has no detours, no branches, and incidentally no rough spots."[12] The rapids may not have looked formidable from thousands of feet above, but viewed from a canoe at water level, they were wild, powerful, and alive, white water boiling over barely submerged boulders. Anyone who had paddled or tracked the river would have taken exception to Crowley's comment about "no rough spots" and made a few corrections to his advisory—especially a trapper who had a canoe full of his winter's food supply flip over and wash away.

National Geographic magazine sent a team to travel from the inland plateau to Lake Melville in summer 1950. Andrew Brown and Ralph Gray hired two "trapper guides"—John Michelin, who by then had likely lost count of the times he had seen the falls, and his cousin, Leslie Michelin. In the magazine article, the river was Hamilton, the official name at the time, instead of Grand, still the preferred name in Labrador. The four canoeists descended from the Height of Land and paddled downriver, impressed by the amount and power of the water: "Our first hours on the lower Hamilton made clear why the natives call it Grand River. A stream of extraordinary beauty, it flows now fierce, now tranquil, hemmed in by bold hills often soaring 1,000 feet or more."[13]

As chief guide for the Barbara Mundy expedition of 1946, Russell may have been a bit put out initially by her decision to hire John Blake to go with them, but he would have admitted it made things easier. Nothing had changed since John McLean's time. Going up that river was work and the only way to do it was to paddle, pole, track, tow, and walk. Russell had done it dozens of times, but never with two inexperienced women. John Blake had travelled the river since he was 15, although not as far as the Height of Land; his trapline was at the lower end of Grand River. For Nora and Barbara, it would be an adventure, and while Russell didn't fear the river, and didn't want them to be afraid, he approached it with great caution. He was responsible for the lives of his half-sister and the woman he hoped to marry, and would do whatever he could to keep them safe.

There was no spirit of apprehension when the party embarked. Barbara and Nora had full confidence in their companions. Between them, Russell and John knew every portage path, all trappers' tilts, and the best camping and fishing spots along the way. They were experts in canoe. For Barbara, it was the realization of her longtime wish to see the interior of wild Labrador. For the men, it was a romp, a quick trip to the falls and back in time to prepare to go upriver again for their winter's trapping.

Like the adventurers who preceded them, Barbara documented every rapid, camp, and mug-up in her diary. Dutiful daughter that she was, she even managed to get a couple of letters carried out by other river travellers to be mailed to her mother. The first day began when Wilfred (probably Baikie) readied his motorboat to tow them, their loaded canoes, and Russell's dog, Flop, across the bay to collect John Blake at Mud Lake. They would be helped as far as the rapids at Muskrat Falls, where the river funnels through a 100-metre-wide channel to drop over a shelf 20 metres high. Barbara had been there two years before when the Height of Land trappers were on their way upriver for the winter.

August 14: Nora, Russell and I started with Wilfred at 8 A.M. Picked up John at Mud Lake. Ike fired a salute at Valley with double-barrelled shot-gun. Much engine trouble and only reached Willow Is., a bit above base. Camped on sand in HUGE tent—moon shining thru'—Flop mad with delight. Wilfred & John went back to Valley for engine repairs—spent night there. (Traverspine, Black Rock, Muskrat Is.)

August 15: Still much engine trouble, but finally got to Muskrat Falls. Four trips over portage—two for girls. On to Lower Tilt for swim and night having boiled a bit above Falls. Geese. Camped on bank, brook winding off to right.

On a map, Grand River appears to be a welcoming waterway, opening the interior of Labrador to travellers starting at Lake Melville, although not by a straight route. At the mouth of the river in Goose Bay, paddlers go southwesterly against the flow. The river turns slightly northwest at Gull Island, then takes a sharp angled turn almost directly south at Horseshoe Rapids, until Mininipi Rapids, where it flows from the west again, making a backwards Z-shape.[14] After Mininipi Rapids, the river valley turns northwest and keeps winding in that direction to the Labrador plateau. There are the less fearsome Mouni Rapids to get through, and Devil's Hole, with its treacherous whirlpool, before reaching 56-kilometre-long Lake Winokapau. From the end of the lake, it is 72 kilometres upriver to the Big Hill portage, where trappers began their final climb to the Height of Land.

It was not an easy river, but a struggle upward all the way. Trappers who went upriver two or three times a year walked as much as they paddled to get to their grounds, for all the portaging and towing they did around shallows, rapids, and falls. They either carried their kit, including canoes, over the hills or, if possible, tracked (towed) their loaded canoes as carefully as they could at the edges of the cascading flow, one man aboard steering, and the other on shore at the end of a 15-to-30-metre-long rope, balancing on jagged, slippery rocks as they manhandled their precious food, axes, traps, guns, stoves, and tents to safer water. According to the published advisories of the late-nineteenth-century explorers, the shoreline was no safe haven. Punishing clouds of mosquitoes and black flies were hovering to chew them alive when they came ashore to camp or portage.

August 16: Blowing hard. R tracked, I tried to steer. Got to Upper Tilt. River getting prettier, flies worse! Rattle Brook, opposite Long Pt. below Sand Banks. Steered Flate's Rapid, Edw's Brook; poled Tom's Rapid.

August 17: Crow Pt., Sandion [Sandy Island] Lake; poled and steered for Porcupine Rapid. Gull Island Lake—strong tide, poling. Fred's Pt. for night. Even Flop was in canoe at one time.

August 18: Grizzell's [Grizzle] Rapid—poled with us in part way. Lowe's Cache. Gull Island Rapid—this one a real one, white water (poled and bow-line with pole). Gull Is. Rapid to Otter Brook I steered. Otter Br., lovely pebbly rocks with water running out in three directions. Lower Horseshoe (pole on bow); Harvey's house, fishing. Hills high on either side. Dewdrop diamonds on fluted leaves. Camped on sand below Harvey's. Horseshoe House. Such wonderful fun!

Russell and John were very alert on the day they went through Mininipi Rapids, the worst on the river. Every trapper had stories of close calls, canoes swamped, food and gear washed overboard—that happened all the time. Recovering from losing grub or equipment was one thing, but Russell and John had both lost friends and family members in the rapids, skilled men who knew what they were doing. Since his childhood, Russell had heard stories about his grandfather, John Montague, an experienced trapper and guide, who drowned while tracking his canoe over Gull Island Rapid in 1902.

August 19: Three Horseshoe Rapids. Poled Bob's Brook between Lower and Middle Rapids which were tracked with bow-line. Smooth sand beach and point for mug-up. Crossed river there below Horseshoe Cliff. Strong tide. Recrossed river beyond Mininipi Island. Long vista to Mininipi Rapid. Sowed seeds for Uncle Fred—R marked it out with rocks and stick. Canoe taken through with bow-line and pole. John's swamped with loss of boiler and paddle. Camped on bank at turn of River opposite Mininipi River; a lovely spot.

John didn't tell Nora and Barbara about the time he saw Raymond Mesher drown at Mininipi. Four men searched but never found the body—John believed bodies were never found in the river.[15] It was worrying enough to know that Fred Goudie had died there just two years earlier. Barbara had a soft spot for Uncle Fred and was glad to plant some flower seeds near that place, in his memory. On August 20, they did the remainder of Mininipi Rapids with a double tracking line on each canoe and made it through without serious incident. On August 22, Barbara paused to write a letter home.

Dearest Ma,

At the moment we are waiting for the rain to stop so we can continue on our way. This is a <u>wonderful</u> trip, my goodness when I think how I always wanted a trip like this I never dreamt it would be such a marvelous one—we are about half way to the Falls—Left NW a week ago yesterday but engine trouble delayed us & we really didn't get underway until late Thurs. The River gets more & more beautiful & it is fun to see the places we have heard about. On Cyril's ground now. The River is low & a bit easier for the boys—but my how they have to work. We will be able to run all rapids except Gull Island and part of Mininipi. Meat & fish are very scarce & we had counted on that—hope it improves as bread & tea will become monotonous. John, Nora & Russell are good to travel with & Flop (R's dog) loves it—getting far more rides than us—as his poor feet are sore & I get R to take him in the canoe. I've steered some & hope to do more but the back of my neck!! gets sore when the tide is strong. Guess I feel quite lonely out in the canoe with R ashore—but with him in I even fall asleep in bad spots!!! We have a big canoe & tomorrow John & Nora will have one too—So far they've had only a tiny one & coming thru' Mininipi it was swamped. Luckily the only losses were a paddle & a boiler. R was tracking it & J had a pole in the bow—around a bad rock it took water & filled so quickly things were floating out when R jumped into her & threw things out while J, N, and I held the tracking line—I wonder how the men do this year after year—it's such terrible hard work—and then the 400 mile walk (round trip) added to it! But they love it. Flowers are ever so pretty and many I never saw before.

R is putting his boots on with the remark "I started for the Grand Falls myself" so I guess we are about to break camp & go on. Arch & Jim Goudie left a few days ahead of us to find some sort of a mine in Lake Winnikapau & we think we'll meet them on the way down today so I'll send this along with them—Mailing letters here is rather like having the Indians give me one last year half way down the Nascopie.

R was with Austy & Bud when they went up & it's fun hearing comments on how they made out around difficult spots. She was wonderful but he was <u>green</u> and was better at the end than at the beginning.

Love to you & H & Cherie & the rest. You'd have loved this trip I think if you didn't mind living in a tent—which I love—and going with friends not just guides certainly makes a difference for these boys go out of their way to make things interesting & comfortable to show us all the things they can. Nora thinks it's a grand trip too & I'm glad for that.

Love again,
Bee

August 23: Mark's clean house, Warren's old canoe on scaffold. The Nostril, Baikie's Nose. Shoal water. Boys poled, I steered. Lots of fun. Shoal River, crossed to south side, poled some more. Arch and Jim Goudie came around bend while we were boiling. Devil's Hole (broke finger)—on to Winnikapau. Mountains still quite high. I paddled a bit—young ducks before getting to Long Pt. at dusk, where we camped "in ashes." Killed ducks that evening. Meant to go on if calm about 1 A.M. but overslept.

Camping "in ashes" or "a night in the ashes" is a night spent without a tent or shelter, waiting for the weather to improve.[16] Upon reaching the camping place at Long Point, where the river had widened into Lake Winokapau, the party talked about paddling on in the night, when winds were usually calmer. Elliott Merrick wrote in *True North* that it was not unusual to be windbound there for three or four days. Trappers in loaded canoes feared being out on the deep lake when the winds blew hard, walled in by sheer rock hundreds of feet high, hours away from a safe shore to haul up a canoe. Luckily, the weather was good for their paddle on the long lake when Barbara and company woke the next morning.

Where Lake Winokapau narrowed into the river again, Barbara noted old bricks on the ground at the site of what was once the HBC trading post, Fort Winokapau, on Wolf Island.

August 27: River getting narrower. Came to Lower House (Edw. Michelin's)—currants and raspberries. Then to 3 Square Is. where we found four canoes—ones we were to have had were chewed up by bears. Boiled, continued on to set trap for bear. Saw bear walking leisurely along shore. R went after him and could have got small one, but waited for big one. All disappeared and we got none. Climbed up sand bank to burnt woods—missed him. Portage—rapids begin above this point and unable to go in canoe much above here. Strong tide, rapids and deep gorge below Falls. Big Hill Portage—new burnt woods, charred trees falling each year across narrow path—general mess. Jacob's Ladder. Camped on top—no brush! Brook for water. Left one canoe and some things at foot of portage; taking only one across. Set net for fish.

The dreaded Big Hill portage was the final ascent to the Height of Land, the Labrador plateau. From the rapids, where they hauled the canoes ashore, they hiked mostly, paddled when they could, and slogged their way toward the falls. Four years later, the *National Geographic* team, going in the opposite direction, took the portage route down around

Grand Falls, and described it as "17 miles of lakes, ponds, brooks, and 10 miles of backbreaking carries."[17] Trapper Horace Goudie recalled the first time he was ever there: "What a hill, what a portage that was!" He said the most difficult part was the path they called Jacob's Ladder, "so steep that when two men carried a canoe uphill, the man at the end had to look up at the blue sky all the time." Goudie said they were climbing at an angle of at least 45 degrees.[18] The *National Geographic* team put it at 60 degrees, "a bad place to find footholds with 100 pounds on your neck. Fires had burned off all vegetation, even moss."[19]

August 28: Next morning John and Russell staggered up hill with the canoe—crossed more burnt woods (3 miles) beyond Louie's kettle and Archie's hill (partridge, ax on Sunday) to first lake. Other points seen in distance to the East. Still, pastel shades. While boys staggered again Nora and I cluttered up the bushes with laundry. Enough water fortunately left in lake for duck-hunting when R & J came. They got some divers [ducks] (we named it Diver Lake) while I swam. I shot partridge on the way over and we had them for supper—then to bed.

August 29: It is raining and at 8:30 I am writing this, J is playing guitar, Nora is putting tops on deerskins and R is being lazy. Left Diver Lake (so-called by us because J got 4 divers for us) about 11:30. Shallow lake, so all but one walked around. 9 minute portage to Muskrat Lake. About a 7 minute portage past a puddle with lovely blue flowers to Orphan Pond—beautiful clear water with grassy islands. Rubber boots marked most portages. Another 5 minute portage to Whitefish Lake, many islands. Left burnt woods when we paddled across it. Strong wind kept us windblown for awhile. Left names on tree with "This may be the land that God gave Cain, but we love it."

Lazing around, playing the guitar, and sewing—what sort of river explorers did they think they were? If only Barbara's diary account could have been seen by Russell's grandfather Montague, who was hired in 1887 by British explorer Randle Holme to guide him to the falls. Holme made the questionable decision to venture upriver in a heavy wooden boat. He later wrote that canoes would have been more suitable: "but as my crew consisted of white men who were less accustomed to canoes, I had been compelled to take a boat."[20] The portages must have been horrible, using block and tackle to haul the boat slowly up the hills. A photograph shows Montague and another man in deep woods, dragging the boat over tree roots and deadfalls.[21] They ran out of food and turned back without seeing the falls, which Holme believed must be spectacular, perhaps 2,000 feet high. He praised Montague as a "fine, strong man" and pronounced the mosquitoes an intolerable plague.

Four years later in 1891, two American groups came to Labrador, each hoping to be the first to photograph and measure the falls. Montague guided one of them, lead by Henry G. Bryant of Philadelphia and C.A. Kenaston of Washington. It was another excruciating trip, again hauling a 500-pound wooden boat with block and tackle over the portages, along with one canoe.[22] Montague was mentioned when Bryant reported to the Geographical Club of Philadelphia about their successful trip, having achieved the goal of establishing accurate measurements of the height of the falls, although they hadn't been the first of the two teams to reach them. Two men from the competing Bowdoin College expedition got to the falls first but almost didn't make it out alive. The Mundy expedition members did their share of struggling, but they knew where they were going and had nearly reached their objective.

August 30: Left Hardshoe—John in rubber boots to hips and Russell in his "rompers" wallowed in mud, pushing and pulling (and saying a few things). Came thru' a muddy, rocky stream to Humbug Lake—cursing and swearing all the way. Humbug Lake—quite a long lake with islands. Killed porcupine Flop found and went into narrow channel winding thru' woods (Humbug Brook) and cutting away sticks to Deershorn Lake. R hacking with ax while balancing on gunnels. Deershorn Lake—lake with rocks and coves. Went up brook a bit (N and I had to walk). Portaged to Sunday Lake. At end we saw 5 geese, but they saw us too. N & I walked over Louie's Ridge while boys paddled canoe thru' brook. Uncle Fred's lower trap—Portage to Big Lake. Paddled up it to far end and camped on Otter Rub. Shot 3 geese (young ones). Heard Falls.

August 31: Went in to Grand Falls—roughly 260 miles from NWR. Path hard to find—really no path at all—Uncle Fred's old marten path. Gummed-over marks showed the way WHEN we could find them. Rocky, mossy, rough country—boulder fields, swamps, and lily ponds every once in awhile. Saw many marten stumps and spray from falls quite far away. Walked around a lake (Lemon Lake, so-called by us for we lemonaded there!). More rocks to come suddenly out on high cliff overlooking Bowdoin Canyon—deep gorge with perpendicular cliffs about 400 feet high—boiling water, snow bank and green fields on south side. Walked to bend of river for view of Falls. Spray rising higher than cliffs and like soft rain in woods. Rapid immediately above falls and drop of 385 feet—right angle turn to left preventing good view of falls on north side. Found bottle lavender with age and read notes. 1891 first one and most recent 1932. Austy's, Hubbard, etc. We left ours—also put names on tree. N & I third and fourth women to have seen falls from north shore. "Next time we see falls it will be from south shore." Smooth rocks right out to water's edge—boiled and lemonaded with water R dipped up—having a bath in the process! Water drew us and made my knees weak! Flop didn't seem to know what it was all about. Returned to camp at sunset—finding morning's footprints in moss. Newish moon.[23]

Either John or Nora snapped a photo of Barbara and Russell, smiling widely, sitting on the smooth rocks of the north side of the river where the water spills into Bowdoin Canyon. Russell is holding Flop tight, the dog probably anxious to get away from the thundering falls.

Recorded descriptions are unanimous about the view. It was an "incomparable sight" that *National Geographic* writers saw in 1950, from their vantage point on the opposite, south side of the canyon: "In rapids just above the falls, the Hamilton drops 219 feet. The falls are 245 feet high; in lashing descent through Bowdoin Canyon the river plunges another 574 feet. In 16 miles the stream hurtles downgrade 1,038 feet— one of the most tumultuous descents of any major river on earth. And the Hamilton here is a broad-backed, full volume river."[24]

Two members of the Bowdoin College Scientific Expedition to Labrador in 1891 named the spectacular river canyon after their college in Brunswick, Maine. When their story was told, anyone would conclude it was astonishing they survived to tell the tale. Four men set out with the goal of "rediscovering" Grand Falls, having brashly dispensed with the need for a local guide, as "Indians cannot stand the pace that our men intend to strike." The Bowdoin Boys, as they were called, disparaged explorers with guides as lazy travellers, unwilling to do the work themselves, obviously referring to the other American explorers on the river that summer. (Hardly fair, considering the 500-pound boat Bryant and Kenaston and their guides hoisted over the portages.) The college team earned full marks for audacity, entering strange country with such confidence. Taking along a few "Indians or half-breeds" might lessen the load, but "it is very doubtful if any living person has ever been to the falls or knows any more about the last, and probably the hardest part of the trip, than Cary."[25]

Six days into the Bowdoin Boys trip, unsecured cargo was swept from a canoe that capsized in the Horseshoe Rapids because of a failure to "fasten the stores into the boats before starting, as had been ordered." The expedition was in jeopardy, with the loss of a quarter of their food and all the instruments needed for measuring the height of the falls. At the top of Lake Winokapau, it was decided two men should go back, due to the shortage of food and one man's hand injury. Austin Cary (Bowdoin '87) and Dennis Cole (Bowdoin '88) pressed on and made good time reaching the Height of Land, even with the mishaps, but the worst was yet to happen. When they returned to their main camp from a two-day hike to view and photograph the falls, they found everything smoldering, including their canoe and most of the remaining food. They had neglected to extinguish the campfire properly.[26]

Elliott Merrick equated the loss of a canoe in such circumstances as "almost synonymous with finding oneself dead."[27] They salvaged what little they could, and then walked and rafted down the river, arriving at Joseph Michelin's house at Traverspine River two weeks later, starved and nearly barefoot, with rags wrapped around their feet. Fortunately, they had a cache of food halfway down the river, which likely saved their lives. On the voyage home, the Bowdoin expedition stopped in Halifax and was welcomed by Premier William Stevens Fielding of Nova Scotia at an official reception. When they arrived in Rockland, Maine, church bells rang in tribute. Although Cary and Cole photographed the canyon and the falls, no photos or illustrations of Bowdoin Canyon or Grand Falls were published.[28] Two weeks later, their competitors Bryant and Kenaston reached the falls, suffering nothing worse than exhaustion from portaging, towing, and tracking their heavy boat upriver. They found the small bottle left by Cary and Cole and left their names and notes in it. On their return home, Bryant published an article in *The Century Magazine* with maps and numerous illustrations drawn from imperfect photos.

On Grand River in 1946, there was no starvation, no exhaustion, and no rags were wrapped around feet. It was more a matter of whether to have fish or goose for dinner.

Sunday, Sept. 1: Lazy day, up at 9; laundry, mending—goose for dinner. J & N wasted it with sleep. R & I went up to Whitefish Falls—a rocky brook, and walked over portage as far as we could which was not far. Fished and had lovely afternoon. Now 'tis time to eat our fish and to bed.

After a restful Sunday, Barbara and her party began the return journey, back over the rocky, or even worse, swampy portages. She said the "tent seems like home now." At Big Hill, she picked berries, "sweetest you ever tasted." Fish they carried with them were mostly spoiled, "good feed for numerous bears which were about." Things were going well between Barbara and Russell. On September 4, they camped on a point among some birch trees on the south shore of Lake Winokapau, "a heavenly night in every way." The camping spot would always be a special one to her. They stopped for a mug-up near Fox Island and Russell was able to show her where he portaged into his trapping grounds in the fall.

Thurs. Sept. 5: Cool, overcast day—Flop asleep on my feet while I write this in canoe. It cleared and was a beautiful day. Boiled at R's fall portage—he and I climbed to top. Spruce and moss, birches and dry leaves, willows every now and again. His camping spot at foot, sat on rock at top for a few minutes and shot at top of trees. Only white woman to have been there. Name and date on tree. Sailed down Lake Winnie—lovely day. Camped near Rabbit's Head on south side on old Indian camping ground.

Friday, Sept. 6: Rest of Lake Winnie—stopping at Gordon's in vain search for salt. Water very much lower since we passed two weeks ago. Ran Devil's Hole on strip of tide—could actually see downhill slope—past Shoal River, Mark's to Mooney's [Mouni] Is. where we boiled. Camped at our Cree Brook spot again.

In early summer 1950, the *National Geographic* writers observed the river was full of water, canoes sometimes going "at express train speed." Andrew Brown and Ralph Gray wrote that after paddling glassy-smooth Winokapau, at Mouni Rapids, the river "picked [them] up and flung [them] 12 miles down the valley."[29] They calculated the distance from Big Hill portage near Grand Falls to the mouth of the river to be more than 200 miles. It took them only four and a half days to come down, swept along "like twigs in a flooded gutter." In summer 1891, it took Henry Bryant's expedition seven days: "the swift current carried us down-stream with exhilarating speed."[30]

Sept. 7: Terrific wind-storm night of 6th. Next day (7th) storms off and on all day. Tried fishing—left note for Cyril—6 geese at John's—wonderful sail—lots of white horses licking our heels. R got 2 gossards[31] at Allan's Is. "Conk" for supper—into small pond to see beaver and his house.

Sept. 8: On thru' tide and rapids to Upper Tilt camping place. Mininipi very low and rough in spots—canoes lowered to middle of it, and the upper part of Gull Is. Middle Horseshoe the loppiest and most fun. Rapids too tame and short to suit me, but am thankful for what they were. 3½ days up to 1 down! Met Indians at Horseshoe and bummed sugar from old Sim.

Sept. 9: Sailed gloriously from Upper Tilt to Goose—what we did in two days going up—about 50 miles. Better fun than rapids as it was choppy and lovely! More Indian tents seen at Lower Tilt—I lowered John's small canoe down sand bank at Muskrat Falls—R helping over rocks at end. Beautiful near full moon and dark, dark hills silhouetted against yellow sky—on to Groves' Pt. for night. This was Monday, and R & I windblown there for several days. Got back to NWR on Saturday on HBCo boat. A wonderful trip but too short. I've been far more fortunate and luckier than most in the things I've been able to do up here. Thanks be for that.

Canoe: 50 cents day	*$15.50*
John: $5 day	*$125.00*
Boat to Muskrat:	*$16.00*
Food:	*$35.00*
	$191.50

The 27-day river excursion, 19 up and 8 down, had ended happily, without serious incident, only a boiler and a paddle lost. The company of four, their dog and guitar, had been to Grand Falls and back by canoe, not to prospect for minerals, make scientific observations, or earn bragging rights, but for the pure fun of it. Their names were on the record, in the weathered bottle, with the others who had stood on the north side of the gorge since 1891.

One hundred and sixteen more names went in the bottle before it was given to Newfoundland premier Joseph R. Smallwood in 1965 "for safekeeping."[32] Most of the people who entered their names in the 1950s and 1960s were geologists, engineers, and surveyors working for Shawinigan Engineering Company of Montreal; 29 were flown in by helicopter in one busy month, October 1957.[33] Shawinigan was the largest supplier of electricity to industrial and domestic consumers in Quebec and owned a 20 per cent interest in Hamilton Falls Power Corporation, a company set up in 1958 to develop the falls.[34]

Over the next 15 years, the Labrador landscape would be altered forever. To contain the water in the plateau, 88 dykes were built "to plug the low spots on the rim of the Labrador 'saucer.'" The dykes ranged from 4 feet to 90 feet in height and from 200 feet to 4 miles in length. Any maps of Labrador were rendered obsolete when Premier Smallwood pressed a button on July 1, 1973, closing "the 250-ton centre gate of the Lobstick [Lake] structure" which started the filling of the main reservoir, named after him. Months later, the third largest man-made body of water in the world covered 2,200 square miles.[35] The mighty falls, with measured output of between 45,000 and 49,000 cubic feet of water per second, were reduced to a trickle, the water diverted to underground turbines.[36]

Barbara, Nora, Russell, and John were among the last people to travel to the falls the hard way, by land and water, before the country was swarming with engineers and bulldozers. Barbara had fulfilled her dream of paddling the river, had seen the falls, and as importantly to her, now understood exactly where Russell would be going for the winter. Back in North West River, she helped him prepare to leave again. Her letters home were fewer, shorter, and showed her disconnection with big city life and new connection with Russell.

Very soon I will be coming home; I'll have to hurry and get out in the next two weeks I think to avoid getting stuck. I hate to set the date for leaving—if I didn't think I'd be back I don't think I could leave. I guess I've really been happy here in spite of the Mission & those connected with it. I am indeed glad to be free of it. My successor didn't last long! She left last Monday & now Doris is in charge—I'm awfully glad for her and Miss Brown, the only really good staff member here in my day, told me over the phone (didn't have a chance to see her at Goose) that she was "glad to get out of the joint"—Outside the Mission I've been very happy—too much so, I guess, I've not been used to it and hate to leave it all.

Our trip was wonderful, but a bit too rushed and the two weeks since our return have been hectic. Russell went off again on Thursday—to be gone 'till March if fur is good and he doesn't lose any food on the way up. I was busy helping him get ready—making duffles, etc. and baking cookies, Christmas cake etc.—all so new to me—but such fun to do for him—For about a week before he left I could hardly open my mouth, for fear I wouldn't be able to speak to him but the actual parting wasn't as bad as I feared 'twould be. We were both smiling and I know we both felt it was not good-bye. Again I got so busy I couldn't think much about it. There were several things I wanted to do for him before I left and quite a few things for myself & I want to help F get C off this week. R's leggings must be done <u>well</u> *and the kind he wants are pretty tricky but I'll do my damnedest! I've felt rather lost today as it's almost the first Sunday since I came down the River the last time that we haven't been together for at least part of the day.* (Letter: September 29, 1946)

Barbara had delayed her departure as long as she could, much to her mother's irritation, making it clear she intended to spend only a winter in New York, and wasn't much looking forward to that. She had been straightforward about her romantic involvement, but suspected her mother would be fervently hoping that time and distance away from Labrador would help her forget a most unsuitable infatuation.

Your letter came tonight and it sure was "a grumble"! It was written the 25th of Sept. and you knew I never intended to leave here till the 1st of Oct. anyway, so why were you wondering at that point where I was? I thot surely I'd get off this week or next but there was so, so much I had to and wanted to do before I left—as it is I'll have to go just before F's baby *comes to be <u>sure</u> of a boat. There'll be many after that but I can't be too sure of when. Have had no answer yet as to what date I can fly out. Cyril goes tomorrow if the wind goes down. Russell left two weeks ago tomorrow.*

... I certainly hope this winter will be happy, for my innards just cannot stand being twisted around. After the peace up here it's going to [be] hard at best to return to all the turmoil outside. I want it to be as good as possible, so I'll know best what to do for the future. (Letter: October 9, 1946)

Chapter Twelve

LABRADOR BRIDE-TO-BE

The bride, for example, who comes from New York or Chicago to live in Bright Meadows and rudely criticizes the smaller town's ways, and who in fact insists upon dragging fifty-story skyscrapers into comparison with Bright Meadows new six-storied building, is being not merely discourteous but stupid in her choice of comparison.

—Emily Post, *Etiquette*

B arbara corresponded with her friends in North West River in late 1946 and during the winter and spring of 1947, but no letters from them are among her collection. She certainly would have written Russell, who may have received letters carried upriver, but none survived. What is known about her time in New York that year can be sifted from the "Alumni Notes" column in *Among the Deep-Sea Fishers* and some newspaper clippings.

Living with her mother and sister in Manhattan, Barbara found ways to keep busy and use her knowledge of sewing and embroidery. She secured a position at America House, a retail shop on Madison Avenue that specialized in the sale of fine handicrafts.[1] She continued her volunteer work for the Needlework Guild, still a large organization, although that winter, the New York branch, established in 1890-91, closed its doors. The ranks may have been dwindling, but Barbara did her best to keep its members interested in the Mission. With more than two years' experience as a fieldworker, she was an authority on life in the north. She visited Guild branches and schools, bringing samples of the beautiful handicrafts done by Newfoundland and Labrador women. Her talks had been written up in the local newspapers, usually with a photo of Barbara modelling an embroidered Grenfell jacket. (Did any of the Guild members ever ask or wonder why donations of handmade clothing were needed for women who could do such intricate work? Did Barbara ever let slip that she was returning to Labrador to marry a fur trapper?)

A reporter covered her visit to a Guild branch in Flushing, New York. Barbara accepted clothing the Guild had gathered to send to the "bleak land of rocks, snow and perpetual ice," the donation bringing a "note of warmth and cheer into the lives of the hardy natives of desolate, isolated Labrador."[2] Barbara would never have described it that way but perhaps her stories of life in North West River were too benign for the newspaper reporter. When she spoke to students at the Demarest School in Bloomfield, New Jersey, she told them about her canoe trip up the Grand River with her "woman companion and two guides." She always brought along a good selection of carvings, embroidered items, and hooked rugs, as well as samples of fur and antlers. According to the *Bloomfield Independent Press*, the students were "thrilled by the stories of the animals and the work of the trappers."[3]

Barbara made notes in preparation for the talks she gave and they show that she still believed the Mission's medical and educational services were essential, even though she voiced other complaints privately about staff and operations. In a speech she gave in Philadelphia to delegates attending the annual Guild convention in May 1947, she explained the Mission wasn't responsible only for a hospital in North West River, but served the whole coast. She told them about life in the community, how hard-working (and therefore deserving of charity) the people were. She described the men's annual work cycle of trapping, hunting, and fishing: "I don't believe I have ever seen men work as hard, nor have I ever seen men happier." She talked about the clothing store and how the women used it.

For a short time one year I took charge of the C.S. It was just before Christmas and I saw how much this clothing meant—not only to actually clothe the people but to provide them with gifts for their families. I remember one local woman in particular who worked hard for the Mission and besides that spent all her free time sewing for the Industrial Dept. or for other people. Only once in 2½ years did I see her without something in her hands! She had a great many grandchildren but she never failed to give each one a Christmas gift, and many of them got a birthday present too. Most of these came from the C.S.—for she seldom took cash for her industrial work. Besides this there was a time when she almost completely clothed the large family of one daughter. I think such people deserve all the help we can give them. (Speech: May 14, 1947)

Some of her audience might have heard about the new air base at Goose Bay and wondered if their donations were still needed when there were jobs to be had. Barbara stressed that there were people who "live as they always lived, who are desperately poor and for whom the Mission can do a great deal" and who lived in places too far from the base to go to work there.

Volunteer work for the Guild and her job at America House helped to fill Barbara's days. She had friends to catch up with and there was the opera, theatre, museums, art galleries, and shops to search for things she'd need next winter. Her mother had not been well and certainly wanted her to stay, but nine months in New York under her roof and influence would not change Barbara's mind. She wanted to be in Labrador, not in New York talking about Labrador. Although it had not been in her history to disappoint or defy her mother, somewhere, perhaps in the power of her love for Russell and her wish to have a family of her own, she found the strength to do exactly the opposite of what Mrs. Mundy wanted.

With a winter behind her at Thousand Nine, Barbara had deftly handled many pointed questions about the man in her life. If her mother inquired about when Russell's family had come to North America, she could smile and say she thought the first ones came about 10,000 years ago. Wouldn't Cree and Inuit ancestors trump all? She had done her best to explain Labrador people and their life, and about the Groves family, emphasizing their honesty, skills, and generosity. She carefully prepared the ground for the day she announced her intention to go with Russell for the winter on the trapline.

The facts had been established. Russell Groves was a 35-year-old fur trapper and salmon fisherman with more than 20 years experience, a skilled duck and deer hunter, a widower with a young daughter, the owner of a modest home in the Bight at North West River. That was the brief outline and none of it impressed her mother, whose living room on Park Avenue could swallow his entire house. Her son, Floyd Jr., made more money in a few hours on the telephone than Russell made thrashing about in the bush all winter. Mother enjoyed eating duck but invoked the Audubon Society when she learned Russell killed dozens in a single hunt. Barbara knew telling her mother about his uncanny ability to find his way in the country, his expertise in hunting and canoeing, his encyclopedic knowledge of the rivers and lakes, the fish, animals, and birds would gain him no points for intelligence, resourcefulness, or toughness, for surviving alone, winter after winter, in a land only recently mapped by expeditions of explorers. Didn't Boy Scouts do all that? She was sure her girlfriends would understand when they saw her photos of him smiling in his well-worn river clothes, a strong, handsome man with his face tanned and hair blown. A man you would trust with your life, if not your investment portfolio.

On her last night in New York, her brother, Floyd, and his wife joined Barbara, sister Harriet, and their mother for dinner, bringing fresh corn and a corsage of lilies. They may have thought she was making a terrible mistake, but they mixed cocktails and toasted her and Russell. In just a few weeks, she'd be in a little tilt on Fig River, preparing a meal of porcupine or partridge.

Barbara probably didn't regale her family with stories of some of the earliest pairings in Labrador. There would be no comfort for Mrs. Mundy in the old tales of women used, abused, and coerced into marriage. The reminiscences of Lydia Campbell (born 1818) shed some faint light on what women endured just a few generations before. Lydia wrote a journal, at the request of a visiting clergyman, which was published in series in *The Evening Herald* in 1894 and 1895.[4] Newspaper readers in St. John's were probably enthralled by the recollections of the elderly Labradorian, a rare first-hand account from the mysterious northern part of the colony. Many of Lydia's descendants lived in North

West River, including her granddaughter, Flora (Blake) Baikie, an expert embroiderer and sewer, well known by Barbara.

Lydia's Inuit mother, Susan, died when Lydia was only seven, but remnants of the story of Susan's marriage (c. 1807) to Ambrose Brooks (one of the English planters listed in the HBC record with Thomas Groves), were told and retold. Susan and her siblings were orphaned and lived with some "older Eskimaux" who "took them and used them very hard." Lydia said her mother ran away one October when she "grew up to be a woman" and travelled by herself, with just her woman's knife (ulu) for protection. She got to Mulligan River and saw a "French boat with 2 people in it." Susan waved her coat to them and they rowed toward her. As Lydia Campbell wrote, "When they came to her they could not understand each other; but they took her in their boat and went back to their trading post, and she stayed a winter with them, and was loved as a sister to one and a daughter to the other."[5]

In Lydia's story, after a platonic winter with the men at the trading post, in the spring everyone went seal hunting. It was when they returned to the French post at Mulligan that she met and 'married' Ambrose Brooks: "they found my dear, good mother and carried her off, and as there was no other kind of women to marrie hear, the few English men each took a wife of the sort, and they never sorry that they took them for they was great workers, and so it came to pass that I was one of the youngsters of them."[6]

Lydia Campbell's newspaper journal did not include details about her own first marriage, but she described the event to Arminius Young, a Methodist missionary who served in Labrador from 1903 to 1905. When she was 16 in 1834, 40-year-old Bill Blake (the son of Orkneyman William Blake and an Inuit woman called Betsy) decided he wanted to marry her, though she "loved another." In Young's account, Bill Blake contrived a way to force Lydia to marry him. He invited everyone to a party at Rigolet, including Lydia and her father, Ambrose. They were very happy to go to the party, travelling by dog team from their home in Double Mer. Everyone was "kind and nice to Lydia" at the main house, but meanwhile, Bill Blake was getting her father drunk. With the old man insensible, Lydia was told to change into a new dress to be married to Bill Blake, and that her father had agreed to the marriage:

> Lydia insisted she would not have Bill. Her feelings were not regarded, and two cruel women began at once to remove her old dress. The girl resisted but it was all of no avail; she was powerless in their hands and was forced to submit to the inevitable. Blake came in and she was compelled to stand beside him, while some servant at the station read the marriage ceremony.
>
> It is unnecessary for our present purpose to follow this marriage further, sufficient to say that her life with Blake was very unhappy. He did not live long, however, and some years later, Mrs. Blake married Daniel Campbell, a young Scotchman, with whom she lived happily for the long period of fifty-four years.[7]

Lydia's first marriage was not a model to follow, but neither was it unusual in its day. Courtship was a ritual for people who lived in more populated places, where eligible young people might see each other on numerous social occasions for months, or even years, before announcing their engagement in the newspaper and then marrying. In Labrador, men like Blake knew if Lydia loved another, she would soon be married.[8]

Available, able women who were not your close relatives were a rare commodity—sought out and fought over. Lydia wrote about a woman whose husband had drowned and a month or two after, "a young man, which was (then) an English half-breed, wanted a wife. He bethought himself why not go and try to get that young widow." She said the dead man's ghost appeared and frightened everyone but the couple did get married.[9] Lydia's daughter Margaret told the story of a pair of brothers who each wanted to marry the oldest of a pair of sisters: "The father told his daughters to go and stand a hundred yards away and, when he would call, the men would run towards them. The youngest brother got to the oldest sister first so the other brother got the youngest sister." Margaret, who had married for love and had a long and happy marriage, knew the grandchildren of the couples who were decided by the race.[10]

The orphaned Susan, Lydia's mother, mistreated by her relatives, took refuge with the French and English men who had come to the coast, then found a husband, but one who also used her hard. Flora Baikie had heard many stories about her great-grandmother and clearly did not approve of Ambrose Brooks's treatment of his Inuit wife:

> Gran used to tell us that before her father would go off anywhere he'd tell them not to let their mother eat any raw meat. One time they killed a caribou and Grandfather Brooks went off somewhere. Gran said she and her mother skinned the deer and cut it up. Every now and again, she said, her mother would eat a piece of the fat. Gran said when her father come home she told him. He took a piece of rope and give his wife a hammering. He hurt her, Gran said, cause she cried. I says it wouldn't be only me that got the cracks if 'twas me he hammered. Raw caribou fat is real good.[11]

Stories about alliances formed less for romantic and more for practical reasons were common. If the couple loved and cared for each other, so much the better. Barbara wanted a loving marriage but realized the work she was taking on by marrying Russell. She was the one coming from outside who would need instruction and kind assistance with local ways. While men were trapping or fishing, women were making sealskin clothes and boots, splitting wood, hauling water, fishing trout and smelts through the ice, smoking salmon, shooting partridges, snaring rabbits, setting traps for foxes, salting and drying codfish, picking berries, tending gardens, cooking meals, baking bread, doing laundry, sewing and mending clothing, and giving birth, sometimes alone and, if they were lucky, with a midwife assisting. Standing beside their husbands in the few photographs that survive, they are stout, work-hardened matrons, with hands folded above full, apron-covered skirts, woollen shawls wrapping their shoulders. Their husbands trapped mink, beaver, and lynx, which were fashioned into stoles or coats and sold in exclusive shops to people like Barbara's mother. Labrador women rarely wore any fur, except for a little bit of trim around a parka hood. It was too valuable to keep for one's own use.

Getting married should have been the easy part for Barbara and Russell, but it turned out to be much more complicated than expected. On August 15, he met her at the airport with a kiss. They stayed with his family at Groves Point, wanting to be near enough to the base so they could walk over to see the military chaplain Russell had asked to perform the marriage ceremony. Over the next several days, they went back and forth to the base, becoming increasingly frustrated. The chaplain, a Baptist, had wired St. John's several times asking for official permission to perform the marriage and had not received a reply.[12]

Yesterday we went up to see the Padre and altho' he had written out a week ago—when he first came in—no word had been received. Just like the Newfies, isn't it? He did not dare go ahead as recently the Am. [American] one married someone and it was declared null and void by the gov't and Tomkins had to go over and marry them again. T. went on Thurs. which is too bad. However this one has wired and we hope to hear tomorrow. (Letter: August 17, 1947)

This was a serious crimp in their plans—they had hoped to be married quickly and then to go camping for a few days before beginning preparations for heading up the river for the winter. While waiting, Barbara spent time with Russell's daughter, Phyllis, and the extended Groves family on the Point. Aunt Betsy had some useful observations about her winter in a tilt with husband, John, and their young son, Wilfred, many years earlier.

She tells me the only thing she was not too keen on when she went up the River with her 2 yr. old was the <u>heat</u> in the tilts. R tells me he built a new tilt last fall, made another one a bit bigger so "I could stand up in it" and has logs cut for a new house. If it is a late fall he will be able to build that this year. I had to laugh when Mrs. John was telling me about the nice little house she had with a proper floor and all—R said "better not tell her too much." (Letter: August 17, 1947)

A couple of days waiting became a week—Barbara was thoroughly discouraged and "completely helpless to speed things up."

We are sick of walking up and down the hill, so the Padre says he will hang out a blanket when word comes and we can see it with glasses from

here. Phyl and I have just been over to look and nothing yet. He—the Pad,
had been down to NW for a funeral yesterday and said—too bad you
can't go down and just set up housekeeping. I couldn't help remarking—
you haven't been here long enough to know NW—the tongues wag at both
ends already without anything like that! Time out to watch huge hailstones
falling and bouncing all over. The Padre says he has no idea when anything
will come thru' and advises us to make other arrangements if we can. R is
at the base now to see if there is a magistrate or if the Capt. of the KYLE
would do. Neither of us want that if we can help it, but a whole precious
week has gone and time is getting very short and we have to be ready for
the winter in six weeks or less and there is a lot to do. I guess our few days
alone with no work is fast vanishing, worse luck. Someone has certainly
put a curse on us. If no word has come by Sunday or Monday we are
considering hiring a boat, taking Nora and Morris with us and proceeding
to Cartwright where there is a minister. We hope we won't have to as it is
expensive and also it might be another week or two out as we could be laid
up for days by wind etc. (Letter: August 21, 1947)

Clergymen of any denomination were scarce that summer. United
Church minister Lester Burry had been in St. John's for over a year as
the official Labrador delegate at the National Convention, discussing the
political future of Newfoundland and Labrador. There was an Anglican
minister based in Sandwich Bay, but Barbara and Russell were hesitant to
travel all the way by boat to Cartwright unless they were sure Reverend
Felix Honeygold was there. After several more trips to the base, they
finally learned that the Canadian Forces minister on the base would not
be able to marry them due to Newfoundland regulations, which did "not
recognize" Baptists as clergy allowed to perform the marriage ceremony.
Instead of writing her mother to say she was married, Barbara vented
her frustration with the delay in her wedding plans.

What do you think of this? Word has come to the Padre (by _mail!_) that
careful search had been made & the end result was "no Baptists" ever heard
of! _So_ to get a licence in Nfld. to marry he has to write to his Canadian
superior etc. etc. etc. & he says it will be _at least_ 2 wks. more. I think far
more than that probably. Herbert is waiting to take us to C. [Cartwright]
& at moment we are on the Am. [American] side waiting for 10 o'clock to

come. We saw Col. yesterday & he has given permission for us to fly to St. John's. R has figured how much he can spend & if we can do it on that if we can be sure of return passage within a day or two we are going. If all goes well it will be sure, shorter & settled. We are not _positive_ that Honeygold is at C. [Cartwright], also so _much_ has gone against us that I'm afraid he _might_ say wait 'till Burry comes for R is not an Anglican. Then we'd end up at St. John's at greater expense. Neither of us really know _what_ to do.

1:30 Papers are being made out and we are going on the 1st plane available with a letter from the C.O. stating they are to return us as soon as "practicable." R remarked yesterday "I call this fighting to get married—off for another dig at 'em today." This "dig" is the _only_ one that seems to have had results. (Letter: August 26, 1947)

On August 27, Barbara and Russell flew to St. John's on an American military aircraft. They took rooms on different floors at the "rummy" Crosbie Hotel on Duckworth Street and went looking for a church and a minister to marry them. Barbara thought the Presbyterian Kirk on Long's Hill was the most attractive, and at least she was Presbyterian, so they met with the minister, who was very accommodating and agreed to do the deed the next day. For their honeymoon, they would move to the much nicer Newfoundland Hotel.

Our wedding day. At 5 P.M. I became Mrs. Russell Groves in St. Andrew's Presbyterian Church in St. John's, Nfld. We were married by Dr. David Lang. The organist, Mr. Bob McLeod, played both wedding marches and "Oh Perfect Love." The witnesses were Mrs. McLeod and Adam Brown—the latter, Peter's brother. I wore a blue linen dress with white shoes & hat. The hair ornament Ma wore and which Grandma gave me to wear at my wedding, I wore against the brim of the hat. Also wore Mother's orange blossoms as a corsage. After the wedding we went to the Manse for a very nice tea—Dr. Lang, Mr. & Mrs. McLeod, Adam, R & I. Dr. L. drove us to our new abode the Nfld. Hotel. R says I "looked lovely" and I say he looked very handsome in his dark blue suit, white shirt & hankie & blue & red checked tie-buff stripes in between. A beautifully sunny day was the perfect start to our new life, and we are very happy. It's a bit hard to believe we are really married, but I guess we are! "Something old (hair ornament, underwear), something new (hat & shoes), something borrowed (orange *blossoms), something blue (dress) & a six pence in my shoe." Tried to call family but no luck. R <u>hates</u> telephones & shakes his fists at "damn fool of a looking thing" & we have laughed ourselves sick over it. He had all he was going to say to Ma ready & then we couldn't get her—by morning he says he will have forgotten it!* (Diary: August 28, 1947)

Barbara and Russell would have been satisfied to have a honeymoon in a tent, but made do with spending their first days as a married couple in the city's finest hotel. Being in St. John's had some advantages; they eventually managed to make radio telephone contact with her family in New York, went to the movies, did some sightseeing, shopping, and enjoyed "feeds of fruits—all kinds."[13] The American Air Force obliged with a flight back to Goose Bay on Thursday, September 4, the newlyweds bringing as much fresh fruit with them as they could. They had hoped to get directly to their house in North West River but windy conditions kept them at Groves Point a little longer. They got back to the Bight Saturday afternoon and by that evening, Russell had made bread and shot five partridges for the next day's dinner.

Wedding presents arrived by mail from New York. Visitors were dropping by with gifts of fresh vegetables. The house was tidied and cozy; the nights were cool with red northern lights, "reflected in water & dancing all over—beautiful."[14] Barbara took some time to go through her photos of North West River and sent some to *Among the Deep-Sea Fishers* in time for them to be included in the October issue. They occupied the centrefold, shots of trappers with sleds and dogs, under the title "Freeze-Up Travel." Russell had work to do on his canoe and tent, Barbara was getting to know Phyllis, whom she said was very cute and observing, "comes freely & wants to bring her friends." On September 21, Russell gave Barbara a ring that belonged to his great-grandmother Groves: "which I am using as a guard—just the right size. I'm glad to have something that really belonged to him."

Monday: R still busy at his tent, another wash day has gone by and I seem to be managing better—but we are only camping compared to what 'twill be with baking, scrubbing, etc., etc. However in time, I'll improve I guess. I'm glad every hour of the day and night that I came back. Some things are hard to get used to, others just plain hard, but I love it anyway;

as long as I have R it's worth everything.

Tues. Sept. 23, 1947. Two years ago today I wrote in my diary: "This could be my home if I so chose"; and tonight I've mixed bread and it is my home. Snowing hard all day and white breakers rolling up—I love to watch them; and I like to see the snow again. I wonder if I didn't <u>know</u> on that log that I would be back—I think I must have. Well here I am, and I'm <u>very</u> glad. I want to always feel as I do tonight—happy, contented & very much in love.

Tues. Sept. 30. R is up seeing if we are <u>really</u> going today. Everything packed & ready. I do <u>so</u> hope this winter will be all I hoped it would. <u>Please</u> make me a help & not a burden. Don't let me be afraid of steering or being alone, make me be ready on time, and learn all I can so I can really be a help. Let me get along on as little as possible & go 'till I drop without showing it if necessary. I don't want him to be sorry he took me in anyway. I want him to <u>want</u> to take me again. Don't let me get sulky or cross or hurt if we get tired—and if I ever do please make me get over it quickly. And please may it not be <u>all</u> work with him; everything is so much easier if R puts his arms around me. I know he loves me or he wouldn't do the million & one things he does to help and to make me happy—but I do like to have him hold me tight and kiss me. And may he get lots of good fur and don't let anything ever happen to him.

A prayer for her future couldn't hurt, and it wasn't much she was asking, to be useful and strong and loved. After all the time she had waited to get what she wanted, let nothing spoil it now.

Chapter Thirteen

LIFE BEGINS AT 37

A crowd of jolly trappers, we are leaving one and all,
The first hard work is started on the portage, Muskrat Falls,
And getting in our canoes, boys, oh, it seems so fine,
Going up Grand River with our pole and tracking line.

—Douglas Best, "The Trapper's Song"

T he house in the Bight was closed for the winter. Goodbyes had been said to family and friends, everyone wishing Barbara luck. Men, dogs, canoes, and all their winter's supplies were piled high on the motorboat that carried them away from North West River to Grand River. The boat brought them as far as the first portage at Muskrat Falls, where everything was put ashore for the climb. Barbara had been there twice before, so she knew how tough the carrying would be. She was nervous and excited and more than a bit worried about doing everything right. On the boat ride to the portage, she wrote to her mother.

You should see this boat—such stuff in it—5 men, me, 4 Huskie dogs, 1 crackie dog, 5 canoes, bags of flour, etc. etc. all over the place. Last night R & I slept head to toes on one bunk, Stewart & crackie on t'other and 3 others on floor. (Letter: October 1, 1947)

She promised to continue writing letters, in the hope they would be carried out from the trapline to be mailed, warning her mother not to worry if she didn't hear anything for months. Details about the nasty weather and the difficult portage were kept for her diary.

Wed. Oct. 1: We left yesterday at 1 o'clock, stopped at the Valley for

Spot [Russell's dog] and then went on to Gibbon's Pt. where we anchored. Raining & miserable. Stewart Michelin took us to Falls. Warren Baikie, Wilfred B. [Baikie] & Cecil Blake others with us; 5 dogs, canoes & piles of things everywhere. Didn't camp as it was too wet, so slept on boat, not bad at all. Got to Falls at 10 A.M. today. Rained all last night & 'tis snowing now—quite a bit of snow on portage. R still carrying loads—I'm taking it easy after two. Cabbage & beef on stove, all is very cozy. I am certainly glad I am with him. I'd feel very lost if I weren't. Camping on top of Muskrat Portage tonight. Steep __muddy__ portage.

Oct. 2: Snowed all night (3 inches in A.M.) and still snowing now (3:30 P.M.). No portaging done. Aside from making work hard it is really beautiful—trees heavy with snow, yellow leaves of birches still on. Walked part way to Falls & was blown up by R as I expected had I gone the whole way. Rocks slippery—(I wonder if R would be as lost without me as I would be without him.) "Your baked bread didn't last long"—and no cookies. If I live I swear next year he'll have so much he'll be mad & say 'tis __too__ much to carry! (Hope I'll be efficient enough then to do better than this yr.—which has been a total failure in that respect. Thank the Lord I made the cake—I just hope it's fit to eat.)

The trip upriver may have seemed haphazard and disorganized at the outset but always followed a well-established pattern, with the most experienced man leading the others. Nobody was declared the leader; it was simply understood. As trapper Horace Goudie explained it, after dozens of trips upriver, they were all "100% qualified" but "the most experienced one was the one that was the most clever in every way, and ambitious." Goudie said there might be seven or eight camps "all in a bunch" and by the time it was light and they had eaten breakfast, they would listen for the signal from the foreman, a bang on his stovepipe with the poker and it was time to load canoes and go.[1] As first man through the rapids, the leader "would tie up his canoe and walk back along the shore to see how everyone was getting along."[2]

Sat. Oct. 4: Tonight we are at the foot of Gull Island Lake, camped on the bank opposite Judson Blake's house. Fr. hen for Sunday dinner. Dogs tired. __Hard__ poling for R thru' Porcupine. I __think__ I am doing better—just hope so, and that it doesn't kill R. I want so terribly to be able to do it, so it won't be too hard for him. R just went for water—he is so darn handsome at times! Funny how he can be old & tired looking at one moment, & then his expression changes and he's all young again! I love to see him with his pipe. Afraid my lips are going to be sore. Glad tomorrow is Sunday—that longed for day I thot about in N.Y.!

Sun. Oct. 5: Quiet, pleasant day, overcast & warm. Cecil went back for his dog, found him asleep in barrel! at Sand Banks—baked, "went cruising," & just lazed.

One rule trappers followed, unless it couldn't be helped, was the observance of Sunday as a day of rest. Some trappers would do light work such as sewing, while others would not even thread a needle. Lee White's brother Gerald, who had been trapping since he was fifteen, recalled Sundays in the country were spent the same way as at home. He'd read a little from the Bible, sing a few hymns, and cook a good dinner.[3] Trappers were steadfast about this rule, even when alone on their trapping grounds. Horace Goudie said, "Never, absolutely never, would a trapper take his gun in his hands to shoot game or go out to check his traps."[4] It was a day when canoes stayed ashore and nothing was portaged, a true day of rest before the wearying work began again.

Mon. Oct. 6: Gull Island Lake & thru' Gull Island Rapid. I tried poling with R at upper end of Lake. A wet job but I liked it. R said 'twas hardest pole he ever had—very strong tide. My pole broke in the end. He steered all the way thru' the Rapid with the Warrens [Morris and Baikie] on the bow & tracking line & Wilfred [Baikie] & Walter [Blake] on rocks. Sometimes he was sitting right on tail with nose up a fall and in real white water too far out for my comfort. Guess there is nothing that would stump him. A bumpy camping site and Tues. A.M. more rain & blowing a gale. Twice yesterday in the tide of Gull Island Lake we had to go back—the first time we were out too far—the second I couldn't reach bottom & her nose swung in … We didn't start today 'till 11 when it cleared—but continued to blow hard. Poled quite a bit, makes the hands icy & numb & very wet job unless you stand up which I finally did. I see now why men lean so far out of the canoe—they can't push hard unless they do … Camping early I had a bath & feel wonderful—but am appalled at the sight of my underwear. Not much I can do about it at this point either!!

The series of rapids from Gull Island to Mininipi were the worst the river had to offer. Russell and the others were extra careful, one man in a canoe steering, two others holding lines on shore, hauling against the flow of the river. Barbara was watching intently from shore, willing everything to go well. Trappers packed their canoes tight, balanced them as well as they could, keenly aware that one wrong move could swamp the boat. Even with two strong men holding lines, everything could be lost.

Thurs. Oct. 9: Today has been beautiful in every way. Yesterday was one of those write-a-letter-but-don't-mail-it days. Tues. A.M. we left Horseshoe House & went as far as Mininipi Island—really between the Island & the Rapid about halfway. The 1st Horseshoe [rapid] R steered & Walter tracked—all canoes were lightened. The Middle one R poled as far as Bob's Brook & from there Warren tracked while R steered. The 3rd one (Horseshoe Cliff) I steered 'till the very end when Wilfred took over. We crossed to the south side there and then the <u>hard</u> poling began. Strong & for a long stretch abrupt drop off along the shore to <u>very</u> deep water which meant we had to hug the shore or lose bottom. Very uphill indeed. Crossed back to North Shore above Mininipi Island. Felt very down all day with constant mental letters going through my head. But before we went to sleep all was well again and today has been a day one really wants to live. Tried to snow and was snowing before we got thru' the Rapid which was excellent. R & Warren took our canoe <u>fully loaded</u> thru' W tracking (with a bit of help? from me) & R with pole on bow. Not often can this be done (R doesn't think he's ever done it before). Tonight we are camped at a lovely spot high on the bank (old Indian place) just above the Berry Banks. As Warren Morris's canoe & our canoe leaked badly & next camping place was far off we camped early. I played hookey & went after berries & got a kettle full & they were yummy. A babbling brook is beside us and it's been clear, cool, and a wind that rumples the hair & I've been singing all day.

Fri. Oct. 10: Slack waters all day—overcast with snow flurries once in awhile. Cold wind—that plus crampy back & front did not make it too good a day—hard to put anything behind the paddle or pole. Tonight we are camped above White Bear Pt. & Sampson's Rub. Porcupine for dinner. Later—the same night—Well it's been said now; and it took only six weeks

& one day! I wonder if I have bitten off more than I can chew—I wanted it more than anything else in the world and now that I have it I've <u>got</u> to make a go of it even if it's going to [be] totally different than I hoped. I guess I just hoped for too much.

Whatever Russell said, when it finally came, was no surprise to Barbara. Things had been rising to a boil, fuelled by two days of tension created by the danger and difficulty of rapids on the river. In white water, the nose of the canoe in the air, "too far out for my comfort"—her diary entry about Gull Island Rapid describes hard poling but then the surprising interjection "we've had a lot of happy times together." She had a bath and felt wonderful. The day after they went through Mininipi Rapid, something snapped. Perhaps Russell felt Barbara did not fully appreciate the danger she was in, and how hard he worked to keep her safe. She was admiring the scenery, picking berries, and "singing all day." She knew he worried the other trappers might resent that he and Barbara were slowing them down. Or maybe it was just that he was not used to having a woman along when he was working. On Sunday, they had a chance to air their grievances.

Oct. 12: Slept all morning, did some washing & about to do hair. R & I talked. I wish we could understand one another better in some ways. I think I've adapted myself well in most ways—he's helped me in the big ways and has done a tremendous amount for me in every way. Some of the little things have been & will be harder for me than the big ones but he doesn't seem to be conscious of them at all. I, knowing both his & my way of life, can see them better, I don't really think he has <u>any</u> conception of what a change it is for me—if he only could know I think he'd think I'd done pretty well too. There's so much—living here, doing without lots of things I've always had, even being married before—that's so awfully new & different for me & for him it's just "old stuff"—And it's all been piled on at once. We haven't really had one day together when we could just be together as we used to be without having to think or worry about something. I honestly wish that once in awhile he'd forget we were married & be as he used to be & call me something else than Barbara!!

Mon. Oct. 13: A hot day in more ways than one! I have more self-control than I thot but I need more yet. Leaves are falling and there is the look & smell of autumn in the air. Our load is smaller—50 lbs. of cabbage (12 heads) reduced to almost nothing & we have left flour at Hayward's & flour, 1 lb. butter, 4 candles at John Blake's. Dogs found lots of little frozen birds among the rocks coming up. Camped tonight at Swift Rocks (Sweat Drops) just above Shoal River—raining. R says I'm steering better—after this A.M. I didn't much care if I steered or not! Less effort, better results as often is the way! Now that we are almost there I'm getting better—and I am sorry to think there'll be little or no chance to practice in the future. I've thoroughly enjoyed doing it & would like to do more. The men certainly get the best part of life in this land.

Tues. Oct. 14: Today we came on thru' the Devil's Hole and R & I are camped at Long Pt. Warren & his adorable pup are "home," Walter, etc. have gone on as has Wilfred. We stayed here and I'm glad for I'm tired. The Devil almost got me below his Hole this time. The canoe went out, sat R down & for the 1st. time I was a bit scared—not at the time (too busy trying hard to get back in) but after! And now we're thru' all tide—Crossed River several times today—full of bends from Shoal River to Hole. Bubbles in lake like black opals. R wonderfully patient today.

Wed. Oct. 15: Long monotonous paddle up Lake Winnie (about 35 mi. today, 6 from end to Long Pt.) stopping at Walter's for little canoe & bags of flour. Lake W is like a letter S. Left small canoe at Wilfred's & went on to camp on other side at R's portage. Both glad to go to bed. One Fr. hen on the way. Spot rode all the way—little canoe was towed from Walter's. It rained and was overcast most of the day. And of course, Mama Nature chose to call again—she always picks the <u>worst</u> times!!

It had taken 15 days to get from Muskrat Falls portage to the south shore of Lake Winokapau, where the trek to Russell's trapping grounds began. Wilfred Baikie's tilt was on the north shore; it was called Fox Island tilt because of the nearby island at lake end. At last they would be on their own and would probably not see anyone else until a planned meeting with the other trappers on the second Sunday of December. Russell surely told Barbara they were still at least a week from home, his main tilt on the trapline. It wasn't such a great distance to cover, if you only had to do it once; it was the repeated portages carrying hundreds of pounds of gear and food in cold, wet, windy weather that would take so long. They were leaving the big river, but still had small lakes and ponds to cross in canoe, and a lot of forested, swampy, difficult, hilly terrain between them and home.

Russell was used to hard work, but the combination of the daily physical exertion and the romantic expectations of his new wife—her need to discuss everything—must have been wearing on him. The more time they spent travelling (and talking), the less time and energy he would have for hunting and trapping.

Thurs. Oct. 16: As it cleared last night and was lovely early this A.M. we thot we had a nice day—but again 'tis grey and drear. I am baking and taking life easy while R is portaging something. Both had a good rest last night. At last we really are alone together & on our own and I am glad. Also glad that the next few months are to be just ours & ours alone. I hope it will be successful in every way and if it is 'twill be happy and something we will both look back on with the happiest memories. That's what I want above all else. Hope the meat situation improves—'tis not good for R to work so hard on bread & tea & occasional cabbage of which we now have no more. Walked in to 1st Pond this aft with R. Took only snowshoes & was pooped. I certainly am no good for carrying at this time and perhaps no good at all.

Fri. A.M.: I guess the last has been said on the subject last night (if I can manage to keep everything to myself)—I was convinced R was different than other NW people as far as I could see—I thot he wanted to be shown affection & wanted to give it. But now we're married it's just as if we must accept the fact we love each other and there's no time for even little reminders. It's a business now—he does his work, I do mine—he keeps his problems to himself & I am supposed to keep mine. That sort of an arrangement seems enuf for him—it's not for me. It's not what I wanted nor what I expected and of all things I must accustom myself to and adapt to—it will be the hardest of all.

Fri. P.M.: Stayed around the tent most of the day—walked into 1st Pond this aft. breaking off willows etc. to top of hill & from there taking the kerosene. I'm still not good for much, damn it. Later went across with R when he changed canoes. And now to bed.

Since they were going back to Wilfred Baikie's tilt one more time,

Barbara wrote a letter to her mother, hoping someone would carry it down the river and it would find its way to the post office in Goose Bay. She wouldn't get another chance to send a letter out until December. The trappers' mail delivery was unpredictable but reliable. Letters and messages would be left at the tilts everyone used, to be passed along in relay by the next man going up or down the river. If they were lucky, there would be treats like cigarettes and candy in the mail from home. Sometimes a trapper would learn if his new child was a boy or girl, or that a friend or relative had died, in those precious notes. At least she could tell her mother they had made it to Russell's trapline safely, but there was not much joy in the letter. She described their journey up Lake Winokapau.

A long, wearisome paddle (about 35 miles). It rained most of the day & I had the curse. Lucky we came tho' as it has blown a gale since & we would have been caught there for days probably. R is portaging and I am baking, etc. for I'm not feeling too good. The portage is only 6 or 8 miles but will take a week at least! This evening we will go over to the Fox Island tilt to get our small canoe & leave the big one. I'll leave this there & it may work its way down in time. We plan, if possible, to come out to meet the three [trappers] above the 2nd Sun. in Dec. Then I'll try to bring a long letter. We have to come out for flour we're leaving here & also we want to get "the news."

Our swollen, aching hands are now reduced, but R's neck is getting it! My hands were so swollen I couldn't even get my wedding ring off! R's presumably did not crack so badly this year. There's no snow here, thank the Lord! and we hope to get to Fig River before it comes or before the ponds freeze.

R is very tired—it is too much for one man even tho' the crowd helped thru' the bad places. He worked <u>too</u> hard trying to keep up, for he knew they'd not leave us but we didn't want to keep them back. I poled & steered a great deal this time—also helped track thru' Mininipi. Some places I steered last year I couldn't this because the canoe was so terribly loaded. She was really much too heavy for me to handle. No mishaps but a "near miss." One place I was steering & I was too far in the tide & had one hell of a time getting back. It took R right off his feet & sat him down—luckily there was a large solid rock near and he braced his feet and slowly he brought her round & in but for a time he thot he'd have to let her go—had he been on his feet he would have gone with her. It was the nearest I've ever been to being scared—not at the moment, but after it was all over. It was not a rocky place so even if he had had to let the line go I would have just gaily sped down the River 'till he could have jumped aboard from another canoe. The dangerous part is over now in that way—but R is feeling the responsibility of taking me—for he not only has to do the right thing but he has to see that I do & if one or both slip up it might be bad—at least thru' the tide it would have been—but that's behind us now.

And we've been married 7 weeks & I'm in the midst of the curse for the _3rd_ time! I'm fed up with it. Got it the day before we were married, had it _all_ the time in St. John's. Then again for the week before we left when we had _so_ much to do (and it was like a flood to boot) and now again. And for a solid week before this time I was feeling rotten because my back chose that particular time to go bad too! So on this portage, I'm no good. Went to the 1st Pond yesterday with only snowshoes (3 prs.), ax, & 2 gals. preserves & was pooped. And there's no meat to speak of and all this heavy work for R on bread & tea & cabbage (of which we have no more) is not very good! Had 12 heads (50 lbs.) and it's gone now. But we'll live if only we do well in fur. I don't know _what_ R will do if we don't. And fur prices have gone down again. I hope all goes well. I'm certainly glad to be with him. I don't know _what_ I'd have done if I weren't! (Letter: October 17, 1947)

If the letter found its way to Thousand Nine, it would do nothing to assure Mrs. Mundy that her daughter had made the right decision. This was not a description of a romantic early morning duck hunt, Barbara cozy in blankets, enjoying the view from the canoe. She was weary, pooped, fed up, aching and swollen with the damnable curse. On top of her physical misery, fur prices were down and there was no meat.

Sat. Oct.18: Last night I felt awful. Wondered how I'd manage even in NW (if R were away) if I felt as badly. Today it came in waves—I could cry at times & then be OK—off & on all day. Went as far as 2nd Pond with only sleeping bag. Took food up to R and had no intention of staying all day, but he didn't seem to want me to come back alone so I stayed and picked some berries while he portaged. Duck for supper & berry cake—good.

Sun. A.M. 'tis raining & I think it's probably for the best—we're both tired & I am so afraid that in that state we'll say things to each other that we'll regret and then it's too late to take them back. We don't seem to understand each other's feelings any more. I try to tell R how I feel but he won't tell me & I don't see—If he'd tell me it would help. I think things I don't <u>want</u> to think and I <u>mustn't</u> think them particularly when I can't talk about them. Slept most of the day as if I were dead. Guess I needed it—the accumulation of exhaustion had caught up with me. Feel fine now after a nice walk up shore for first view of Fig River. Feel much better about life in general. Scaffolded some flour, 1 lb. butter, 4 candles, baking powder, sugar, beans, tobacco, & dog food. (Only enuf of latter for two or three nights.)

Between the south shore at the top of Lake Winokapau and Russell's main camp was a rough portage path, his fall portage. It traversed forest, marsh, and bog, broken up by four large ponds. Barbara and Russell were engaged in a difficult relay with the small canoe, carrying everything up steep hills, across the bogs to pond edge, then stuffing as much as possible into the canoe, paddling across, then getting it all out again and portaging to the shore of the next pond. From the start of the portage, it was "a bit over a mile—then almost another mile of stumbly stuff & willows to 1st pond—a tiny one connected by channel to a small lake—about ½ mile from there to 2nd pond." Barbara used a head strap: "so much easier to carry things—takes the strain off the back."

Mon. Oct. 20: Ready to move yesterday but rain and my innards kept us here. Still raining this A.M. P.M.: Camped tonight at 2nd Pond—thot it was going to clear & left River at 12:30. As soon as we got to top of hill & out of woods, it came down in torrents & we were wet to the skin, cold & miserable. Cold wind blew too! Spot found us a porcupine & 2 partridges. The latter, rice & red berries our first really decent meal since we left.

Tues. Oct. 21: We woke this A.M. to find an inch or more of snow on ground, trees, etc. It is now aft and 'tis still snowing a bit. R got the canoe from 1st Pond & has taken one load across this one. Intends to clear portage & perhaps take flour thru' to #3. Willows slubby, swamp to knees or more & all very "dirty." I wanted to go too but it seemed stupid to get wet all over again. One person's clothes are enuf to try to dry! So I am still in pj's—slept all A.M. How do I do it? esp. when we go to bed so early! I'm feeling swell again—a very pleasant change.

By Wednesday, October 22, everything was at Fourth Pond. The physical work had taken a toll on them, made worse by 10 days of poor food. They had a single meal of duck, a couple of partridges, and a porcupine (thanks to Spot) between October 10 to 20, eating mainly stove bread, oatmeal, and thin pea soup. They killed two beavers along the way, "one a fine big one," and were looking forward to a meal of meat. Making camp while wet and exhausted, all their remaining energy was needed just to prepare and cook it. When the portaging finally stopped, Barbara hoped they would have a chance to recover.

Thurs. Oct. 23: Here we are at Fig River and R is "home" and happy about it. Camped on his usual spot. What a day—the Lord ordered up the right kind for me for last night was a nightmarish jumble of weird dreams & I woke all tense and full of funny shivers—unable to relax. I had to work it off some way & I have, with many a laugh! Crossed the 2nd & 3rd Ponds & portages to the 4th & last—snow all gone.

The last portage long, boggy and trees heavy with snow. Wet moss & leaves are slippery but with snow on top, they're something. How R knew <u>where</u> he was going was beyond me—we seemed to be wandering around amongst old burnt woods, scrub trees, swamp, & Indian tea. The "road" when visible, only a rut. Finally came out to see the Fig River (would be a good view in good weather) and then a slide almost down to it. I had kettles, buckets, & pans of all kinds trying to balance them on my neck & R & Spot hauling a beaver left a lovely slippery path for me to fall about in. Glasses steamed up—snow drifting from frowzy hair & each tree I embraced to catch myself unloaded its snow on my head. It was funny & the sure cure for what ailed me! R's present opinion of me: as he slid down by the tent with a stick of wood breaking a picket I asked "What's up"—he replied "if I knocked the tent down you wouldn't know it"—I asked if he thot me that stunned & he said he "didn't know"!

I'm learning things the hard way as usual, but I suppose 'tis the best way tho' rather tough, as it leaves a lasting impression—things are not going to be "let's-get-it-over-with-in-a-hurry" idea with me—it's worse that way than not at all. I do wish it were different. But still I'd not change back—it's wonderful to be here & the snow & all (to look at) makes it almost like fairyland. I've loved today. Delicious beaver for supper—and now 'tis time for what I hope will be a better sleep.

Fri. Oct. 24: Here am I with everything I've ever wanted—a husband to love & do things for who would return that love, a house of my own, a life I've always longed for, living in a country & in a way I love—everything about it is what I've wanted <u>all</u> my life & yet I've failed in it all. I'm not making R happy, I'm not happy myself as a result & I can't seem to learn the things that I must to live here & be a proper wife here. They say "where there's a will there's a way"—I have plenty of will, but I haven't found the way. Well, I'll be alone with my thots this winter & perhaps I'll find it yet. There's no one to help me now but myself & I'll have to figure out what to do about it … Why is it when you're in love <u>everything</u> seems possible, even the impossible? I want this desperately & I've got to keep it & make it a go. I've just got to. Walked along the shore a bit, ret'd to tent, bathed & made myself feel better with a bit of lipstick! Mended R's & my things and now all my chores are done, including the baking. At least I <u>think</u> they are—perhaps there are more I'm shirking—wish R would tell me.

Sat. Oct. 25: Portaged all day from 8-6 for R. I didn't go back the last time and for a bit while he carried I tried to clear out some of the path— perhaps if I am not much help carrying that will help in years to come— will try to do more tomorrow. R says this was an old Indian portage but not used by them for years or it would be cleared out … Roast beaver on stove again & cakes ready to bake. R is putting out net. It's been a good day.

Sun. Oct. 26: The moon came out last night, geese kronked flying overhead & the shadows on the tent were lovely. This A.M. was glorious, sun shining. We got to the top of the hill just as it rose—but in afternoon, snow again! This portage is a series of hills & marshes to the Pond which was frozen this A.M. R feeling rotten but portaging just the same, Sunday & all, to get advantage of our one supposedly (!) fine day.

Breaking the taboo against working on Sunday meant Russell was determined to finish portaging. Barbara wrote, "R is back from his last load & <u>all</u> the portaging is over. 'Tis 5 P.M. & we can now relax for the evening. I'm very happy." They had made it to one of his camping places on the Fig River trapline, though still not at his main tilt, and Russell immediately set a few traps. They had been married two months.

Mon. Oct. 27: This has been a lovely day—wind blown, so we went beaver hunting in the A.M. down the lake to where the Fig River comes south from Grand River & flows east (or rather flows the other way). The lake is off to the south, just at the bend. Very pretty there, little points & coves. Several small ponds dammed up by beavers just inside. Found one house being used & R set a trap … Back to tent now for a beaver supper & berry cake. I wanted to hug R! I've had such a nice day, but he doesn't look in a very huggable mood, darn it!

Tues. Oct. 28: Up bright & early to get off up the lake—as soon as we got up down came the rain, black as pitch out. When rain stopped it began to blow—but at daylight we started anyway. (R was in a talkative mood last night & I loved it—I love having him tell me about himself etc.) Just as we reached R's lower tilt (which he built) it really blew & we had to come ashore in a hurry. White caps in no time. The little canoe was very top heavy (altho' we scaffolded 5 bags of flour at portage) & most tippy. This tilt is high on a bank across the lake from a wonderful waterfall. Did the bears ever have fun in it! Roof partly off, some things thrown outdoors (corks from net all the way down bank) and the mess inside! When R left, can of flour, box (closed), stove etc. were all neatly on bunk, net hung up, etc. Bears had ripped part of bunk down, & everything was helter skelter in a heap. Net too, completely rotted. Could hardly get in for the junk. We boiled outdoors & then set to work. Everything thrown out. While R got new birch bark & logs & brush, I cleaned what could be salvaged with moss & chips & then hot water & soap. Some things had completely disappeared and now all is cozy and neat & clean again, but still a bit damp due to leakage. Not too messy outside either, thank God. Then we walked along shore to look for Fr. hen R had shot but lost this A.M. Found him but had to give him to Spot as jays had been at him. Tilts don't have doors & bears tore down canvas! Celebrated our housecleaning with tin of beef we found, kindly left by bears.

The next day, the wind blew hard, keeping them at the tilt for the morning. When the winds calmed, they walked part of Russell's winter portage path, another trail leading back to Grand River. From the hills, they could see "the distant mountains & about where the house is."

Barbara wanted to see where they were, to get familiar with Russell's paths and camping places.

Oct. 29: Guess this will be the best winter of my life in more ways than one. R wanted to go alone I think but I was afraid I'd not get another chance before snow came & it is good for me to go with him & notice (or try to!) how he gets about, also the more I go the less tired I'll be when I <u>have</u> to go—but I suppose it's because I love it so that I want to go every chance I can get. And being "lonesome" I have been & will be again far, far more lonesome in NWR & NY than I could <u>ever</u> be here with R. How could one be lonesome in a spot like this? More washing on return (not approved of!) and not done very well, I am afraid but best I could considering all things. Supper is on & it is getting dusky. What will tomorrow bring, I wonder?

Thurs. Oct. 30: At R's wee tilt he built last year at entrance to North Path. It is about 6 x 6½ feet (tent was about 6 x 7, & tilt on lake about 6 x 8). To get in here I have to really crawl—not straddle & duck as at other & legs must be stretched out or I hit my fanny! Cozy & warm. It was blowing hard again this A.M. but R took one load up to point & then came back for me & second one. We boiled there—a lovely mossy point with scattered spruce ... This tilt is on a point by a gurgling brook, across is an island and up a quiet turn—almost a cove—still and reflecting a lovely pink sunset. It was again a grey, cold day with an icy wind blowing and ice formed on paddle above the blade. But tonight is gloriously clear—full moon and sparkling stars and dark trees against the sky (up here they are more shapely somehow) like the wonderful nights R & I had sometimes in NW; the best night since we left. Every once in a while there's a crackling sound—R says 'tis the tilt cracking as it dries out. No bears here except to nibble at R's sled, but rabbits or something chewed up all magazines, Xmas box, etc. One bit of reading matter left as at last tilt. It's a <u>lovely</u> spot.

Russell had two main trapping paths, north and south of Fig River. The North Path went from the tilt by the "gurgling brook" on Fig River, to Elizabeth River, another tributary of Grand River. There were at least five bodies of water large enough to be called lakes along the path and a tilt at the end. The South Path went from the main house—his biggest tilt—south to a camping spot at a lake below Mount Montgomery. There was a tilt halfway to the end of the path and many lakes along the way. Russell also set traps along Fig River, especially where there were beaver houses.

Fri. Oct. 31: We moseyed along setting traps on the way up. Calm but cold. The river is lovely, bending & pretty. A rapid a bit below the house and one above. House on south side in a clearing—looks north & west to a cove, rapid & burnt woods at next bend of river. The door was still in place but bears or wolverines or something had gotten in thru' the window & everything was topsy turvy but not <u>too</u> bad. Sealskin gone but bottle snitched last year returned! (Foxes once stole a boiler from R!!) First we looked in box to see what was in it—then to work—everything thrown out; I dusted with wing & R fixed leaks & brushed tilt. Then I scrubbed everything including box and what wasn't clean was left to do later. Found moss & chips excellent for cleaning at tilt but an old shirt here is fine. Water rising fast—R says 'tis strange when it's cold. Full moon rising thru' trees. Both fell asleep while bread was baking, then got settled on floor as bunk is too narrow for two but R is going to fix that. The house is about 8 x 10, has 2 windows & a door I can walk thru' if I sort of duck my back at the proper moment. Coming up everything was grey with frost. While cleaning up water would freeze!

In the month since they left North West River, Barbara had swung between feeling "a total failure" to being ecstatically happy. Her note that Russell was talkative one night was a sign that at last he was relaxing, having reached his trapping grounds, both of them safe, tilts repaired, food supplies dry and stored on scaffolds. With the portaging done, at least for a while, there was great relief on both their parts. Now he could concentrate on trapping and she could figure out how to keep house in tiny log cabins and canvas tents.

Chapter Fourteen

INDIANS FOR NEIGHBOURS

I was one of those who used to go to North West River along the route through the Atikonak and Winuakapau lakes. There were English-speaking trappers there, living and trapping out in the bush. They always built their log cabins a one-day walk from each other.

—Mathieu Mestokosho, in *Caribou Hunter*

The domestic situation had calmed, but something else was causing Barbara and Russell anxiety: the frequent sign of Innu around the trapline. Russell's paths were close to the border with Quebec and the route Innu families, whole clans from infants to elders, travelled from the north shore of the St. Lawrence deep into the interior of the Ungava Peninsula, intersecting with the migrating caribou herds. Over the years Russell had met many of them and was always finding old scaffolds, pieces of canoes, and remains of campsites on what he considered his ground. Some of the trappers, especially the older ones who went as far as the Height of Land, had Innu friends, traded with them, and spoke a little of their language, but meetings could be tense. The Innu were nomadic hunters, whose survival depended on caribou; their hunting effort was spent on finding and killing as many animals as they could. Their trapping method was more opportunistic than systematic, with greater interest in finding fur-bearing animals that could also be eaten. They knew the white men maintained numerous cabins and trails, but never acknowledged anyone's ownership of a path on the land.

Fur trader Raoul Thevenet tried to bring attention to the potential conflict over land in the Labrador interior in 1921, warning that the Innu "are becoming very bitter against the white trappers and any year trouble may break out." He said the Innu had been using the same hunting ground "for generations past, but these last few years the co-called Natives (half-breeds) and Newfoundlanders have been making a regular business of trapping, some of them having as many as three to six hundred traps set during the hunting season." Thevenet said the hunting grounds were "overrun," that Innu were getting poorer every year, and without relief from the Canadian government, some would surely have starved. The Newfoundland government gave little or no relief to the Innu.[1]

To the trappers, the Innu were unpredictable competitors who did not play by the rules, who drove the animals, and sometimes helped themselves to things they found in cabins. John Blake described the Innu way of trapping: "trap so long in one place, get the fur caught up and move on to some other place."[2]

Another view of the Innu way was explained in an article published in the Goose Bay air base newsletter, *The Honker*: "They do not seem to understand the white man's ideas of game laws or game conservation programs for they kill whatever they require whenever they require it, regardless of condition of fur or mating seasons, etc. And the Indians also deal in furs, which they obtain while on the trail. When they have made a large kill of caribou or bear, they remain on the spot for some time, and it is not long before fur-bearing animals are attracted to the spot. So by finding themselves a meal, they also find themselves valuable furs, which in turn means hard cash and food at a later date."[3]

For millennia, the Innu had survived in small family groups, killing and eating what they needed. Little wonder they paid no attention to anyone telling them to do it differently, especially people they viewed as interlopers, who had only recently appeared in the country with the notion that they owned it. And as for the white man's hunting laws, Thevenet said, neither Innu nor "natives" paid any attention to game and fish regulations unless a game warden or customs officer was in the area, which happened only occasionally.[4]

Barbara had become acquainted with Innu women who came to the Industrial Shop, some who had been patients at the hospital in North West River, and those who camped at Groves Point. From her room in the hospital in North West River, there was a good view of their canvas tents on the opposite shore, with tin stovepipes puffing smoke through the top, women preparing meals, men building canoes, children playing on the beach. When autumn came, whole families and all their belongings were packed into canoes and they paddled away, not reappearing until the following summer, after a winter hunting in the interior. The Innu near Russell's trapping grounds would be a new group to her—the so-called Canadian Innu, from communities on the north shore of Quebec at Natashquan, Mingan, Musquaro, and Sept-Îles, heading for North West River or the coast, to sell some fur, get supplies, and meet up with relatives. The summer was spent making canoes at their camps around the HBC trading post. In August or September, they put their canoes in the rivers that flow from the Height of Land south into the Gulf of St. Lawrence, the waterways that brought Innu into the same territory occupied by Labrador trappers.

On November 1, Russell saw tracks near a beaver house. He told Barbara he was worried about the food left at their main tilt, when they'd be gone on the path for a day or two. Trappers would sometimes conceal their food supplies a distance from their camps.

On the house R thot he saw a man's track. We went on & found the dam broken. Indians had been there very recently with snares. We found where they boiled. R says Seven Island [north shore of Quebec] ones & probably north in the woods as no other sign on the River. Coming down we stopped at another pond. I loved coming down the Rapids—awfully glad I went with R in case there's not another chance in open water. Because of the Indians we will now have to scaffold things away from the house, at least 'till we know where they are. Twice R has been cleaned out by them—once after he [had] been away 2 years & once while he was at Fox Island—that time he had to go home! If they should do that to us after the work of getting it here, we'll <u>have</u> to do something. R says he thinks they won't do it if they know we're here, but he's going to be on the safe side anyway. When we got back I made a berry cake & R added a stick to our bunk. Now he is cleaning beaver & I am mixing our first yeast bread since we left. It's been a grand day.

Sun. Nov. 2: A most unSabbath-like day. R putting up shelves & making bunk bigger, sorting things out, & I baking and washing!! Results are lovely tho' and I think we're looking much more settled and cozy—R feels the loss of space! Almost broke my spine on door & R had to take the ax & make it a bit bigger with the remark—how was I going to get into the tilt where he had to make the door bigger to get his snowshoes in!! Laughed his head off as he patched my poor skinned back. Gosh, it is sore! Tomorrow we go down again and don't know just when we'll be back. R is uneasy not knowing where the Indians are. Would like to find out & give them a good scare by making a funny noise at night nearby! Almost made himself sick on my _good!_ yeast bread and porcupine, peas-pudding dinner!

Mon. Nov. 3: Here we are at Lower Tilt again—left at dawn, moon still shining. R broke bunk by heaving sugar on it—thank the Lord _he_ did it! Sun not much good to us these days as he skims over the hills, rises late (9) & sets early (5)—over the hills that is. Got a bit tho' nearer the lake below Little Tilt, where river widens out & hills rise more gradually, farther from the river. Set traps all along, got 2 muskrat above tilt. Left some food at 1st trap below house in case Indians call while we're away.

Tues. Nov. 4: Off early this A.M. to set up lake. Went down so. [south] side. Beaver in trap set last time. First fur in trap & first to share with Uncle J. [John Groves]. So far R has 2 beaver, 3 muskrat, all shot, so all his own. Picked up flour and are now caught by wind at Long Pt. (Had to break thru' ice twice in river below lake.) We are camped at pt. just below Long Pt. by a bubbling brook with a lovely waterfall cascading down the rocks above. I'd like to know what's on top! I wish I didn't have such an insatiable curiosity about what is just beyond, above, or around!! Tent is up, R is chopping wood & I am sitting by the fireplace where we boiled ... Last night I started out on bunk in summer underwear & sleeping bag. R on floor fully dressed. At 1 we woke, he frozen, I practically roasted & running away in perspiration. We changed places & all was well. It's going to be fun to be in tent again tonight.

The Innu regarded the trappers' way of life as needlessly difficult, building and maintaining many cabins, carrying so much heavy food into the country. Innu hunter Mathieu Mestokosho, from Mingan, Quebec, had probably been on Russell's trapping grounds, so close to the Canadian border, on the numerous occasions he passed through with his family. He knew a lot of trappers from North West River and had observed their habits: "These hunters took huge quantities of provisions with them. They lived in log cabins. It's amazing how much flour they'd have stored away. We'd visit these white hunters and, as we entered their cabins, they'd hide their flour. But they always asked us for meat. They especially wanted caribou."[5] While the trappers felt insecure without a large quantity of supplies for the winter, the Innu carried a scant amount of provisions and lived off the land as much as possible. But as much as they depended on wild meat, the Innu enjoyed stove cakes too, and even nomadic Innu clans had picky eaters, according to Mestokosho, "some of our children refused to eat meat."[6]

Nov. 5: Windy, loppy & cold (overcast) 'till we passed the Lower Tilt. R set his net just above there to freeze in; 3 fish so far, hope to heaven there will be some next haul. Clear & cold & beautiful from there up. Second bridge of ice coming down still there & with load R unable to drag her [canoe] over, so we had to camp & R is now making a rough catamaran to take her across. Made a good camping site out of nothing. Wish I had watched him but I was washing dishes & fixing horrible nails & chin—first good chance in daylight for ages. R is now taking a load up to the water on cat with Spot. From the sounds they are not getting on well … It is so beautiful out I hate to go into the tent. I wonder if ever again in my life I'll live such a wonderful way.

Nov. 6: Again at Little Tilt … It was 2 when we arrived so we boiled & R went hunting & to look again for Spot. I took kettle to berry pick—Soon drove 2 partridges & yelled for R who was out of earshot. So I came back for rifle & hoped I'd know how to shoot it! Actually found my way back & shot head off #1, couldn't find other then walked on a bit & found another pair! "Off with his head." At that point R arr'd with the 22—he had come back not knowing what was up … My hunt is now on stove! Feeling very proud of self. I wish to heck I were petite tho'—I'm outsize for this country & I can't help it tho' but wish I weren't reminded of it so often! I love this little tilt—perhaps because I was so very happy here the first night we spent here.

Nov. 7: I am now at my 4th house—each one gets cuter than the last! R & I both can look down at the roof as we are taller—my shoulders hit the ridge pole when inside & I sit on the bunk (which is almost on the floor) and all I can see of R outside is legs to the knees! The roof is a bit open in spots but R says a lot of snow will seal that! Today we left almost before daylight, cloudy all A.M. but frost making everything white—junipers just fairy like … Honestly, I just can't believe I'm here sometimes. It seems like a dream—too good to be true.

Nov. 9: This Sunday has been busy too. I washing, R puttering about doing all sorts of odd jobs—refurbishing floor, wood, another shelf, tapping boot leg, etc. I also baked quite a bit as we are off again soon. Yesterday we came here from the tilt in the North Path. No sign of Spot 'till after we passed the fireplace & then we saw his footprints in the frozen moss pointing riverward & there he was waiting at the tilt … And there R & I stood looking about & no one anywhere near. I love that!

Nov. 11: Tonight we are at our 5th house (the tent makes our 6th). It is about the size of one in North Path, 20 yrs. old and like an old lady settling in all directions! Very hunchbacked or round shouldered with braces front & back to keep her up. R shook her before we entered to be sure she'd not collapse … Patched up our leaky roof with canvas from & bits of old Indian canoe left up the brook a bit. Boiled by Silver Brook (R shot a silver fox there once.) This is where the Indians stole R's things & left their old stove in payment! … I washed the family's clothes, baked 2 <u>huge</u> loaves of bread which crackled, washed my hair & did several other odd jobs—too busy even to eat. Oven smoked me out & when I took it off the stove pipes made horrible noises & steamed & sizzled and the stove burned so furiously I didn't know what to expect. R says it's "nothing" but I had fits! I love it when R speaks of "our" things—Before I left I put our frozen laundry in the tilt. I had to laugh trying to get in thru' the door with it and breaking icicles off the sleeves. A frozen sleeve could knock you out, I think, & I seem to see myself struggling with sheets in NW. I bet I end up smashing a window with one!

This A.M. (Nov. 12) we woke to find just enuf snow to cover the ground. We went down the river to the lake & came out on it just west of the islands which almost cut the lake in two. Everything was grey with frost & fog. It is a pretty lake, low shore line & beaches. Saw old Indian scaffold & campsite ... I wish I could take pictures galore but not enuf films & I mustn't use them all at once—but I want to remember all this <u>*clearly*</u>*. Tomorrow we plan to leave Spot & go to the mts. for a deer hunt.*

Today (Nov. 13) We had a nice walk—not a mouthful of meat to even <u>*see*</u>*! Went up the river 'till it was open, cut in north & followed a brook, then across a pond & back to river ... Back to river & hit it* <u>*exactly*</u> *at R's last trap! He tried to make me think he knew that's where he'd come out. He's smart, I know, but* <u>*not*</u> *that smart! Wish it had been clear—I'd love to get in the mts. proper—and a deer would have meant a lot to our tummies!*

Food was a preoccupation on the trapline. Barbara recorded nearly every partridge, beaver, and porcupine they killed—they would have been doomed to a nearly meatless diet without partridges. In mid-November, when she was wishing for a meal of caribou, she may have wondered if the Innu way of doing things made some sense after all. Russell would have killed a caribou if he had seen any, but he wasn't spending much time hunting. Some trappers found caribou too heavy to haul around, and didn't bother hunting them.

When Innu found caribou, they would kill as many as possible, eat as much as they could, and harvest all edible or usable parts of the animals before moving on. Mathieu Mestokosho recalled a great hunt in 1925 when they killed 30 animals one day and 77 a few days later: "We had more than one hundred caribou to eat."[7] Meat was stored on scaffolds, if they had any left over when it was shared. Caribou skins were processed, the hides used for boots, clothing, and bedcovers, and to make babiche, thin strips of rawhide used for the webbing in snowshoes or to lash fur boards and toboggans. They pounded every bit of marrow out of the bones.

Innu knew what it was like to be hungry. People had starved to death, and nearly starved, when hunting was poor. During the winter of 1930, Mestokosho's grandfather told him to "look around the area" for other Innu families who may need meat. They climbed a mountain near Lake Keshikaskau and spotted a tent beside the lake. Two families from North West River were there, with hardly any food. They made a plan to meet a few days later to share what they had.[8] Sometimes the circumstances were desperate enough to be brought to official attention, although with little good result. In 1928, HBC factor John E. Keats wrote to Roman Catholic Reverend Edward J. O'Brien from Davis Inlet to warn him he would find his flock in bad shape when he came to Labrador in the summer. O'Brien was a priest from Newfoundland who went to Davis Inlet and North West River to minister to the Innu.[9] Keats wrote:

> I am sorry to say that we have had a very very poor year. Far inland the Indians barely caught enough to pay their fall outfit, and some of them have been living on Nfld. Govt. relief this spring to keep from starving. Hope you will find conditions better at North West River although I imagine the Indians that hunt to the North will have very little.[10]

A few years later, in 1933, things were no better when HBC's district manager for Labrador, Hayward Parsons, wrote to Father O'Brien. Parsons had received a telegram from HBC factor George Budgell, who advised him "that destitution was rife in the Rigolet district." Parsons passed along the information to the Secretary of State. Parsons had also received a telegram from the HBC factor at Davis Inlet telling him "natives have no means of support," the fur hunt had been "almost a complete failure," and the Newfoundland government was not forthcoming with assistance. Parsons thought the authorities may have been influenced by "those who write articles which to say the least of them are very misleading, particularly when coming from those supposed to be conversant with living conditions of the Labrador Natives, who brand them as a lazy and irresponsible lot."[11]

O'Brien tried hard to advocate for the Innu, who were not always offered the same meagre relief available to people in Newfoundland. In August 1938, he went to *The Daily News* in St. John's to tell the story of the "distressed condition" in which he found the Indians, the worst he had seen in 18 years. O'Brien told the editors he was "heartily sick of nit wits clothed in the symbolic dress of Authority," probably a reference to the Newfoundland Ranger in Davis Inlet. In January 1938, O'Brien had heard that several families were "at the point of starvation" in Davis

Inlet due to a scarcity of caribou and fur. He contacted the authorities and a wireless message was sent ordering the Ranger in Hopedale to investigate. The matter was handed off to the Ranger in Davis Inlet, who doled out amounts of flour—25 pounds for a large family, 15 pounds for a small family—to families who would go to Voisey's Bay, where deer were "falsely reported plentiful." A man who refused to walk the 50 miles (80 kilometres) with his wife and children was given no supplies. The others left for Voisey's Bay and arrived there after a week of extreme hardship to find no relief and no work. It was "an emaciated band of Indians who staggered in to the Hudson's Bay Company Post" at Davis Inlet in March. O'Brien complained to the Commissioner of Public Health and Welfare about "the inhuman treatment of approximately forty starving Indians."[12]

A letter written to O'Brien, dated August 31, 1948, by HBC factor Max Budgell for Joe Rich, the Chief of the Davis Inlet band, told the sad news of the previous winter when children died of starvation:

> We have left Davis Inlet and are going to live in Nutak. We don't know yet whether it will be better or not but we are going to try it and hope to get more deer than there are in Davis Inlet. We are sorry to leave the church and we are sorry because we haven't seen the priest. Last year we had a hard winter, three children starved because we were too far in the country and bad weather stopped us before we could go to Davis Inlet. We ask for your blessing. We don't forget you and we ask you to pray for all of us. Everyone very well now. We ask you to try, if you can't come yourself, to send a priest to see us. Some of our babies are not baptized and some of our young people want to be married. I buried the children who starved, we had to leave them in the country. We have no books now, prayer books, and wish you would send some.[13]

When there was starvation, it was never because people weren't hunting and sharing, and when families were desperate, food in a trapper's tilt would be taken. The Innu people Barbara and Russell saw signs of that winter were not desperate though; they were actively hunting and perhaps having more luck than their trapper neighbours.

Barbara and Russell planned to spend a couple of days exploring and hunting for caribou at the far end of his South Path, an area he hadn't visited in two years. They found his tent site as he left it, stove hung up on pickets.

Tonight (Nov. 14) We are camped in the snow at the foot of Mt. Montgomery, the highest lump around here ... While boiling we heard 4 shots—Indians are somewhere & that's probably why no deer yesterday. Signs of them here tho'. We also got 10 partridges on the way in ... It snowed most of the day & was bad for camping but we are quite comfy now—using our plates for frying pans & baking dishes—wonderful bread as a result.

Mon. Nov. 17: We left our tent on Fri. altho' it was still bad weather. R was afraid there would be a big batch of snow & we ought to get back to our snowshoes. We had a very comfy night even tho' we had no sleeping bag. Kept fire on & alternated between cold, frying & just right ... Altho' the next day was Sunday we ret'd to house as it was <u>still</u> bad & we didn't know how long it might last & food would in time get short. Saw Indians' camp on lake & stick showing they'd gone into mountains—where we heard them shoot. They must have seen our track but never went to tilt ... Today R went "up around" and I baked, did laundry & mended <u>all</u> day. My first struggle & battle with long undies took all my strength and they are <u>still</u> not clean. I'm beginning to understand what those dread words "river clothes" mean—and I fear it will take all our soap & all my strength to keep them even moderately clean. My "woolfoam" [soap for washing woollens] is almost gone ... The Indian(s) had tea & candles & I said I guess they'd not steal our food as they seemed to be supplied. R's retort to that was "No. Unless it's ours they're using." When R went up to beaver house today he found they'd been there again & had "written to" him on a tree. He says with them around he's afraid everything is driven & his chances poor as they have been here a long time. Funny, they've not been down here yet. Tomorrow we expect to be off again.

Barbara's housekeeping skills were being put to the test. She had heard women speak of the work it took to get "river clothes" clean and decided to tackle the problem before it got to a critical stage. Trappers mended and cleaned their clothes when necessary but would never have spent all day heating water, laboriously washing filthy garments, and then hanging things to dry.

With their long underwear at least passably clean, Barbara and Russell ventured out again to check the traps along Fig River, finding "not a skin of fur." Getting as far as Lower Tilt, they had to haul the canoe sometimes, as the lake was freezing. Russell shot some fish through the ice, finding nothing in a net he had set. The ice wasn't thick enough to walk on—"ax went thru' with 1 blow"—so they checked traps along the north side of the lake and got one mink. On the fall portage path, at a beaver house at the fourth pond, they saw that the "damn Indians" had been there before them, and cleaned them out. Barbara was quite indignant about it. As far as she was concerned, they had no business being there.

Wed. Nov. 19: Saw man's track coming down—they must be everywhere & what chance has R got? It isn't fair for them to even be in the country, let alone on someone else's ground. And they're keeping away from us. R says it may be so we won't know who they are and after we're gone they can clean us out.

Fri. Nov. 21: Hauled canoe from Lower Tilt to point & found river fast except for some quiet dark holes—so we abandoned her & walked rest of way to Little Tilt. I was glad for I can't bear to hear R curse as he does at ice etc. … Walking over rocks, pebbles, frozen lumps, etc. in skin boots is hellish—might just as well be barefoot. My feet are sore at this point. Had to bridge one brook with log & R actually gave me a hand across—seemed like old times! And now we are in Little Tilt.

With the river and lakes frozen fast, the small canoe was finally more trouble than it was worth. They had been pushing, pulling, and hauling almost as much as they had paddled, since thin ice began forming on the water early in November. Safely stowed at the point between Lower Tilt and Little Tilt, the canoe would be retrieved later in the winter.

Sat. Nov. 22: We went into tilt on [Northern] path. The darn Indians have been on that path too. Cut sticks and footprints. Their aim seems to be to wipe out all beaver & to find houses on people's paths first. Otter *tracks on the lakes—4 feet & a <u>long</u> slide. R lost one—got his toe only—2nd otter loss. Got 1 weasel, 1 mink, rabbit, which we are having for supper & porcupine, which Spot stole cleverly & ate completely. He's a devil … This time we went on into Elizabeth River … R can't remember the river being open so late. (Says we shouldn't have gone on lake ice we did!) Got 7 partridges, so we have meat for 3 more days.*

Hunting along the way for fresh meat took time and sometimes yielded little or nothing. The days they got seven and 10 partridges were good days indeed. Travelling the paths with her husband, Barbara learned how success in hunting and trapping was only partly about how much effort was made. A trapper could work hard and still end up with very little because there were no animals to be had, or another hunter had got there first. Russell had years of experience with the weather, the river, the abundance and scarcity of animals. He felt sure of his ability to deal with whatever nature might throw at him, but, that winter, the unknown and worrying factor was the presence of Canadian Innu. He kept track of them as much as he could, listening for their gunshots, sniffing for their campfire smoke, watching for their snowshoe prints. He couldn't predict what they might do—if they would stop by one of his tilts and relieve him of essential supplies. He hoped to hear no more shots, smell no more smoke, and see no more signs.

Heavy snow was falling and Russell and Barbara decided to head back to their main house, as Russell said, it was "gathering fast." They were free of the burdensome canoe but the going was wet and rough. To get back to their main house, they would have to cross Fig River.

Mon. Nov. 24: I slipped all over the ice and hills & finally hit my kneecap on a rock & can hardly walk as result. It hurts like hell—I just hope nothing much is wrong. My elbow has picked now to act up again (not much thank heavens) so I feel very much crippled at the moment. R has been sweet & done everything besides cutting up a lot of wood—for I can't possibly go with him in the path with this knee … Just after I hurt my knee we literally took to the water—only way to get to house. R knew we could wade it at the rapid above house, of course, with usual luck even it was getting fast & channel left open was deeper as a result. R took my load & I took stick to help me across & in we went … Spot, by this time, had come across river again and was howling as he saw us take to river. R says Indians would wonder what was up should they see our track emerging from it!

Tues. Nov. 25: R spent day sawing & splitting wood, & I washing, darning, & baking. R was up to knees getting new brush for floor. I shovelled paths to clothes line & my <u>super</u> little house—soon to be surrounded by snow banks & sheltered from above by a large spruce 'twill be most cozy, I feel sure!! Rained this aft. so what next? Knee <u>much</u> better. Good supper; partridges with rice & onions, peas pudding, and new bread with redberry jam for tea before. We feel <u>full</u> when we have such meals. R has just put our bread on boards above us to keep it (we hope) from mice. The little devils have not only gone at our flour, but even our sleeping bags! Sign of fur to come, says R—wish it were here <u>this</u> year.

Thurs. Nov. 27: I went out this A.M. to see the full moon setting & vapor rising from the rapid ... Our little house looked so cozy too—smoke rising & lamp in window hung with "ice candles"—a lovely name for icicles.

Sat. Nov. 29: The last two mornings we have started out in full moonlight and it has been beautiful. Yesterday we came from home to tilt in [southern] path—beautiful day—snowshoes most of way & I got along far, far better than I expected to after such a long time & it was a good distance for my 1st try again. Actually I guess it's the farthest I <u>ever</u> walked in them in one day. Feet were sore at end and for the first time I was tired—I think a lot of my being tired is worry etc. & nervousness that I'll keep him back etc. He has enuf to curse at now & I don't want <u>me</u> included—also going with glasses I'm terrified of willows, sticks, etc. in my eyes ... Ice forming under feet made them sore & my knee went on the bum again. I stumbled & got hooked up & gen'lly made a mess of it—the one woody spot we had. I was completely choked & in tears about it & all the thots of other things on my mind when a little redpoll came to my rescue. R picked him up in the middle of the lake & he was almost frozen. It gave me something else to think about. I held him in my hand under my jacket & could feel him gradually come back to life. He seemed OK when I put him in a tree in a sheltered spot & soon after the sun came out. Perhaps Mr. Audubon will smile on me for that <u>good</u> deed!!

We boiled on ice today. Got back early & R went in to brook—one weasel only. He is discouraged & so am I—for different reasons tho'. Our three days at "home" were grand—if only it could continue. Hunting is <u>everything</u> to R and he doesn't seem to realize that <u>he</u> is <u>everything</u> to me. He even said he could have been perfectly happy to have left me a month after we were married & he can't see that I would <u>not</u> have been happy with that. Imagine being separated from someone you love 11 mos., returning & aside from the week in St. John's having him to yourself for exactly 1 day and 2 nites & then being separated again for about 4 mos. I'd rather have waited even longer to get married! There's an <u>awful</u> lot I'm discovering that's pretty hard to discover. I just hope somehow I get the courage to take it—if only R would not consider as "silly" the little things that mean almost more to me than anything else. A word, a touch or a smile would do <u>so</u> much—I could go thru' hell for him then, I think.

Barbara couldn't bear the thought of a winter apart and was dreading the time when she would have to spend a single night alone in a cabin in the dark forest. Her knee was no good for walking: "So tomorrow I'll be alone for the first time in my life both day & night. Wonder how I'll like it?" On the subject of being alone in the country, she would have been in full agreement with the Innu, who thought it a dangerous and lonely way to live. In the trappers' view, more men working in the bush meant fewer furs for each. They were friends who helped each other without question when necessary, but they had a competitive spirit. Nobody wanted to be the one who came back to North West River with the smallest haul. According to the Innu way of thinking, the more hunters there were, the better chance they had of finding and killing animals, and whatever was killed was shared. Innu were not much impressed by the lone trapper's hunting ability, especially when it came to caribou. Innu "are never alone," and if one was unable to hunt "someone else hunted for him and his family."[14]

Most trappers got accustomed to a solitary life. Some claimed to enjoy the solitude and found the transition difficult when they came home to a small house crowded with noisy children. After months alone, North West River was too busy, with too many people.[15] (Russell had been alone on his trapline for over 20 years and now had to accommodate a woman in his domain, one who wanted him to talk to her!) Max McLean trapped with his father, Murdock, and then alone in the Nascopie River district in the 1940s. He admitted being lonely at times, "but there was bugger all [he] could do about it." His father advised him: "never lie on the bunk and stare at the ceiling. When you get like that get up and do something or go somewhere."[16] They adjusted out of necessity, but even hardened old-timers like John Montague admitted to going out of their way occasionally to seek some company:

> You'd be out all day, then you'd come back, chop your wood, get your water, skin your fur if you had any, bake your bread, and p'r'aps you'd have to sew your shoes. There was always something to keep you busy 'til about 9:30 or 10 in the evening. Probably you wouldn't see nobody for two or three months and you'd be glad if you could see somebody, somebody come along. You might track an Indian or somebody, you know, somebody to talk to.[17]

Gerald White recalled the loneliness when he first went trapping by himself in 1931 at age 15. After months on his own, when he saw Harvey Goudie, another North West River man, "The sound of his voice was almost as good as fiddle music to [him]." Gerald once went on a cruise [hike] to visit Innu he knew were camped near his trapline. As he approached their camp, they saw him coming and lunch and tea was ready: "I wasn't even in the tent door proper and the old lady was haulin' off my mitts and shoes, puttin' patches on them and sewin' up my mitts." His father had Innu friends and Gerald understood enough of their language to know the old lady was "tellin' [him he] was too young to be all that ways from home by [him]self." He said, "It was so good to see people and someone else's smoke coming up." The following summer, a young man from the family came to his house in North West River to make sure he had gotten home safely. Gerald was visited by another Innu boy and girl that summer and he remembered the girl saw his mother's accordion, "picked it up and went right to town" playing "all kinds of French tunes." He said they were "awful nice people," the Innu from Sept-Îles, Quebec, and knowing they were near was a comfort to him as a young man trapping far from home.[18]

Barbara understood trapping was a solitary occupation but she had gone into the country to be alone with Russell, not alone by herself.

Dec 1: Today I think I will write several times as this is a brand new kind of day in my life! R went off this A.M. at five minutes to seven & he's not coming back tonight. He's been gone 2½ hours & it seems ages. I suppose because I know he won't be back 'till tomorrow—it's sort of a queer feeling, that. Last time he was away, Hayward was there, but this time there's no one to talk to. I've tidied up, soaked & rubbed my feet which seem OK now, read a bit & am about to bake. Went for water & it was a mauvy, peach dawn, but 'tis overcast. I hope it doesn't snow before R returns—I want a clear night. He suggested going to house today, but it would have been awful had he had to give up going to tent & anyway my knee is not good yet & it's the 1st day of the curse. By tomorrow I hope my knee will be OK. I certainly am glad it's to be only one night at first—but I guess it'll be the only time. I can't imagine 4 mos. of it—gosh, what a dose. It seemed to me I baked all that day. I wanted to go out, but for some reason found excuses not to. But about three I did—walked down river to "2nd" trap, saw white partridge tracks (drove 2). Even if I hadn't driven them, the gun being on the blink, I probably wouldn't have got them. I was gone about 1½ hrs. & ret'd to find tilt still there! I had just hacked up the porcupine, got water, etc. when I heard an "hello" & there was R. I couldn't believe it! He had got to lake at sunrise, tent at 12:30 & back in 10 hrs! He says he didn't run, but it must have been close to it. It was good to have him back but now it's got to be gone thru' again! and keeping a fire in all night would have been good for me probably! We came back to house on 2nd—a glorious, cold, clear day—at lake at sunrise. (Rising water at rapid made us take to the woods.) Came very slowly & got here at 3—walking more "hooky" than when we went in and deer tracks on ours bet. river & lake! Why don't we see them?

She had avoided spending a night on her own but that would change on December 4. A day without Russell was manageable; she had work enough to keep her busy and distracted, but the cursed stove in the tilt threatened to do her in completely. Every loaf of bread came out burned.

Today R has really gone. I went back to sleep 'till 9:30 then had bath & made jam, tapped a shoe & generally cleaned the house. 'Tis now 12:30 and the stove is smoking <u>everywhere</u>—door, stovepipe, even out of the oven itself, & R only put that back this A.M. I don't know <u>how</u> I'll cope with it. I <u>can't</u> take it off & on every few hours, nor can I be smoked out. While it's mild & decent weather it's not too bad but <u>what</u> will I do when it isn't? I wish R could & would do something to it. 'Tis now a quarter to five & I suppose R is all settled & snoozing—pipe in mouth—at Elizabeth River. It's been a dull ½ snowy day. I think (and hope) all my outdoor jobs are done. I have water, splits, wood, shavings, (+ birch bark) all in house. Partridge is picked (finally had to do it in the house as my fingers got too cold & feathers flew everywhere). Spot—who was looking hopefully up the River for R—is fed. Oven—which I finally <u>had</u> to take off (& rabbit wire broke) is outside door. I'm leaving it as <u>long</u> as possible. Gosh, I hope R can fix it, & tell me <u>how</u> to make bank less slippery for going up & down. Down is worst—heavy buckets help keep me in one spot coming up!! Soon I'll have to light lamp—think I'll go to bed early—or would it make the night <u>too</u> long? 6:30 It's dark, the partridge is frying, I'm hot & have just woken up. I wish I could keep cooler in tilts. It's awful to feel (& look) like a grease pit all the time. Guess I'll have supper, mix, struggle with the oven & to bed. I am so terribly sleepy. 9 P.M. I'm going to sleep. The oven got back on with a struggle with the fire <u>out</u>—heaven help me when it's too cold to do that.

To keep herself company, before she put out the lamp, Barbara started writing a long diary-style letter to her mother. She wanted it ready to take to Fox Island tilt for their planned rendezvous with the other trappers, who would carry it down the river to be mailed. She and Russell would not return to North West River with the group, but would stay in the country until nearly spring, or as long as their food lasted. She had so many things to tell Mother and Harriet. By early December, she had been over all of Russell's paths, seen each and every tilt and tent site, and knew exactly how hard he worked and how far he walked, for every fur he brought home. She was getting used to the daily routine of struggling with a finicky stove, sharing the country with Innu, and using outdoor toilets.

Outdoor plumbing isn't as dreadful to get used to as I imagined if it can be in the form of a "little house" or restricted to one spot (a natural little house of trees as I have here) but at night in rain, snow & wind it is <u>awful</u>. I almost died at NW it was so cold & there we have a fine "little house"—getting there is bad. R says "stay in" but I think that would be almost worse to accustom myself to but I think I'll have to come to it some blizzardy or drenching night. Must get up & give the bread a punch.

I don't think you need to fear I'll be cold in a tilt. So far I have about dissolved into a grease spot. I have woken in the night in the tilts—I on bunk R on floor in draft (but next to stove) just running streams of perspiration and ever since I've been married my face has looked as if it just came out of a grease pot—Horrible! But I can't do anything about it. The heat these stoves give off is Terrific—and they're all so low, even in NW—that you have to bend double over them so you can get the full blast of heat right in the face. R is amused & a bit disdainful of all the "baths" I take. I take them as often as is possible & <u>not only for comfort</u>. I can't stand that clammy perspiry feeling if I can possibly avoid it but I also think about the long backbreaking hours of washing this heavy underwear etc. & the cleaner I can keep my clothes the fewer backaches & aching hands I'll have. (Letter: December 4, 1947)

It was a vivid picture she painted for her mother, who probably read her letters while being served coffee by the maid at Thousand Nine. Going to the "toilet" in a snowbank under the trees, washing river clothes by hand, and bathing in a chipped enamel basin—how much worse could Barbara's life possibly be?

Dec. 5: R is back again and with bad news. Indians have been to tilt & taken some of our food, so now we <u>are</u> going out on the 14th to let the boys know we may run short of food. Think perhaps Walter & Warren may have flour to spare & Wilfred too, might offer some. If they (the Indians) take more R is going after them, but they've been clever—staying clear of us and we never see a fresh enuf track to know where to look for them. Even slept in tilt & messed it up. Hope freezing kills lice, etc. I shudder at the thot of returning here some day & perhaps finding they've used our sleeping bags! R is now going to bury some of our food for we're afraid they may just clean us out one day. And they seem to keep track of us and carefully miss meeting us. They've been on his paths, taken beaver from his *ground and now they're stealing our food—And they're the darn Canadian Indians which are flown in here. Some say the HBCo flies them in—also there is trader named Ross who does. And Labrador men are allowed only 8 beaver a year.* (Letter: December 4, 1947)

Newfoundland authorities had set a limit of eight on the number of beaver pelts a Labrador trapper could sell per year. Like the Innu, trappers resented any restrictions on their hunting, although Horace Goudie recalled the beaver populations fell due to over-trapping and eventually "vanished completely."[19] More than a few trappers found a way around the rule by trading beaver pelts with the border-crossing Innu, who had no such limit in Canada. Mathieu Mestokosho remembered buying pelts from North West River trappers, paying 50 cents for a small one and $2 for a beautiful large one: "I got thirty dollars a beaver pelt in Mingan, and as much as sixty for the nicest ones. Beaver that I didn't even kill myself and that I'd paid two dollars for!"[20] The money made from those few beaver pelts was an unusual windfall for the Innu hunter.

Dec. 7: Cut R's hair—not bad at all & think with practice I can do a good job on him. R cut wood, fixed path & read.

Mon. Dec. 8: R went to beaver house & I did the usual—wash, bake, mend, etc. Tomorrow we go down for possibly a week + at Fox Island.

Arranged meetings with other trappers were always kept—if someone didn't show up, others would likely go in search of the absent one—they would never leave the river without checking to make sure all was well. Before leaving for Fox Island, Barbara and Russell buried what food they could, hid their berries in the woodpile, and laid fresh boughs on the floor of the tilt used by the uninvited guest. Barbara commented that at least he "had been decent enough to throw his tea leaves <u>outside</u>." Arriving at Lower Tilt, they found it had also been raided. Their nuisance neighbours were closer and Russell's fears about losing more food were realized. This time the raider left a token payment.

Dec. 10: He, however, took <u>all</u> our flour, most of tea, pork, etc. Left a black, shot-up no good beaver skin. That makes over a bag of flour, to say nothing of other food gone. And he has a dog (able perhaps to unbury our things). We had counted on this flour & our choice is return to house or go out a day early & use our Fox Is. flour & wait for Wilfred. Certainly

hope he'll let us have some. A peachy dawn & sunset—but overcast &
warm all day. It is <u>wonderful</u> to be out all day again; & every dawn I see—
which I love—I think of all the things R & I have seen together—but most
especially the one when we ret'd from Mud Lake. It was beautiful & I was
so comfy with my head on his knee.

Dec. 11: R went around lake but I stayed behind because of knee—
came home with a fine big beaver (which the rest of the family had buried
in mud!) I went across lake for porcupine we got last time, poked at a
couple of traps on this side & seeing no sign of R came back to have tilt
warm & ready for him as it was blowing & snowing a bit. I had intended
to go meet him but didn't. Have just reckoned food & have to move on
tomorrow as the Indians left us <u>one small</u> mixing.

Fri. Dec. 12: We moved on to find our scaffold rifled—beans, 2 candles,
some dog food left & tarp just thrown across! So we had <u>nothing</u>. Came up
winter portage to 2nd lake, then cut down across to 3rd Pond trying to find
Indians. Came out fall portage from there—much sign & when we got to
lake fresh tracks to scaffold and along shore. We looked down from top of
hill & to our surprise lake & river were fast—lake all bumpy looking with
rough ice. We saw Wilfred coming down & met him at foot of hill. He told
us Indians were camped on Pt. & who had taken our stuff.

Crossing each other's trails for weeks, fearing the loss of their
food—finally it had happened and something had to be done about it.
Barbara put the details of the confrontation in the long letter she was
writing to her mother. She must have thought about the anxiety the
story would cause Mrs. Mundy, her defenseless daughter in the wilds
being tormented by Indians, but it cast Russell in such a good light. Any
woman reading the letter would understand Barbara's pride and utter
confidence in her husband.

We had to either go back to house today or come out here as we had
no food. My knee was bad again, & R felt it had been so mild we might
not get across to meet W. But we chanced it & by gosh our scaffold—food
for going down—was cleaned—<u>everything</u> gone. We were fit to be tied.
As we got to River we met W & discovered the Indians were camped right
here & he told us one Philip Nona had told him he'd taken "a little" flour
from us. Well, 2 bags (a mos. food)—to say nothing of pork, tea, tobacco,

candles, butter, etc. etc. We hardly considered "a little"! We went straight to the tents & were there before they knew we were handy. R went up bank & a girl sung out "white man come"—R made straight for Philip & lit into him. We both were pretty mad—out came a tiny bit of our flour in a <u>hurry</u>. Philip's ma-in-law (who I think was scared to death) produced deersmeat. More coming tomorrow & they say our flour will be ret'd Xmas Day as they return from Matthew Anthony [Canadian fur trader]. They again say it is the HBCo who supplies them & I think we put the fear of the Lord in them—the "boss" came out & said it would be ret'd then he asked us into his "house" and we were served up a swell meal of deersmeat & tea—better kitchen ware, china than we have—a blanket is put down for me to sit on & even a table cloth spread out on brush. Wilfred tells us the "boss" says Philip is a "bad man." I say if they're out of food and don't bring enough why don't they go home—why should they force us who came prepared to have to go? Lucky we came out today as they are moving on Mon. (Letter: December 12, 1947)

Through all the anxious weeks spent watching for them, Barbara probably hadn't pictured herself sitting on a blanket in a tent, having a "swell meal" with an Innu family. Meeting them and spending time with other women for the first time in nearly three months was a welcome interlude, even under the testy circumstances. After sharing their caribou and tea, her comments about the family, living the way their people had for hundreds of generations, were somewhat moderated, though she still believed they were encroaching on Russell's ground.

We're staying here [Fox Island] tomorrow if we have enough food to take us all the way back to the house—or if W will give us some. The letter I left here in Oct. is still here—and so alas is our big canoe which we hoped would be run down [the river] a bit. Wilfred isn't coming across—he's done some canny bargaining with Indians & he has no extra food. We hope Warren & Walter may not come back so we're staying today to see them & ask. I don't know <u>when</u> we're leaving. We plan to stay as long as we possibly can. If the Indians do return what they took and the other crowds leave us alone (the place is lousy with Indians) & W & W can give us their extra we may be able to hang on into March. If not, we may be out far sooner. It just depends on food. There is no fur so R wants to stay as long as possible to *get what he can. We have our food here & we live far better than we could at NW, for we do get meat which we wouldn't have there. So it is better in every way to stay. Wilfred is doing no better than R and I feel much better about it, but R doesn't—he said he was "ashamed" to come out he'd had such a poor hunt. I told him I was sure it would be the same with the others and thought we'll hear from below & know. It's just a rotten year in every way—no bait, little meat, no fur!* (Letter: December 12, 1947)

Writing bits and pieces over several days, the letter Barbara had started on December 4 was finally completed on December 13 at the Fox Island tilt, while the three men smoked and talked in the background. This letter, and the recital of complaints she had written in October, would be carried out and mailed together, probably reaching New York by mid-January. They would be the last ones her mother ever received from Barbara. Mrs. Mundy had suffered a disabling stroke in early September, on the same day Barbara and Russell had flown from St. John's to Goose Bay, two weeks before they left to go upriver. Her sister, Harriet, and brother, Floyd, made the decision not to tell her, knowing she would probably cancel her plan to spend the winter in the country with Russell, and go immediately to her mother's bedside in New York. Perhaps they thought their mother would recover by spring; she was receiving the best care available. As Christmas approached, Barbara had no way of knowing her mother was critically ill and not expected to live much longer.

Chapter Fifteen

I WISH THIS WINTER WOULD NEVER END

I never saw a Christmas tree from the age of 12 years old 'til I was 30-something. Never went home and even today it don't affect me much, for that reason, I guess. I'm always glad when it's all finished. I can't get with it at all, Christmas.

—Horace Goudie,
"Lobstick Lake Was My Trapping Place"

Trappers at the Height of Land were never home for Christmas. They were too far away, had worked too hard to get there, and wanted to spend as much time as they could on the fur paths before heading back. They usually got home sometime in mid to late January, after a long return trip with a new set of obstacles and dangers. Loads of fur and maybe also canoes would be hauled on komatiks over raggedy sharp ice while the men looked for open holes or soft spots in the surface and listened for the sound of ice dams breaking in the tributaries or on the river. Temporary ice reservoirs were created as rafted ice was pushed downstream, piling up until the pressure of water smashed the dam. Squirrel River (on maps as Cache River) was notorious for exploding three times a winter, according to Elliott Merrick, blasting a wall of ice into Grand River. Dan Campbell, one of the trappers going home with Merrick in 1931, warned, "we always runs across here." On both banks of the Squirrel River, and on the other side of the Grand River among the trees, Merrick saw "huge blocks of blue ice eight feet thick, tossed there by some terrifying force."[1] There was no end to the cautionary tales. Ike Rich trapped up Grand River for years and told about the time he and three other men were making their way down through Horseshoe Rapids, over good ice with snow on it, when "suddenly there start to be a rumbling and noise of ice cracking and banging." The older trapper he was with commanded him to jump to shore. They just made it, getting their sleds up over a bank, "and the river was just the clear water from one beach to the other." The deluge of backed up water had completely swept away the ice they were walking on minutes before.[2]

It was safer to go as a group, but Russell and Barbara would make the trip down by themselves in spring, while there was still some good ice on the river. The pre-Christmas gathering would be their last visit with fellow trappers for months and everyone was comparing notes on their luck with fur.

Dec. 13: We are staying here to hear what news we can. Only Warren came as they've not had much to eat & Walter is hunting. They've not done well either & they are going home on Friday. Had a letter from Doris, that was all. The [Innu] "boss" came over with Wilfred & we had both deermeat & bearsmeat—very good. Boys below lake seem to be doing better than them. I feel much better about things & wish R would not be so discouraged.

After a short visit at Fox Island, it was time to head back to Fig River. Barbara estimated the distance from the meeting place to "our own ground" was 12 to 14 miles and figured it would take about seven hours to get home. It had become normal to walk long distances in snowshoes, just as it was to visit and barter with Innu. She was quite comfortable with the people she had been so apprehensive about only weeks before—now she knew them as neighbours. On Sunday, December 14, they went back to their lower tilt, with some bear meat from Wilfred, stopping at the Indian tents for a little trading and visiting. Barbara wrote that the "boss," Joseph, had commented that her snowshoes were in poor shape so his wife gave her some babish & tapish for mending. They were also given "some deersmeat to pay for butter." Time was spent admiring Philip's 10-day-old baby; "the mother was lovely looking and gave me a can of Klim!" The Indians planned to drop by on Christmas Sunday.

Days of heavy snow drifted up by wind kept Russell at the main house, so they dug paths and Russell cleaned his beaver skins. Having a few days at home, with regular meals of meat, must have done them good. Barbara wrote, "Everything's been grand recently." Finally on December 20, the weather calmed enough for them to get back on the path. They checked a beaver house and got one, bringing Russell's total to the limit of eight.

Stashed safely away on the scaffold at their main house, Barbara had special things for Christmas, the fruitcake she had made and presents from her family. In her experience, the holiday season was much anticipated, fully observed, and celebrated. She knew it wasn't like that for Russell, who probably hadn't had a proper family Christmas since he was 15. She wanted their first one to be memorable, but it was looking like they might not even be together.

Mon. Dec. 22: 4:45 P.M. Have just come in & lighted the lamp. Am again a widow. R was to go into So. path this A.M.—not returning 'till Christmas night and if bad weather maybe not then. 'Twas a very dismal outlook—it's been so unlike anything Christmasy & then to think of not even having a soul to say Merry Christmas to was indeed queer. I had so counted on this Xmas with R—perhaps the only one I'd ever have with him, but last week's weather balled things up. I tried not to show it but that & being all alone for the best part of a week wasn't cheering. Guess R saw how I felt for at the last minute he changed, took Spot & went down the lake. I do hope he gets something. Now he will be back Christmas Eve & I must try to have everything done so I can go & meet him. From now on I guess he'll only be home a night between rounds so I won't see much of him. Thank God I'll have him for Xmas even if not for New Yrs. Neither day seems to mean anything to him & they've always meant so much to us; more than any other days anyway. I've done a lot today. Finished lengthening sleeves on jacket, cut out R's presents, baked, made jam, washed something, knitted, shovelled, thoroughly cleaned or tidied up house, picked partridge & now wood, water, etc. are in & I'm soon going to have supper & then work at R's presents. Glad the moon will try to shine—don't like going out [to latrine] on dark nights—not so bad here but little house at home is in trees & it can be dark there. Wonder what

R is doing now. Lying back having a smoke, I guess & perhaps wondering what I am doing.

Tuesday Dec. 23: 10 P.M. Just finished a bath, will write R a wee Xmas letter & then to sleep. It's been another busy day. Making & wrapping R's presents, getting brush, cones etc. and must up betimes to make wreaths, etc. & be able to go meet R. Baked again so wouldn't have to when R is here … As I walked thru' the woods today I could hardly believe that I was here—it's so peaceful, quiet & unbelievably beautiful. Trees just laden with snow & no one (not even R!) near. So far I've not minded being alone except I miss R … I think I am more content & happier than I've ever been in my life or ever will be again. I wish this winter here would never, never end.

Christmas Eve: Finally got up and had all daily chores plus laundry, plus baking done by daylight! Even washed windows! Have made wreath, cones at windows and it looks a bit like Christmas. R may think I'm a silly fool, but I'm sure I don't care this time for I've had lots of fun. He, poor dear, has never known the fun of getting ready for Christmas and this must be the first Christmas he's had with anyone since he was a little boy. I want it to be a nice one—perhaps he'd still prefer it alone & just have it an ordinary day. Must finish dessert, do over some laundry the jays messed up, get meat in, rebrush house & then I'm off—won't bother to eat. I'll mug up with R when he comes. Went down & met R just below rapid—a most heavenly day. Met Indians who are camped where we saw otter. Joseph's wife gave R some deersmeat for his wife! They (Indians) expect to come up Sunday. Good to have R back. He opened harmonica Christmas Eve & I think he likes it. Good.

Christmas Day 1947. It started at 12:30 when R woke & we opened presents and sampled cake. Knives from Ma—good ones R says, particularly mine. R gave me a new pair of snowshoes. About six we had breakfast of deersmeat & a bit of hoarded bacon and good butter. Back to bed again 'till about 9:30—delightfully lazy but I've been feeling horrible. Headache, knees that "swim" and generally lousy. Another mug-up then— every time we eat anything we end up with cake! R is now sawing wood & I'm getting dinner ready—'twill be bearsmeat & deersmeat, peas-pudding, red berries & cake & coffee. Really going to town today! We did alright!

Dinner at 4 & just barely recovering now at 6:30! We were <u>full</u>. Beautiful cold, moonlight night, trees lovely in it. Wish I could get a picture of our little home with lamp, icicles, cones, etc. I love it.

Barbara would have given a thought to her family that day, celebrating at Thousand Nine, enjoying eggnog in the living room while logs crackled in the fireplace, a perfectly decorated tree sheltering piles of beautifully wrapped gifts arranged underneath. The cook would have a fat turkey roasting, all their favourite side dishes in preparation, and pies and cake ready in the pantry. The ritual of gift-opening over, everyone would be dressed in their best for a formal dinner in the dining room, the table glittering with silver, crystal, and porcelain. Barbara didn't miss one thing about Christmas in New York. Russell was outside sawing wood, her fussy stove was smoking and hissing. Their cozy tilt at Fig River, candlelight shining from its one window, spruce bough wreath on the wee door, looked like a pretty gift box, tucked under snow-covered trees. Even though feeling "horrible," she loved her day of lazing, eating, and then eating more. The cake she had baked in September was a great success—the bacon and butter she saved for the day were a wonderful treat. Their first Christmas together had been perfect.

Dec. 28: On Friday the 26th, R was off again to the North Path. I had more or less of a lazy day—a bit of wash, wrote letter & read. Spot demanded new brush and at 5 I was "in," reading by lamplight as it was getting dark. Then I heard an "hello" didn't sound quite like R, but I thot it must be—bad going and he was back. Again I heard it & got up to see Philip (of all people) at the door! He had brought a bag of flour plus a <u>few</u> other things. So in he came and I produced tea & on & on he stayed. It was obvious he wished to "seeum Russell Groves" so I forthwith had a night alone with an Indian! We talked and stared at each other until about 8 when we gave up & went to bed. I was almost sorry I'd chinked a few holes that day & <u>did not</u> suggest the wrapper for the door! He kept a fire in but was cold. At five we arose & again chatted in Indian-French-English! until about 10 when he thot he'd go hunting which I thot an excellent idea! He was gone 'till 2 when he ret'd. I never knew a longer 24 hrs! Nor did he, as he told R he found the time long! R <u>finally</u> turned up about 4 and by 6 Philip was off for home by glorious moonlight. A very deliberate &

slow man in every way—polite, took his cap off for meals, & in spite of distinct Indian smell he wasn't too dirty. Didn't relish the idea of being alone with him, but R says he'd trust an Indian more than a white man & if all are like Philip I'd agree. He wanted to know "how many moons" we are staying. And the mouse appeared that night too! So I was not alone. R thot from P's track he'd been here for the night & I think he was amused & wondering how I was taking it! What next, I wonder? Today is Sunday, frost is falling and we've had our "5 o'clock," then another snooze & deersmeat at 9. Partridges on for dinner. I think our food will last 'till April—we'll see.

On New Year's Day 1948, Barbara began another long, chatty letter to her mother. She kept adding pages, planning to leave it at Fox Island tilt, hoping Wilfred Baikie would bring it downriver and mail it for her. It would be good to think her mother read this letter, written by a much happier woman, comfortable in her surroundings and coping, even with unexpected overnight guests. The joyful description of the Christmas scene at the Fig River tilt, decorated with spruce wreaths and cones, their pleasure in a few gifts and appreciation of some specially saved foods, would be a reassuring tonic for worried family members.

All would be well, if only there was more fur—Russell wasn't happy with the amount he had. Every trapper wanted to go home with a good haul but he had another reason for making an extra effort. Since he began keeping company with Barbara—canoeing, boiling up, and hunting for ducks—he was well aware of the chatter their activities had caused in North West River. Now married to an "outsider," a woman generally believed to be rich, he was determined to provide no ammunition for sly comments that he was slacking off and leaning on his newly acquired trust-fund wife. The only way to get more fur was to keep to the routine of travelling the paths, checking and resetting the traps. That meant he'd be gone many nights, sleeping in one of his little tilts, miles from the main house, and Barbara would be alone, unless she walked the path with him, during the coldest time of the year.

Jan. 7: We are at Lower Tilt again—came down today & set a record! Not even a jay or squirrel or mouse in trap and nothing for supper either— 'tis terribly discouraging. Only occurrence of day was when I fell into hole of water (covered with snow) just below Fanny's Is. On Mon. R went to his beaver house in the woods & came home with a middle-sized one; has 2 large from there & says if he gets the other middle one he'll let the young ones go (for another year he hopes). Yesterday we both went looking for a new house & the one in burnt woods is empty now (R says) between him & Indians. Went up river that comes into Fig River at burnt woods & found one in first. Calm spot—knew it was occupied by breathing hole thawed thru' top. Saw a marten deadfall & empty (worse luck) bear's cave. Hair still on sticks nearby where bears had rubbed selves. 'Twas a very leisurely pleasant day.

Although Russell had "his" eight beaver by December 20, he continued to check the beaver houses and kept his traps baited. Beaver was good meat and if the furs were better or bigger than any of the eight, he could substitute the best ones in order to get a higher price. Barbara didn't mention it in her diary, but he may also have traded with the Innu, as other trappers did, or perhaps he planned to keep the extra furs until the next year when he was allowed to sell them. Great care was taken with all the furs. The slightest nick or cut in the skin would reduce their value.

There's still no fur—R has really nothing and says he's ashamed to go home—but how can he catch it if it isn't here to catch? He has his beaver, 4 minks, about 20 weasel (which he doesn't count) & one otter. We've seen 1 fox track since we arrived & several cat tracks but he says he thinks the latter are old residents & know the traps by now. He's done wonderfully with beaver but poor luck with otter and there are some of them around here, altho' the other men said they'd seen no sign where they are. He has a good dark cross (almost a silver) and several red foxes he didn't sell last spring which he can sell this year—but there's not going to be much money in the bank. (Letter: January 1-February 6, 1948)

On January 12, Russell went by himself to the north path and, the next day, he came home with a mink and the liver, leg, and skin of a caribou. He had seen fresh sign, so tracked and killed an old stag. Two days later, he and Barbara went back to retrieve the rest of the meat, which turned out to be "very tough" but it was a good hide. Barbara may have felt she had written too much in her letters home about difficulties, poor food, cold, and hardship. In the diary-letter she started on January 1, she noted the days were noticeably longer and time was going "so terribly quickly."

I keep forgetting to put in here that when I first walked in here & saw a new ax mark on the wall by the bunk & there R has written the poem I sent him a year ago—I sent it because it was what I'd felt about some of the heavenly Sunday nights we'd had together. I hope we'll often go again & lie out under the stars & northern lights with a nice fire to keep us warm & cozy. "Like an opal was the moon that night; a soft, white glowing jewel safe-guarded by the stars; the glory of the sky's great miracle sank soothingly upon the souls of men and for just a little while forgotten was the war." It made me feel all nice inside to think he'd put it there and it still does every time I see it!

… We are now the only people up here as all other trappers have gone home. The Indians, of course, are somewhere but they've moved in towards the mts., so we feel we're quite alone. I don't mind a bit & for some reason the fact the nearest people are 250 miles away doesn't bother me at all! (Letter: January 1-February 6, 1948)

Memories of the blisters from her new snowshoes and a well-justified fear of frostbite kept her close to home for a few days. On January 16 she started out to meet Russell but "hardly got 5 steps." The next day was windy—Barbara figured it was minus 40°—although Russell told her "he's never seen such mild, calm weather & so little snow for this time of year." They took a few days off from their routine to walk to a lake he had named for her. Russell had a couple of traps there for his wife and daughter.

Sat. Jan. 24: Wed. & Thurs. we had more good sleeps—cold & blowing and traps in order so R took his week off! The first time since we've been married that we haven't had to run someplace or other—it's been lovely. Friday was a clear, cold day—blowing and drifting after we started off for Barbara's Lake. Froze my face a bit going up lake & did I <u>ache</u> on return; legs barely functioning. I'll have to get over that & get hide on my toes or I'll be crawling home on all fours! To bed at nine but slept from 5 to 7 and never would have thot of supper if R hadn't gotten it.

Tues. Jan. 27: This has been a <u>wonderful</u> day, bright & almost spring-

like. As the days are longer, we were able to start after sunrise, take our time & get back early—before sunset. No fur. Lake all drifted in swirls, ridges, & patterns & second brook smooth with snow. Snowshoes in woods left deep, well-defined marks. Days like this are what I used to remember & connected with Labrador. It's been lovely today.

Wed. Jan. 28: Tonight we are again in the tent (now in a hole of snow—R says sometimes it is over the ridgepole). I just love this part of the path and wish I could adequately describe it so I'd never forget it. It is all thru' woods, up brooks, (some open in spots with paper thin ice edges flecked with snowy feathers) and across lakes. The trees are white with snow and drifts on them & rocks make all sorts of humps and figures, sometimes the snow seems to go around in layers almost like trimmed box hedges. The rocky spot in the woods was particularly lovely. Fresh otter tracks and twice they just went into the snow making little tunnels. While R was fixing up the tent I made an architectural masterpiece too. As no little house [latrine] had been made here before & no naturally sheltered spot was available I had to put up windbreaks and even a floor as this one must be reached by snowshoes. I think I could give Chick Sales [1920s comic actor who had outhouses named after him] a few pointers now!

… Was amused at R, who would happily go unwashed & uncombed for <u>days</u>, when he looked at me, announced my hair was a sight, would I please wash my face & comb my hair!!

Barbara's description of cold in the continuing letter to her mother and sister would have brought a chill to a centrally heated Manhattan apartment. She added some information about her daily activities, typical accommodations, and toilet habits, knowing her details about trapline johnny paper and trips outside to do her business would cause horrified shrieks of laughter back home.

I made a mistake in the size of our house—'tis only 7'10" by 8'4"!!! and seems most huge after a stay in one of the wee tilts! We were laughing about how simply we live but how <u>adequately</u>—a spoon, knife, fork, cup & plate each, frying pan, small kettle & boiler—that's all! In our house we combine bedroom, bath (except for john which despite the cold we <u>still</u> have outdoors), living room, kitchen, (even guest room?), storage room. We hang frozen clothes up to thaw, we dry meat by the stove—what fur

there is (almost nil) is cleaned & dried there, etc. etc. etc. and once we got
settled & everything in its place it isn't bad at all—at first tho' everything
seemed to be in everything else's way!

R had a piece of his sleeping bag which he cut off hanging in a tree &
the uses that has been put to! The outside part became patches on knees &
seat of trousers, the wooly inside lining for mitt cuffs & the combination
of the two lengthened my dickie sleeve. The wooly inter-lining is now R's
johnny paper! Last night I dreamt I flew to NY on a visit from here—&
Gerda was ironing all the things that sit at home waiting to be ironed and
when you asked me what I'd like for a present I said—2 rolls of johnny
paper & 2 cakes of soap! We are getting <u>very</u> low on both—the j.p. & my
Kleenex will definitely not last and so far I can think of nothing to take its
place except the gauzy stuff that held the interlining of R's sleeping bag in
place & an old pair of his underpants. 'Tis most distressing. I try not to
think about it! For H's edification (and 'twill shock you no end) tell H that
I've never been in the predicament of her doggie but I've had plenty of little
icicles which tickle like hell! (Letter: January 1-February 6, 1948)

They were back at the main tilt by January 31 and Russell started
building a catamaran sled for hauling their two canoes down river.
Trappers usually made their own canoes and the men going all the way
to the Height of Land, past a nearly vertical, overgrown portage around
Bowdoin Canyon and Grand Falls, made them "as light as they could,
just enough to last a year." Many canoes were not brought back. John
Blake said it was too far to haul a canoe from the Height of Land to
North West River or Mud Lake so the trappers would scaffold them, or
try to reuse the canvas, maybe as a tilt cover. Three Square Island, just
below the Big Hill portage on Grand River, was a popular place used
by Height of Land trappers to scaffold canoes. The island location was
chosen because it was "clear of bears"—bears were notorious for tearing
canvas off canoes and ripping up tilts.[3]

Russell's canoes were heavier and not meant to be disposable. His
trapping grounds stopped short of the Height of Land and he intended
to return both canoes to North West River and use them again next year.
The big one was on a scaffold at Wilfred Baikie's tilt, while they used the
small one to transport their supplies to the trapline and to travel the

lakes and rivers near their paths before full freeze-up. He wanted to get the small one back to Wilfred's and from there, if possible, both to the lower end of Lake Winokapau. He would scaffold them until the final run downriver in late March. First, they would have to beat their way into the bush and find the small canoe, "abandoned" near their lower tilt on November 21, and haul it to the new catamaran. They had several hard days ahead of them, but first, a relaxing Sunday.

Sun. Feb. 1: We lazed all day—the beautiful weather continues and if it holds we are off to Lake Winnie with canoe on Tues. Coming back from So. Path we saw a perfect "angel" snow pattern where a partridge had taken off & spread his wings. Birds most common here are: white (& pink) spruce partridges—Canada jays (whisky jacks), red polls (willow lennards) and northern chickadees (tom tits). Latter & jays are fearless & brazen and at times all frosty about bills & eyes. And my R is wonderful looking when he gets frosty—his eyelashes & brows all white with it. I love to see them that way and then add his shawl & he is something!

Getting the small canoe and new catamaran to Fig River portage was a bitter battle, through deep, drifting snow and tangled woods, the path fully buried. When they set out on February 3, Barbara felt more clothes were needed, "for the 1st time I wore my extra jacket & shawl and felt the wind behind thru' all, even my overhauls." Russell said it would have been too rough to face, wind that would "shove you almost off your feet at times." On Wednesday, they were still beating the snow into a trail, Barbara pushing the canoe from the rear. They managed to get as far as the second pond on their fall portage but had to give up, leaving the canoe there while they sought refuge at the Fox Island tilt. Russell went back to retrieve the canoe by himself on Friday; Barbara's job was to "do some clearing" of the trail. At least the last day was "glorious" with no wind. Barbara wrote that Russell had once done the same journey in three hours, by himself with just a gamebag on his shoulder.

With both canoes under control, they started down Lake Winokapau, using a track left by trappers who had gone in late December, the wind helping them along: "R put small canoe across big one & sailed down—had to even run in spots." Barbara got a patch of frostbite on her face but there were plenty of trappers' tilts to shelter in. She was quite disapproving of the state of the cabins.

Sat. Feb. 7: Walter's left like a pig sty but between us we got it fit to sleep in. Ancient newspapers cracking on leaky walls make it look worse than ever! They have a fine new window tho'. Thank God R isn't filthy as the majority of the others seem to be. I couldn't stand him if he were. Animals are cleaner in their habits than some of these men seem to be! In fairness tho' their pots & pans were clean. We found the cache clearly marked as WM said he'd mark it—got coffee, soap, matches & some flour (but squirrels had been at it). Lake cracked like thunder sometimes—could hear it rumble on for ages. Ma's handsome skating pants have walked the length of lake now—a bit rotten with age but going strong & amuse R!

This was one Sunday they could not rest. There would be no resting until they got the canoes stowed, and returned to their own tilt. Still towing the catamaran 16 or 17 miles a day, they had "excellent going—came all the way down lake without snowshoes." They made it to Gordon Goudie's tilt not far from Long Point. Ice-covered rocks looked like waterfalls, vapour from a brook appeared to be smoke. Spruce needles changed colour as they thawed in the rising heat of a campfire. Barbara must have been nearly frozen and hungry for a proper meal, but she was always impressed by how the country around the river had been so altered by the winter weather. On Monday, the wind blew a gale so she stayed back at the tilt while Russell wrangled the canoes as best he could. He told her he "had to run to keep up with them & rode [on the catamaran] sometimes." He arrived back at the tilt with a spot of frostbite on his forehead. Tuesday was another frigid day at the lower end of Winokapau, too cold to start for home, but not too cold for hunting: "R has gone off to see if he can find something to eat as we're out of meat. Hope he succeeds. He didn't! So we fried out our last bit of pork & it was our supper."

At last the wind relented and they could start their way back, progress marked by the tilts they stopped in or passed.

Wed. Feb. 11: The wind gave up for a bit and it was much milder, so we started early for Jimmie's. We boiled just above Gordon's upper trap & again at Walter's where we picked up what we'd left and went on. It was a good long walk and from Walter's on the wind was blowing again and it was hard sometimes to walk against it. Had several shots at an owl that kept flying ahead of us and was perching on the highest trees, much too far a shot. His ear tufts stood out wonderfully. He finally tired of the game and flew in over the hills. It was a good 25 or more miles the way we went along the shore.

Thurs. Feb. 12: Was another mild day and overcast a bit—and another longish walk for we merely boiled at Wilfred's and went on into the tilt. Cats had crossed & followed our track in several places. Most of the spots where the water had "quarred" over the bank (quarred ice is the ice where the tide or wave has come in and formed ice and then gone back out and left the ice) was brownish, but there was one perfectly lovely place above Jimmie's where it was blue-green flecked with orange & white.

It was the day her mother died, February 12, although Barbara had no way of knowing it, when she scratched off a quick letter to leave at Wilfred Baikie's tilt for him or another departing trapper to take downriver. She decided to keep the long letter, the one that had taken her a month to write, with humorous stories of her daily routine, thinking she and Russell would mail it when they got to Goose Bay. She was afraid the letter, if carried out by other trappers, would be "hung up" in North West River, taking even longer to get to New York. In the shorter note, she told her family briefly about getting the canoes to the eastern end of Lake Winokpau and that she'd be glad to be back to "our river for several reasons. We like it best & we want some meat. We've had three days now of bread & tea—also our houses are cleaner!"

Fri. Feb. 13: I stayed home [lower tilt] while R went around the lake—cold again & all he got was one owl who apparently killed himself as he was found head down among the willows!

They got to their main house on February 14—a whole two weeks had been spent transporting canoes. She described the walking on that last day as "juggling to the innards—on & off snowbanks (hard) into crust (soft) never knowing what the next step would produce." Early Sunday morning a proper blizzard blew up. Russell told her he had never seen it rougher. She was glad to be home and it wasn't so bad to be snowed in. "Recently we've had lots of fun reading murder stories aloud.

I never really liked reading aloud before but I do now and R, who says he never liked it, is doing some and it's wonderful! I hope we'll always like to." There were plenty of chores to keep her busy indoors: "washing, mending, darning & patching. I think R must now be the most patched man in Lab!"

Russell went to the north path on February 18. The next day she and Spot headed out to meet him at the tilt, noticing the gale of wind had blown the river bare to the ice in places. She arrived just as Russell did and was pleased to see he had left birch bark and splits for her in case she got to the cabin ahead of him. He got a lynx from one trap and later that evening, they were sorry he had brought it into the tilt.

Thurs. Feb. 19: R had a cat at Elizabeth River and it's been in the house in a bag for only a few hours & I already have had one flea! and he jumped away from R and will probably be back. Horrors! When R had one on him the cat soon got thrown out! During dinner & the evening we picked them off each other but by nite we seemed to be free of them.

They planned to leave for North West River about March 20, depending on food and weather, which "has been so heavenly lately." According to Barbara's diary entries, life generally was going pretty well and she was beginning to realize the winter was coming to an end.

Sat. Feb. 21: Again a glorious day—how does it do it? We've had almost continuously beautiful (but cold) weather since the only real batch of snow we've had all winter (in middle December). We went into beaver house in woods—nothing, so R struck up. It's hard to believe that it's almost five mos. since we left N.W. and only a month more at most to be here. I hate to think of it being all over, especially now that the days are longer & lovely and I am so much more used to it all. I think I could be quite happy just staying on & on! But perhaps I'll not say farewell but only au revoir & then I must make the most of every second of it. I've been very happy here.

They began preparations for leaving, although departure day was a month away. Russell was "striking up" some of his traps as they made their last visit to the paths, checking each one, leaving them shut and clear of old bait. Trap houses, the shelters concealing traps for mink, marten, weasel (ermine), and lynx, might be found buried in snow, traps sometimes frozen in place. When the traps were first set, effort was made to put them under large bushes or overhanging tree branches to keep them from snowing over. Squirrel and muskrat furs weren't valuable, but their carcasses were good for bait or to feed the dog. Beaver traps were placed on sticks underwater, near the entry to the beaver house. They would be taken up and hung in a nearby tree until needed the next year. Fox traps were positioned where the animal might run, up a rise in the ground. Barbara scarcely mentioned foxes that year. Russell counted none amongst his haul of fur. The beautiful silver fox he had given her two years earlier was a trophy animal. John Michelin used to say that good silvers were worth $1,000 when he started trapping. The first one he ever sold fetched $550.[4]

Barbara walked the south path with Russell one last time. On February 24 she wrote it was "a magnificent day but no fur" and traps were badly snowed up. The next day they were at their tent, now "too far down in a hole," so Russell moved it to a new location, unacceptable to Spot, who "is in the former place & doesn't seem to care for it." They got a mink but most traps were "drifted up badly."

Russell had another chore in those last weeks at Fig River. He started building a bigger, more comfortable tilt for next winter.

R started to put walls of tilt up and today (Fri. 27th) he has finished that & sawed out door (I did a bit of that). It's bitterly cold, too cold to go downriver to traps. So I have baked & knitted most of day. Went into 1st brook in aft. but found nothing.

Sat. Feb. 28: 'Tis six months today, a whole half year! While R finished cutting the "rifters" for the new tilt (which is to be spacious! present one 6'4" x 6'4" x about 4'—when standing or rather bending to put on pants one's fanny almost lifts the roof—new one several inches larger & we'll be able to stand up with room to spare) I went down river to traps & for an anniversary present I found a mink & a weasel for R. The poor little mink was still alive. I could hardly look at him let alone kill him & the weasel was frozen so R had to go down, but at least he didn't have a trip in vain.

Sunday we loafed & ate too much.

Mon. Mar. 1: I washed & R worked on his sled. Still cold & beautiful, the sun now comes in our window about 10 A.M. Had R's birthday dinner: bones with duff & pudding—our last; also last onions & red berries.

Tues. Mar. 2: R's 37th b-d. The bacon I saved <u>was</u> a surprise. Having no present for him I knitted him 2 pr. mitts out of <u>his</u> wool! We came down to Lower Tilt.

Wed. Mar. 3: We both went around lake—nothing! Most brooks are frozen to bottom & R had to go out to 3rd net picket for water (says I've drained lake by using so much!). So little snow has made thick ice everywhere. R says he has never known it possible before to walk about without snowshoes at this time of year. I'm getting a good tan—R says he's almost ashamed to take me out among the "white people"—that I'm as black as Penami! He has no dark glasses & made a pr. out of match boxes. Some sight! Tomorrow we are going to Fox Is. & back in search of mail & we hope a dog & a cake! Who knows!

They hoped Wilfred Baikie, who had come up river for a second trip, had brought an extra dog to help them home. They hadn't seen another soul in weeks, so were probably sorry to find that Wilfred had come and gone, leaving no dog, but there was a cake. There was some mail and Barbara was somewhat puzzled that there were no letters from her mother or Harriet, but Russell got "a cat going up hill so it was worth the walk."

Fri. Mar.5: We started off for home [main house on Fig River] but, for the 1st time this winter, we had to turn back. Hadn't been gone 10 mins. when R turned & looked at me & my right cheek was frozen—quite a big place extending down to my chin along the edge of my shawl. So we went back & stayed in tilt. 'Twas a <u>bitterly</u> cold day—R said <u>he</u> probably could have faced it had he run a good part of the way.

Sat. was overcast & milder & we got home—a day very similar to the one we had last time we ret'd from Fox Is. 3 wks. before. Blind walking! looking at ground everything seemed to dance & it was impossible to tell where snow banks etc. were. In our absence a large cat had visited our clothesline. Quite a nerve!

Sun. Mar. 7: I didn't feel too hot & never got dressed—spent most of day in bed & R, like an angel, got meals etc.

March 8, 1948
Dear Ma -

Have just finished drawing you a picture of our house here. Altho' it is no masterpiece it will give you an idea—'tis very cozy and I am sad to think of leaving it in about 10 days. If the weather continues fine (and it's been beautiful except for a day or two ever since mid-Jan.) we plan to leave for home Thurs. of next week. But we have enuf food to hold on a bit longer if the weather gets bad. It's hard to believe we will have been gone six months from NW—and have been here 4½. The time has flown. R's figured we'll be at Goose Easter Sunday if the weather remains as is.

Last Friday (we were down at the Lower Tilt) we went out to Fox Is. to "hear the news." We figured Wilfred would be up for his canoe and would have brought some mail. Also R thot perhaps Hayward might have sent a dog up to help us down. Wilfred had come & gone again! but we found <u>all</u> our mail including bills but not a word from you or H! What happened? I thot you were going to send a letter c/o Emmy (Mrs. Wilfred)? But I guess you're OK for a letter from Floyd mailed Jan. 20th didn't mention you so I presume all is well. I was surprised to get all but R had told Noel (who handles the mail) to send it up if he got a chance to send it all the way with one person, but not to send it if it had to be passed from one to the other.

The only letter from family in New York was nearly two months old, sent weeks before her mother died. Barbara's brother and sister had written with the news of Mrs. Mundy's death but that letter was being held for her at Groves Point and nobody was aware of the devastating message it contained.

Fur had "picked up a bit recently"—Russell had seven mink and two cats "besides his beaver & the weasels he doesn't count." Everything would be clean for their trip home; Barbara was washing out all the bags they used to carry flour, sugar, beans, peas, and tea. She tackled their river clothes and was dismayed at how damaged her things were after daily, rough use. The purple skirt she had worn "every day I've been here" had taken a terrible beating.

Sat. Mar. 13: R says if we live to be a 1000 we'll never see another winter like this for clear, cold weather and wonderful going—on track that is. More snow makes better going otherwise as it packs and one can bear up with snow. Snow now is all icy & one sinks to bottom off track. Worms in our yeast & bread for second time tonight!!

Sun. Mar. 14: Our last Sunday here for this year. We had our two breakfasts getting up about 9:30. I washed hair & made tassel for Spot's harness which R bound with old pants to make it softer. *[Spot would tow a load wrapped in a seal skin.]* A _beautiful_ day, but blowing quite hard.

Mar. 16: R & Spot off to strike up the So. Path early yesterday morning. Afraid I've waited too long to take picture of house from across river. No new snow came and now 'tis overcast again. Darn. I'll have to trust to next year!! "Yes I have ... very, very happy"—gosh, how much a few _words_ can mean! I'm _still_ waiting and longing for R to _say_ he loves me etc.! ... Whew! It's _hot_ today—have just ret'd from across River & it's _running_ down me—I put my hand in my pocket for a hankie to mop my brow & to my disgust find it & one duffle mitt gone, so I'll have to climb the hill again as I might need that mitt. Spring is here! The snow is wet, heavy & sinky—right to the bottom. My deerskin shoes & mitts are both soaking—am sitting on the chopping block now trying to cool off! Snow is dripping and this time R _can't_ deny it! Tonight it is raining—R has his wish—I don't care for it but if it will make better going it's a good idea—I suppose if it rains _too_ hard R won't get back tomorrow.

Wed. Mar. 17: Another beautiful, clear, cold day (probably raining in NYC for the policemen's parade!) The rain turned to snow during the night and I looked out this A.M. to find a white blanket over everything—all ugliness now hidden ... It seems a pity to be leaving now when it's so lovely here. Have shovelled dock and paths & gone for water. Now I must pack, I suppose! The sun set tonight in a golden cloud and it's clear as can be with a newish moon. R got home _very_ early and had his best haul! three mink & a cat. If traps hadn't been full of jays & weasel he would have had 2 more mink. Fur is coming & we are leaving! Had we enuf food R says he would have stayed on. But this is our last night & I am sad to leave. I love this little home and it's beautiful up here. We have scaffolded some things & buried flour. I hope 'tis only au revoir & that I'll be back again. I've been happy here. (Forgot to say R saw track of Indians in South Path—they left a cigarette for him on the stove at the tent!)

Chapter Sixteen

DOWN RIVER TO HOME

But when the hunt is over and we are homeward bound,
Feeling very sorry for to leave our trapping ground,
And going down the river we are almost blind with sweat,
But when we see our friends at home we'll be happy then,
you bet.

—Douglas Best, "The Trapper's Song"

Mar. 18: Today the Groves' caravan set forth about 9 A.M.—clear, cold & blowing a gale behind us. Didn't get to tilt [Fox Island] until about 5:30 but R says that's good considering the going and the load. Among our things were: a hind leg of deer (about 40 lbs.) and six <u>huge</u> loaves of bread. I, with my funny little sled was first, then Spot & R with the big one. My sled certainly looked like a runt beside his—I had to laugh every time I looked at it! Where there was new snow it was hard hauling, and where it had blown off (on the banks) it was like glass & almost impossible to stand up. We're really on our way now. R said this A.M. he was glad he'd brought me, and I am certainly glad I came! It's been wonderful in every way.

Barbara had no idea what the trip downriver would be like. She had paddled and trekked upriver twice and down once, but that was in late summer, not over a mostly frozen river, hauling a loaded sled, hoping the surface was strong enough to support their weight. She was used to the cold by now, but as Douglas Best wrote in his song, the hot work of hauling a load made one "almost blind with sweat."[1] To hear Russell say what she was longing to hear, that he was glad he had brought her, probably gave her a tremendous boost, just when she needed it for the ordeal ahead.

From Fox Island, they hauled along Lake Winokapau, its high edges now sheathed in ice. They clambered up the glazed banks to boil the kettle or to get to a tilt for the night.

Mar. 19: The lake is so icy on the banks now that it looked like open water in the early morning sun. R is now taking one load up the hill on "Shorty" [Barbara's small sled]. Yesterday we boiled at Wallace's where we once had to climb a bank at least 2' high—the water has "quarred" & frozen again & our boiling spot was right level with the ice! Some difference in the clothes I wear now & what I used to when I was a passenger & not part of the crew! Once I wore 9 or 11 layers duck hunting—now walking I wear 3 and usually perspire freely!

Mar. 20: Up the hill & on our way. Until we reached Shorty who had been buried on the top of the hill, I walked behind R pushing. Then Shorty & I started our adventurous trip together. She hooked on & pulled me over backwards, once she ran ahead between my legs & I sat down plop in her middle! Going down the hill I pushed with one hand & steered with t'other & in the brook I pushed her ahead sometimes & she pushed me ahead at others! I say she's 4' but R thinks shorter. Anyway, she's 11" wide & in her day was bigger & better than R's present one which is 12' long, 14" wide & ½" thick (this to make her supple). 'Twas a mild, wet, snowy (almost rainy) day & we got to tilt thoroughly soaked.

Sun. 21: It cleared with lovely powder puff clouds & we went on to Walter's—this time cutting across lake from cliff to 5 mi. Pt. & back to Walter's Pt. At cliff below Wilfred's we found a hole of water! It blew a gale & drifted something fierce. Could lean against wind & the lake was so slippery it was almost impossible to stand up. A very pretty sunset—clouds & color.

Mar. 22: At Warren's tonight … Found both canoes left for R—pretty mean I think. Hole of water started with bridges at end of lake—very pretty—contrast of black water & ice. Rocks had layers of heavy ice on them—sun brilliant all day & sparkling on water. My lips are going to be a mess! Warren's house is most tidy & cute—a good floor, corner cupboard and wee window sills and the cutest log house for his dog—with brush floor—you ever saw. His house also has a table with shelf & a box the right height for a chair. All in all, very complete & comfy!

It was a great disappointment to find both canoes still there; Barbara hoped the small one would have gone ahead with the other returning trappers. Russell likely expected they would have to manage both all the way home. He knew trappers who hadn't brought canoes downriver because they were difficult to transport weren't likely to take one as a favour for someone else, adding more weight to their load. If anyone had needed the canoe, it would have been taken. Their big canoe was lengthwise on the sled, the smaller one balanced across its gunwales.

Where the river was well frozen, they hauled the canoes. Where there were "runnable" holes of open water, they put them in the river and balanced the sleds across the gunwales. They had a sail they could use on either the catamaran or canoe. The trip down would be nerve-wracking and dangerous, jumping from sled to canoe, sometimes sliding and other times paddling. As Barbara quickly learned, river conditions changed in an instant.

Mar. 23: Came only to Mooney's [Mouni Rapids] today. <u>Beautiful</u> day for running in canoe; towed little one. Found bridge of ice above Devil's Hole but we hauled around that. End of hole above here a bit. A few bridges between here and there. Hauled little canoe here & then R went back for big one, as he couldn't leave it safely there. When he went back the bridge was almost gone & the ice we hauled over <u>was</u> gone—and certainly no more than two hours had passed! The Devil's Hole was "rough as the dickens" and we hit one wopper, which took in a little water coming thru'. River very different looking in winter but contrast of open water & ice is beautiful & rocky cliffs with snow are too. Burnt wood bank across from here very pretty. River certainly turns about a lot between here and Hole, right back on itself at times. "Shorty" was left at Warren's. At least R didn't have to haul over banks—I have now joined the match box tribe. I wear over my sore lips—R with his big blue eyes & I with my big blue mouth are something to see.

Mar. 24: We didn't get very far today! We're camped between Squirrel River & Shamrock Is. It has rained, snowed, hailed, been beautifully clear, also cloudy, been calm & blown a gale (in both directions or even more). It has been soupy & wet underfoot & now it's freezing! R could get nowhere with the catamaran—it got wet, then sank thru' the soft snow & froze on. We are in the middle of rough ice which we met just above Squirrel River. A beautiful billowy cloud appeared in the notch and I hope I got a picture of it.

This was the place Elliott Merrick had mentioned, where ice dams formed in tributaries and broke several times over the winter. Horace Goudie described crossing a place like that when he first went trapping with his father. He said the crossing place was open water when they arrived with their sleds; several other trappers had made camp, waiting for the river to freeze enough to allow them to cross. The next morning, there was "still an open space in the middle of the river about twenty feet wide." Three men had long rubber waders, which they used when tracking upriver in the fall. They decided to cross the river in waders, carefully walking over the slippery rocks, making numerous trips with all their gear, sleds, and finally carrying six men across, one by one, on their backs. Goudie figured it saved them three days waiting for the river to freeze over properly.[2] Stories like that may have convinced Russell of the wisdom of having a canoe for the return trip.

Mar. 25: It's nice to be in a tent again—the wind _roared_ last night & today it continued—almost blowing me down at times. Rough ice & breaking thru' crust most of today. We had a few wild moments with a sail on the canoe but the sail broke. 'Twas too windy and not many level spots either. _Very_ cold; first time I've worn my heavy jacket (over dickie) when not in canoe. Got to Dan's & found house in a _mess_—too dirty to stay in so we're camped next to it. Slept on deerskin—warm & soft. The sand banks now are grimy looking where the sun is beginning to blow off—gives a funny impression of some tannish shade.

Fri. Mar. 26: Got to John Blake's quite early but stayed as he & Mark are still up here altho' in the woods now. Found a note saying Mark was due back tomorrow and R thot he _might_ come today. They don't leave 'till next week, so they will take over shutting up the River for this season from here on—looked as if it was to be our job. House all newly brushed and tidy! Had sail up all the way today and had to run to keep up quite often & sometimes I was left behind! The canoe tipped over 3 times much to R's *annoyance—he, at those moments, completely forgot that that <u>same</u> wind was what saved him a day's hauling! It's funny in a way, but when R gets angry at anything he gets angry at <u>everything</u> & I wish I could then just vanish as I hate seeing him in those moods—besides the fact I get a share aimed at me even when I'm trying to help. Today I tried to run ahead to keep Spot going straight. R kept right on & as I passed him I slipped and my snowshoe got on his. All the thanx I got for my efforts was a glare & "don't step on my snowshoe—isn't the river big enough for two of us?" Remarks like that just paralyze me. I guess I've seen the worst of R sometimes this winter and he has certainly brought out the worst in me at times. At least I <u>hope</u> there's no worse in either of us!! Pretty good walking all today, odd holes of water here & there and some rough ice around Elsie's & Allan's Islands (discovered he has 2 today). Also have discovered that "Sandion" Lake is really Sandy Island Lake!*

Barbara was getting used to her husband's temper—and giving back as good as she got. It was too much to expect to get all the way downriver without at least one exchange between them. Her comment about "shutting up the River," refers to the custom that chores were left to the last trappers to come downriver in the spring. It fell to the last ones using the cabin to make sure everything was in order, which could include taking the door off a tilt so bears wouldn't break it to get in; taking down the stove pipe, so rain water wouldn't accumulate in the stove and rust it out; and making sure nothing edible was left around for animals. You might also leave an armful of split wood for the next person to come along.

Mar. 27: Tonight we are camped on Mininipi Is.—quite a pretty spot with large, tall trees. R used sail all the way from John's—a large part of the way was on hard ice along the hole of water (couldn't run as there were bridges). Some places hole was wide, others just a strip like a canal. Very bright, tho' hazy day. A note at Min. tilt said Harvey Montague had left there this A.M. so we ought to see him tomorrow. Altho' R said coming along the Rapid and the Slip were <u>good</u> I thot it very sliding in spots & it looked most difficult to me—but we're here. Ran from foot of rapids. Had to get out here as it was too rough by island to run in a small canoe, (John had written to warn R). The ½ sand ½ snow banks don't look so bad now—sort of coffee soda shade. We each had a peppermint candy from John's & I made mine last 1½ hours! Our shoes worn right thru' from the crust, & R's snowshoes (my ex-ones) are a <u>sight</u>—held together with string, rabbit wire, & sealskin. I was a masked bandit today trying to get my face fixed up. Gum seems to have done the trick for lips & neck but I'm ashamed to be seen—my face is so covered with bumps—and this A.M. my hands suddenly swelled to huge proportions & I wondered if R would have to file off my rings. Tonight they're OK! What was it? Three months today since we saw Philip, the last person we have seen.

Easter Sunday Mar. 28: Ran [canoed] from Mininipi Island to just above Horseshoe Cliff where hole ended—very cold with vapor rising, slob ice & an occasional white ice floe. Good going around cliff. Open again thru' to Bob's Brook but we didn't run—too rough for two of us in small canoe. Stopped at Harvey's to boil & he had apricot jam, Klim, & <u>one</u> chocolate candy which R & I divided. Got sugar & butter from him but he never offered to take a thing & he had 3 dogs! Went on to Porcupine as going was not bad & we thot we might catch Hayward or at least have mail & goodies there. Arrived about 6:30 to find house empty & dirty and no word & not a scrap of anything. We were disgusted! From Horseshoe down there were occasional holes but none runnable. Gull Island Rapid I'd never recognize. Some rough ice there and at Fred's Pt. but almost roads thru' it. Poplars on lake turning green and as we came down the river we find less & less snow. River opens out & hills recede all the time from about Elsie's Is. down. From foot of Gull Is. Rapid to Fred's Pt. there was a channel of water straight down the middle of the rough ice. Going not as good down here—breaking thru' crust. Counted 7 canoes—so Warren never had one. <u>Why</u> didn't he take our small one?

The canoes, and who did or didn't take one, would trouble her no longer. They had come as far as they could by water or river ice and left their canoes stored with the others. Russell would make a quick trip back after the ice was gone to bring them home. From here, Spot would haul the large sled, with their assistance.

The lower part of the river was more populated and busier. As expected, they met Harvey Montague.

Mar. 29: Didn't leave 'till 9:30 A.M. and came only to Sand Banks—

took a tender look at our camping ground at Upper Tilt where I first saw the shadows on the tent made by moonlight. Harvey caught us just before we got here & I rode those last few minutes. He has gone on & notes here say Hayward left the 26th & Cecil passed yesterday. Walking down the river has made me far more conscious of its various twists & turns & I feel as if I could better visualize it all now. And one can see the downhill parts even more clearly than in a canoe—especially just before reaching Mininipi Rapid coming down.

Mar. 30: Today we came from Sand Banks to the lower drop of Muskrat Falls where we are camped on a snow bank beside the Falls. It looked as if it might snow but it's clearing & there's a pastel sunset. The Fall portage looks absolutely perpendicular with snow on it. There are huge chunks of ice at the foot of the Falls. Great piles of it. Down here where the river is wide & the hills lower there are some that are all birch and they give a very tannish tint—soft & rather nice. We met Rank Hope and bro. going up just above Falls today.

Everyone in the upper Lake Melville settlements knew who had gone into the country for the winter and would be mentally ticking the names off the list as each arrived home. They were naturally curious to hear how the New York City girl had fared after six months on a trapline, beating a path in snowshoes, living in tilts and tents, eating partridge, beaver, and even owls, day after day. Was she exhausted, bundled in the back of a komatik like so much luggage? How had she managed the solitude, the cold, and unending hard work? Were she and Russell still loving newlyweds? Or were they at each other's throats?

The story of their safe return quickly made its way around the bay. The designation of "outsider" might never be shaken, but that winter, Barbara earned the respect due anyone who worked as hard as she did in such conditions, the same respect Labradorians gave each other. Those who assumed she would gratefully hang up her snowshoes and tie on an apron, staying home like other trappers' wives, were soon corrected. She hadn't gone with Russell to prove anything to anybody. She loved the life and intended to go again next winter.

Mar. 30: Well it's all over now—our honeymoon, if such it could be called, for tomorrow we probably get to Goose; we will have been gone 6 mos. to the day. It has been a wonderful six mos. in most ways. At times, when R was overworked & tired because of the extra work of having me along, we had our difficulties, but perhaps it's just as well to see that side of each other early in the game. I wish they hadn't been, but since they have, I only hope they will leave no mark for the future. R's patience is very short at times & he _has_ a temper. I've tried hard to take it the best I could & sometimes I've not been too successful, I'm afraid. R has worked _very_ hard esp. going & coming, but I _do_ hope he has been happy to have me with him and has felt it has been worthwhile. _I've_ been happy to be with him even if some times have been hard and I'm sorry in many ways that it is all over. Labrador life _really_ begins for me now so those who care say a prayer!

EPILOGUE

O n April 1, Barbara read the letter containing the news of her mother's death. Her sister, Harriet wrote, "I hope Russell can comfort you." Four days later she flew to New York and spent the next three months with Harriet, sorting out Thousand Nine and the estate. In June, the sisters flew to Montana to bring their mother's ashes to Glacier National Park, a place the family had enjoyed on holidays. She never had a chance to tell her mother that her married life, even with its difficult times, made her happy.

It was best that she go for her eyes & speech had been affected & life could never have been the same, but I do so wish I could have seen her once again at least. R's letter had made her happy & I hope she knows that all is well with us. The next three months were hard in every way; physically, emotionally & mentally. It's heartbreaking to break up a home you've loved & get rid of things that have meant a lot. It just tears your insides out, and it left both H & me groggy with exhaustion & lack of sleep. It was good to get back on July 15th. Mrs. J was right when she said. "Never mind, soon you'll be in yr. husband's arms & everything will be alright." Everything is alright when I'm there! It was wonderful to be home again. (Diary: not dated)

Barbara and Russell spent two months together at their house in North West River that summer. She must have been itching to get her hands on it, occupied by Russell alone while she was away. Two days after returning from New York she "was very lucky to get a girl for a few days to houseclean—and it needed it!" All winter clothes and blankets were hung out on the line. Curtains were up "in all rooms except the living-room and porch, leaving that for next year." Barbara thought the house looked "very nice now that it is fixed up." Her furniture, silver, linen, and dishes had arrived from New York and were put to use. Flatware and linens were not reserved for special occasions. The table was properly set for daily meals, even breakfast, according to Russell's niece. Shirley Chaulk Hefler recalled visiting her cousin Phyllis and both girls being put to work on Saturday night polishing silver, a chore unknown in most North West River homes.

Her house in order, Barbara had much to do to get ready for another winter on the trapline. This time, she knew what they would need and how to pack it. She vowed that Russell would have no complaints about not having enough bread. She baked "2 kinds of cookies, pork buns, prune cake, plain bread, and 2 Xmas cakes, one regular and one small!" Six days before going upriver, she lined up her stationary and carbon paper to type a farewell letter to Everybody. They had decided to go earlier than the previous year, with the first group of trappers to leave; "life seems to get more hectic all the time."

It has been mad ever since—the sewing machine going steadily— patches, darning, cutting out, washing. When I leave the machine for a spell, R takes over and starts in on flour bags. I think I have attended to all except the gathering up of our things—this year will be harder than last, as last year I took everything I had—having nothing else, but this year we are settled a bit and things are scattered and in their proper places. And planning for 7 months in every little detail is hard on the brain—just try it sometime and you'll see. (Letter: September 4, 1948)

A different standard for housekeeping was set at the house in the Bight and her return to Fig River demanded a larger, more comfortable tilt. Russell had work to do on it when they arrived that fall. They moved in on October 23, "in time for dinner." It was a proper cabin, almost big enough to call a house (nearly 10 by 11 feet), with shelves, a table in front of the window and two stumps for chairs. Russell built her a "darling little corner cupboard." A cheerful, coloured oilcloth topped the table; it was all "very elegant." She was pleased to be able to walk around without hitting her head.

Everything was easier the second winter. Diary entries were fewer and shorter, more about daily events, the fur they trapped, their luck in hunting, and the weather than a lack of attention from Russell. The trip upriver was routine, still difficult and physically testing, but no surprises. She helped with the trapline, setting and clearing traps. She wasn't afraid to be alone in a cabin when he went on the path, but still missed him when he was gone for a night or two. She succumbed a couple of times to teary written conversations with herself about how he seemed to love hunting more than her. One day in January 1949, she asked him not to go on the path. For sure, she was sorry she had mentioned it: "R was to go down around today but I made a fool of myself & he wouldn't go. I <u>must</u> somehow control myself 'till he's out of sight. I begged him to go on but he wouldn't."

They really were alone during that second winter. Innu families were elsewhere and without them, they had no near neighbours, which was exactly how they liked it. From early winter, she seemed to know it would be her last one with Russell in the country and that she would be in North West River next winter, a prospect that did not appeal greatly.

If I could only store up the beautiful things & the wonderfulness (if there is such a word) of these two winters. There'll never be anything like them again for me as long as I live. I wish NW had brooks & places to explore—It's so horribly uninteresting in comparison—and you certainly can't feel that you're really living as you do up here—Well I'm far luckier than most & I mustn't forget that. Just let me remember it all, tho'; to carry in my mind so I can fall back on it when I get sick with longing for it in the future. (Diary: November 26, 1948)

The things she loved about it were plain, simple, and well described. Since her first winter in North West River as a Grenfell wop, she had savoured the comfort of a tent in the trees, a fire crackling, and a kettle on the boil. None of that had become routine or boring. Barbara fondly recalled one of her favourite camping spots near the end of her second winter.

Back to our camping spot—there are old stumps chopped off here—showing Indians camped here at one time—a long time ago tho'. Everything is so cozy—tent banked with snow, lots of brush, nice smelling juniper in stove, and outside everything put away—sealskin on brush, traps on stump, birds hung high out of Spot's reach & brush bed for the old boy himself. I'm very happy—this is what I love! (Diary: February 15, 1949)

Late in March she wrote, "Well, so to bed for my last night in my little home—How I shall miss it! These have been the 2 happiest & best winters of my life—and I shall <u>never</u> forget them." [1] She sent some photos of trapline life to *Among the Deep-Sea Fishers* and they were published in the July 1950 issue.

Barbara became pregnant early in the summer of 1949. Two happy winters behind her, she began to contemplate what the next stage of married life would bring. She had the home she always wanted, a husband she loved dearly, and a baby on the way, but she was already anticipating missing the freedom, and even the excitement of life in the country. Berries were picked and made into jam, ducks were killed and bottled, bread was baked. It all had to be done but "constant hard work" wouldn't make for brilliant conversation the next time she attended a wop Alumni dinner. Her letters to Everybody would have no more stories about setting traps for beaver, encounters with Innu, or hauling canoes downriver. Maybe what she had always wanted would not be enough.

Others knew what I surely realize now—that once I had to stay home & stop doing things with R it would be the real test of whether or not I could "take it." I wonder if I can? Will I just become old, uninteresting and uninterested in anything as most of the women here have become simply because there's nothing in their lives except constant hard work. Or can I manage to hang on to something so that I will still have something to offer should I ever get among my old friends & relations again. I feel I haven't much to offer now for any length of time. (Diary: January 24, 1950)

Their daughter, Marjorie, was born in March 1950. Russell's daughter, Phyllis, who had been living with her grandparents, or in the Mission dormitory while Barbara and Russell were on the trapline, moved in with them, staying until she went away for her final year of high school. In 1960, Phyllis married a Canadian serviceman she met while working on the military base.

Russell kept up trapping for a few years, although making shorter trips, usually coming home in time for Christmas. The whole family went salmon fishing every summer at Long Point, near Rigolet and The

Narrows, on the south shore of Lake Melville, where they camped in a tent. They would come home in late August with fish for the winter and gallons of partridgeberries. He was still cutting cords of wood, hunting ducks, geese, seals, and caribou.

Barbara was active in the community and the church, a member of the school board, and enjoyed socializing with their friends, but she and Russell were talking about the future. In 1961, they decided to leave Labrador. Russell said it was because they wanted better schooling for Marjorie, but there was probably more to it than that. Trapping was over for him, and for most Labrador trappers. Fur prices had been poor for years and 35-plus years on the river was enough. At 50, he had no interest in working at the military base as many other former trappers were doing, taking orders from someone else, or going in the country as a guide for prospectors. Whatever he decided to do, he would be his own boss.

They went to the United States, visited Barbara's sister, Harriet, in Palo Alto, California, and agreed they didn't want to live there. An old Mission friend of Barbara's was living on Vancouver Island, in the Comox Valley, and coaxed them to visit. They found a house on a beach, surrounded by tall forest, with a view of the mountains across the water on the British Columbia mainland. Russell said it was much like the view from his house in the Bight. He bought a fishing boat, got a salmon licence, and started his second career fishing along the coast of Vancouver Island, the Queen Charlotte Islands, and the north coast of British Columbia, until he was 75. He had deckhands for the first couple of seasons and after that, Barbara fished with him. When they got the urge to see wild country, they took their camper truck up the Alaska Highway to go moose hunting. They both enjoyed travel and took tours and cruises to Europe, Asia, South America, Mexico, and Hawaii.

Keepsakes and reminders of their Labrador life were displayed around the house. Barbara kept carvings, hooked rugs, and other Mission handicraft items. Their shelves were full of Labrador books. They were the full width of the continent away from "home" but were always interested in hearing the news from North West River. Barbara sometimes gave talks about Labrador, showing her slides of the trapline to Comox Valley community groups.

They returned to Labrador numerous times to visit family and once chartered a small plane to bring them to Fig River, flying low over their old haunts. Russell found some of his abandoned traps still hanging up in trees. They had a lot of relatives in Labrador and were welcomed home fondly. In Barbara's first years in Labrador, she had worried so much about fitting in. Years after her death, she was remembered as "Aunt Barb" and stories of her generosity, kindness, and strong opinions were recalled with smiles.

Russell and Barbara lived together in their house on Vancouver Island until she died at almost 84 in 1994. Russell lived to be 96 years old, spending his last nine years living next door to Marjorie in Kelowna. He read the newspaper every day and enjoyed a glass or two of his favourite red wine. One night at the dinner table, talking about the two winters he and Barbara spent together on the trapline, he said she "cried and cried" when she realized she might never go up the river again. "She was a good help to me," he said. After Russell's death, his ashes were brought to where Barbara's had been scattered years earlier, their salmon fishing place at Long Point, about 4 kilometres directly south of Eskimo Island in Lake Melville.

ENDNOTES

Chapter 2

1 "Copartnership Notices," *NYT*, January 1, 1908, 13.

2 Henry Bryant, *My Financial Adventures* (January 1930), unpublished manuscript in private collection of Anthony Bryant, 1-2.

3 "The Late Henry Keep—The Millionaire's Will," *NYT*, September 14, 1869, 2.

4 "Mrs. Schley's Bequests," *NYT*, July 1, 1900, 14.

5 Thirteenth Census of the United States (1910), s.v. "Mundy, Floyd."

6 "Notes of Social Activities," *NYT*, April 18, 1928, 29.

7 Cruise Diary, 1929, Barbara Mundy Groves (BMG) Papers.

8 David M. Kennedy, *The American People in the Great Depression: Freedom from Fear, Part I* (New York: Oxford University Press, 1999), 40.

9 "Mundy on Excelsior Bank Board," *NYT*, November 15, 1932, 36.

10 "2,000,000 Children's Jobs Sought for Adults," *NYT*, November 28, 1932, 1.

11 "5 Girls, 3 Jobless, Live on $33 a Week," *NYT*, November 15, 1931, 18.

12 "Miss Rodman Entertained," *NYT*, December 1, 1929, 8N.

13 *KOINE*, Connecticut College Yearbook, Class of 1933.

14 "Stock Exchange News," *NYT*, September 27, 1931.

Chapter 3

1 "Operas That Will Serve Charity," *NYT*, October 26, 1930, x13.

2 H.W. Tamblyn and John Adams Brown, *The Grenfell Mission: A Survey, Analysis and Recommendations*, 23. The Rooms Provincial Archives Division (RPA), IGA, MG 63.2031. All references from this document will hereafter be cited as Tamblyn and Brown.

3 "In Grenfell's Labrador," *NYT*, November 7, 1930, 24.

4 Ronald Rompkey, *Grenfell of Labrador: A Biography* (Toronto: University of Toronto Press, 1991), 234, and "A Few Facts about the Grenfell Missions of Newfoundland and Labrador" (1937), 1-3 (Centre for Newfoundland Studies, Memorial University Libraries [CNS], file).

5 Starting in 1769, Moravians were given what amounted to "rent-free leases without term" for large tracts of land at three places on the north Labrador coast for the purpose of converting and "civilizing" the Inuit. J.K. Hiller, "Moravian Land Holdings on the Labrador Coast: A Brief History," in *Our Footprints Are Everywhere: Inuit Land Use and Occupancy in Labrador*, edited by Carol Brice-Bennett, Alan Cooke, and Nina Davis (Nain: Labrador Inuit Association, 1977), 83-93.

6 Grenfell was an irritant to the Moravians for 30 years. In the Minutes of the London Committee of the Moravian Mission, February 1, 1901: "Dr. Grenfell is strongly of the opinion that we ought to give more for the skins & furs we take from the natives & on the other land, that we ought to reduce the price of, at least, some of the articles we give them in exchange. The sympathy of our people was, he felt sure, being alienated from us by the present system" ("No. 476, Interview with Dr. Grenfell on Trade Matters, February 1, 1901," *Moravian Missions Documents [1768-1921]*, CNS, microfilm 513, reel 4). In October 1930, Moravian missionary Paul Hettasch wrote to his superiors in England, expressing his suspicions about Grenfell's intentions: "You are aware of the reasons why visits of Dr. Grenfell to our stations have not been welcomed in the past. In many cases they have not been Mission trips at all, but advertisement, and collecting of material for advertisement. In his lectures and reports Dr. Grenfell has been in the habit of intentionally avoiding mentioning the existence of the Moravians on the coast" ("To the Brethren of the Mission Board, London, October 1930," *Records of the Moravian Mission in Labrador [1764-1944]* [Public

Archives of Canada, Ottawa, 1960, 10249], CNS, microfilm 511, reel 8).

Relations between the two missions improved greatly when Dr. Harry Paddon and later his son, Dr. Anthony Paddon, made regular medical visits to the north coast.

7   W.G. Gosling, *Labrador: Its Discovery, Exploration and Development* (New York: John Lane Company, 1911), 466.

8   Archbishop M.F. Howley, quoted in *The Grenfell Obsession*, edited by Patricia O'Brien (St. John's: Creative, 1992), 21. With his staunch anti-sectarian philosophy, and as an advocate for non-denominational schools, Grenfell won no friends in the Roman Catholic hierarchy.

9   Rompkey, *Grenfell*, 120-124.

10   Wilfred Grenfell, "The Land Vision of a Sailor," *Among the Deep-Sea Fishers (ADSF)* 30.3 (October 1932), 97.

11   In 1935, a delegation from the IGA board travelled to Newfoundland to meet with the Commission of Government in St. John's and also to inspect Mission facilities in St. Anthony. They met with E.N.R. Trentham, Commissioner of Finance, who described the forgiveness of import duties for many years as "a large invisible contribution" to the Mission from the government. It was his idea for the Mission to pay duty and receive an equivalent grant from government, about $30,000 a year (Cecil Ashdown and T.A. Greene, *Report of the Commission Appointed by the Directors of the International Grenfell Association, April 13, 1935, to Confer with the Commission of Government for Newfoundland and Survey Conditions on the Coast of Newfoundland and Labrador*, 6 [RPA, IGA, MG 63.1951]). Their final report was submitted November 26, 1935. All references from this document will hereafter be cited as Ashdown and Greene.

12   "Financial Report of the International Grenfell Association," *ADSF* 37.1 (April 1939), 21.

13   "Schedule of Sir Wilfred's Lecture Tour Abroad, Autumn of 1928," *ADSF* 26.3 (October 1928), 118.

14   "Sir Wilfred's 1929 Lecture Tour," *ADSF* 26.4 (January 1929), 172.

15   Rompkey, *Grenfell*, 206-208.

16   Tamblyn and Brown, 28.

17   Grenfell, "Warm Hearts in Labrador," *The Rotarian* 47.1 (July 1935), 9.

18   Harry Toland, *A Sort of Peace Corps: Wilfred Grenfell's Labrador Volunteers* (Bowie, MD: Heritage Books, 2001), 14.

19   Toland, 71-72. A Mission file in St. Anthony showed 2,800 names of volunteers from 1903 to 1976, 89 per cent of which were American.

20   "Report of the Staff Selection Committee," *ADSF* 27.2 (July 1929), 91.

21   *Encyclopedia of Newfoundland and Labrador* (*ENL*), s.v. "Birdseye, Clarence."

22   Grenfell, "Story of Labrador Medical Mission," in *The Empire Club of Canada Addresses* (Toronto: The Empire Club of Canada, 1923), 295-310. Grenfell's speech was delivered on November, 17, 1921.

23   Grenfell, "Story of Labrador Medical Mission," 301.

24   Harriet Mundy was listed with the summer staff for the Industrial Department at Indian Harbour in "Report of the Staff Selection Committee," *ADSF* 26.2 (July 1928), 68.

25   Annie Baikie (Watts) went to Philadelphia University and studied Occupational Therapy. She was in Indian Harbour in 1927 and in 1928 worked at the Industrial Shop in North West River. Her sister, May Baikie (McLean), was sent by the Mission in 1916 to St. John's, Newfoundland, for teacher's training. As the school had not yet been built in North West River, she worked as an itinerant teacher, living with families in small communities for a few weeks at a time.

26   Lilian Schieffelin Sanger, "A Temporary Industrial Shop in New York," *ADSF* 29.2 (July 1931), 59.

27   "Open Shop Tonight to Aid Grenfell Work," *NYT*, March 24, 1931, 24.

28   Grenfell, "Varick Frissell," *ADSF* 29.2 (July 1931), 57. Frissell was the first person to shoot moving pictures of Labrador's Grand Falls. See Frissell, "Explorations in the Grand Falls Region of Labrador," *The Geographical Journal* 69.4 (April 1927), 332-340.

29   "For Grenfell Units," *NYT*, November 6, 1932, xx8.

30 "Many Bazaars," *NYT*, November 28, 1932, 12.

31 "Charities to Gain by Flower Show," *NYT*, March 19, 1933, N3.

32 Burke MacArthur, *United Littles: The Story of the Needlework Guild of America* (New York: Coward-McCann, 1955), 22-24.

33 "Garments for the Poor," *NYT*, November 20, 1891, 8.

34 "The Needlework Guild," *NYT*, February 21, 1892, 8.

35 MacArthur, 116-120, and "Needle Guild's Jubilee," *NYT*, April 21, 1935, 16.

36 "Needlework Guild Column," *ADSF* 31.2 (July 1933), 99.

37 MacArthur, 114.

38 "Grenfell Makes Plea for Labrador People," *NYT*, April 25, 1931, 21.

39 Grenfell to Barbara Mundy [BM], April 10, 1934, RPA, IGA, MG 63.2959.

40 "Grenfell to Explain Work in Labrador," *NYT*, April 7, 1935, N7.

Chapter 4

1 "Award to Mrs. Mundy," *NYT*, January 5, 1934, 24.

2 It was a frequent enough occurrence that in 1936 Clare Boothe Luce wrote *The Women*, a popular Broadway play about wealthy Manhattan socialites spending the required weeks together at a dude ranch. The likeable central character's cheating husband found his new life with a pretty perfume-counter sales clerk not what he expected, and begged his wife to take him back—a hilarious and thoroughly satisfying outcome. The movie by the same name, directed by George Cukor, came out in 1939 and starred Norma Shearer, Rosalind Russell, and Joan Crawford.

3 "Eleven College Boys and Girls Sail to Work with Grenfell Mission," *The Boston Herald*, June 27, 1935.

4 Diary, July 1935, BMG Papers.

5 Grenfell, "Newfoundland and Labrador," *Journal of the Royal Society of Arts* 82.4250 (May 4, 1934), 661.

6   Grenfell, "Labrador—Lesson in Humanity," *The Rotarian* 53.6 (December 1938), 25.

7   *A Brick for Labrador* (London: Grenfell Association of Great Britain and Ireland, [1930?]), 18-19.

8   Ashdown and Greene, 29.

9   Grenfell, "Sir Wilfred's Letter," *ADSF* 30.4 (January 1933), 143.

10   BM to Mother and Harriet, July 10, 1935, BMG Papers.

11   Rompkey, *Grenfell*, 277.

12   BM to Mother and Harriet, July 10, 1935, BMG Papers.

13   BM to Mother, October 1, 1935, BMG Papers.

14   Dora Elizabeth Burchill, *Labrador Memories* (Victoria, Australia: The Shepparton News Publishing Co., 1947), 62.

15   "Glasgow to St. Anthony with the Scots," *ADSF* 33.4 (January 1936), 147-149.

16   BM to Mother, July 26, 1935, BMG Papers. An IGA directors' report in 1935 mentioned the "Scotch Wops have already built about 400 feet of this road in one month at the time this report is being prepared" (Ashdown and Greene, 24).

17   Names of all volunteer and paid staff, and the duties assigned, were published in "Report of the Staff Selection Committee," *ADSF* 33.2 (July 1935), 58-59.

18   Burchill, 30.

19   Burchill, 82.

20   BM to Floyd Mundy, July 27, 1935, BMG Papers.

21   Rompkey, *Grenfell*, 286.

22   Rompkey, *Grenfell*, 276.

23   "Needlework Guild Column," *ADSF* 31.4 (January 1934), 182-183.

24   "Needlework Guild Column," *ADSF* 31.4 (January 1934), 185.

25   "Needlework Guild Column," *ADSF* 31.4 (January 1934), 183.

26   Elisabeth Hamilton and Shirley S. Smith, "All Offerings Gratefully Received," *ADSF* 39.1 (April 1941), 15.

27   Charles Curtis, Report of the Superintendent to the Board of Directors, November 1950, 20, RPA, IGA, MG 63.113.

28   Grenfell, *Forty Years for Labrador* (London: Hodder and Stoughton, 1934), 257.

29   Grenfell, "Warm Hearts," 10.

30   Arthur Rich, "My Grandfather Came from England," *Them Days* (*TD*) 26.4 (Summer 2001), 41.

31   Curtis, "St. Anthony in 1932," *ADSF* 31.1 (April 1933), 6.

32   Paula Laverty, *Silk Stocking Mats: Hooked Mats of the Grenfell Mission* (Montreal & Kingston: McGill-Queen's University Press, 2005), 7-8.

33   Laverty, 71.

34   Laverty, 30.

35   This is one verse of a long song complaining about the Mission. MacEdward Leach, *Folk Ballads and Songs of the Lower Labrador Coast* (Ottawa: National Museum of Canada, Bulletin 201, 1965), 91.

36   BM to Mother, October 1, 1935, BMG Papers.

37   Albert T. Gould, "The New Cluett," *ADSF* 39.3 (October 1941), 67-69. The Mission had four vessels bearing the *Cluett* name. The first, *George B. Cluett*, was a 135-foot 3-masted schooner launched in 1911 and named after its American donor. It was sold in 1917. The second ship of the same name was condemned in Barbados in 1920. There was no *Cluett* for seven years and then the Mission bought *Giant King* in Lunenburg and renamed it *George B. Cluett*. It was decided the vessel wasn't large enough and, since no vessels were available for charter during wartime, the Mission commissioned a larger ship. *Nellie A. Cluett* was built in Lunenburg in 1941 by Smith & Rhuland Ltd. She was 145 feet with a 500-horsepower diesel engine. The *Cluett*s were used to bring supplies and staff to St. Anthony. Captain Kenneth Iversen of Lunenburg supervised the construction of the fourth ship.

38   Harriet Mundy to Matilda Bryant, n.d. 1935, Mundy and Bryant Papers.

39   "Alumni News," *ADSF* 33.4 (January 1936), 167.

Chapter 5

1   "Alumni News," *ADSF* 33.4 (January 1936), 167.

2   Grenfell to BM, June 13, 1936, RPA, IGA, MG 63.2959.

3   "Two Fashions Shows for Charity," *NYT*, March 29, 1936, N4, and "Social Service Auxiliary of Stony Wold to Give Benefit Luncheon and Style Show," *NYT*, February 20, 1938, 71.

4   "Many Offer Help in Grenfell Work," *NYT*, December 11, 1939, 65.

5   "Needlework Guild Column," *ADSF* 37.4 (January 1940), 153.

6   Rompkey, *Grenfell*, 290.

7   Anna Kivimaki, "Hard Winter Ahead," *ADSF* 37.3 (October 1939), 83.

8   "Alumni News," *ADSF* 38.2 (July 1940), 57.

9   Barbara Mundy, *The Twentieth Annual Report of the Coast-to-Coast Labrador Branch of the Needlework Guild of America* (New York, 1940), 24-25, RPA, IGA, MG 63.227.

10   "*Parsifal* Will Aid Grenfell Mission," *NYT*, February 25, 1940, 44.

11   Grenfell, "Dr. Harry Locke Paddon," *ADSF* 37.4 (January 1940), 123.

12   Grenfell to BM, June 24, 1940, RPA, IGA, MG 63.2959.

13   "Wilfred Grenfell of Labrador Dead," *NYT*, October 10, 1940, 1.

14   Schweitzer was a medical missionary in Africa from 1913 to the 1940s. Like Grenfell, he was a self-styled evangelical Christian. Schweitzer was awarded the Nobel Peace Prize in 1952.

15   Mundy, 5.

16   MacArthur, 120-121.

17   Cecil Ashdown to BM, March 2, 1942, RPA, IGA, MG 63.2959.

18 Tamblyn and Brown, 23.

19 Kathleen Young, "Labrador Calling," *ADSF* 40.1 (April 1942), 7.

20 Young, "Our Staff," *ADSF* 39.2 (July 1941), 41.

21 "Alumni News," *ADSF* 41.1 (April 1943), 22, and "Needlework Guild Column," *ADSF* 41.4 (January 1944), 124.

22 "Mundy-Burt," *NYT*, January 4, 1944, 15.

23 BMG Papers.

24 Peter Mundy, interview by author, June 7 & 8, 2008.

Chapter 6

1   Richard H. Jordan, "Inuit Occupation of the Central Labrador Coast since 1600 AD," in *Our Footprints*, 43-45.

2   Randy Ames, "Land Use in the Rigolet Area," in *Our Footprints*, 281.

3   Davies described planters, or freemen, as men who had come to Labrador to work on contract and stayed after their contracts expired, in "Notes on Esquimaux Bay and Surrounding Country," a paper presented to the Literary & Historical Society of Quebec, February 19, 1842 (www.morrin.org/transactions/docsfromclient/books/130/130.html, accessed February 10, 2012).

4   Randle Holme, "A Journey in the Interior of Labrador, July to October 1887," *Proceedings of the Royal Geographical Society and Monthly Record of Geography* (April 1988), 190-193.

5   Post Journal of North West River, June 11-12, 1837, Hudson's Bay Company Archives (HBCA) at Archives of Manitoba, Winnipeg, B.153/a/1-11, Reel 1M105.

6   Post Journal of North West River, July 21, 1836, HBCA, B.153/a/1-11, Reel 1M105.

7   Henry Connolly was one of six children of HBC trader William Connolly and a Cree woman designated in court documents as "Suzanne Pas-de-Nom" or "La Sauvagesse." In 1832, after 28 years together, William

abandoned Suzanne to marry his English cousin, Julia Woolrich, declaring his marriage to Suzanne had no validity. In 1864, after William's death, his eldest son sued Julia for his rightful share of his late father's estate. Bruce Peel, "Connolly, Suzanne," *Dictionary of Canadian Biography Online* (www.biographi.ca, accessed May 23, 2013). Henry Connolly went to Esquimaux Bay in 1843 as an apprentice postmaster, and stayed until 1872, having advanced to chief trader and postmaster. "Connolly, Henry," *Biographical Sheets*, HBCA. HBCA is a division of the Archives of Manitoba (www.mb.ca/chc/hbca/biographical, accessed May 23, 2013).

8   The Goudie family tree was compiled by Bernie Heard for Labrador Metis Nation, now NunatuKavut.

9   Russell Groves, interview by author, May 22, 2003.

10   Morris Chaulk, interview by author, September 28, 2007, and Derrick (Dick) Chaulk, interview by author, September 14, 2007.

11   Sylvia Blake, interview by author, October 10, 2007.

12   Morris Chaulk, September 28, 2007.

13   Morris Chaulk, September 28, 2007.

14   Parish Record of United Church, Labrador, 1932-33.

15   John Montague, "Fur Traders," *TD* 4.3 (1979), 25.

16   Isaac Rich, "John Montague," *TD* 23.4 (Summer 1998), 58.

17   Vaïnö Tanner, "Outlines of the Geography, Life and Customs of Newfoundland-Labrador," *Acta Geographica* 8.1 (1944), 719.

18   Elliott Merrick, "Escape to the North," *ADSF* 30.3 (October 1932), 114.

19   Merrick, *Green Mountain Farm* (New York: MacMillan, 1948), 171.

20   Merrick, "Escape," 111.

21   John R. Toop, "An Incident at Northwest River Recalled," *ADSF* 31.3 (October 1933), 129.

22   Richard Budgell and Michael Staveley, *The Labrador Boundary* (Happy Valley-Goose Bay: Labrador Institute of Northern Studies, Memorial University of Newfoundland, 1987), 8.

23 Affidavit of Joseph Michelin. No. 1619, in the Privy Council (Great Britain), in the Matter of the Boundary between the Dominion of Canada and the Colony of Newfoundland in the Labrador Peninsula, September 10, 1909, vol. 8, 4211.

24 Voluntary Statement of Malcolm McLean of Carter Basin, Lake Melville. No. 1425, in the Privy Council (Great Britain), in the Matter of the Boundary between the Dominion of Canada and the Colony of Newfoundland in the Labrador Peninsula, July 19, 1921, vol. 8, 3745.

25 Budgell and Staveley, 10-11.

Chapter 7

1 "Obituary, Floyd W. Mundy, 77, Securities Executive," *NYT*, November 17, 1953, 31.

2 Cecil Ashdown to BM, March 24, 1944, BMG Papers.

3 BM to Everybody, June 2, 1944, BMG Papers.

4 BM to Everybody, June 2, 1944, BMG Papers.

5 BM to Mother and Harriet, May 22, 1944, BMG Papers.

6 Spencer Dunmore, *Wings for Victory: The Remarkable Story of the British Commonwealth Air Training Plan in Canada* (Toronto: McClelland & Stewart, 1994), 228-340.

7 "Amtrak's Downeaster," www.american-rails.com/downeaster.html, accessed January 18, 2013.

8 Duncan Anderson, "D-Day Beachhead," www.bbc.co.uk/history/worldwars/wwtwo/dday_beachhead_01.shtml, accessed June 22, 2009.

9 Diary, May 24, 1944, BMG Papers.

10 Michael Hadley, *U-Boats against Canada: German Submarines in Canadian Waters* (Montreal: McGill-Queen's University Press, 1985), 23-24.

11 Paul Collins, "Other U-Boat Encounters," www.heritage.nf.ca/law/uboat.html, and "Sinking of the Caribou," www.heritage.nf.ca/law/caribou_

sinking.html, accessed June 23, 2009. The civilian vessel SS *Caribou* was torpedoed and sunk in the Cabot Strait on October 14, 1942, with the loss of 137 lives.

12   Ames, "Land Use," 281. The Army contingent was reduced during winter when ice prevented navigation.

13   Peter Neary, *Newfoundland in the North Atlantic World, 1929-1949* (Montreal and Kingston: McGill-Queen's University Press, 1988), 155.

14   Neary, "The Diplomatic Background to the Canada-Newfoundland Goose Bay Agreement of October 10, 1944," *Newfoundland Studies* 2.1 (Spring 1986), 40-41.

15   Neary, *Newfoundland*, 131-133.

16   BM to Everybody, July 15, 1944, BMG Papers.

17   Eric Fry, "Search for the Goose," *TD* 12.4 (June 1987), 5-11.

18   Fry, "Search," 9.

19   Alexander Forbes, *Quest for a Northern Air Route* (Cambridge: Harvard University Press, 1953), 5.

20   Elliott Roosevelt, "Report to Washington, D.C.," *TD* 12.4 (June 1987), 18.

21   William Guy Carr, *Checkmate in the North: The Axis Planned to Invade America* (Toronto: MacMillan, 1945), 105.

22   Isaac Rich, "We Grabbed the Chance," *TD* 12.4 (June 1987), 32.

23   Robert Davis, "Memories of the 'Other' Labrador," *Dateline Labrador* 2.2 (June 1967), 11-13.

24   Mercer Davis, "The Days Leading up to Confederation," *TD* 27.2 (Winter 2002), 43.

25   Gerald Dyson, interview by author, January 27, 2008.

26   Neary, *Newfoundland*, 156.

27   Robert Davis, "42 Years on the Goose," *TD* 12.4 (June 1987), 77-81.

28   Melvin D. McLean, "The Epic of Goose," *The Honker* (Christmas 1945), 5.

29   Russell Groves, May 22, 2003.

30   W.J. McFarlane, "First Commanding Officer Report: Sept. '41-Mar. '42," *TD* 12.4 (June 1987), 34.

31   McLean, "Epic," 4.

32   Tom M. McGrath, "Ferry Command Begins," *TD* 12.4 (June 1987), 86.

33   McLean, "Epic," 5.

34   Merrick, "War Comes to Hamilton Inlet," *TD* 12.4 (June 1987), 70.

35   Carr, 86-88.

36   Jenny Higgins with Luke Callanan, "Goose Bay," www.heritage.nf.ca/law/goose_base.html, accessed June 23, 2009.

37   Carr, 52.

38   "The War Years," *TD* 12.4 (June 1987), 43.

39   Carr, 95, and "The War Years," 43.

40   BM to Everybody, June 2, 1944, BMG Papers.

41   The hydroponic gardens were started as an experiment by the National Research Council and Army Medical Research. In 1943 the Royal Canadian Army Service Corps ran the gardens, which grew lettuce, radish, and tomatoes. The greenhouses were located on "the farm," a 30-acre patch on the base ("And They Grew and They Grew," *The Honker* [Christmas 1945], 23). Dick Budgell said after the war ended he and others from Happy Valley continued caring for the plants and harvested the vegetables, but the gardens were never planted again (Eric [Dick] Budgell, interview by author, October 1, 2007). In an effort to keep the mess halls supplied with fresh meat, American commanding officer Col. B.R.J. Hassell started a hog farm on the base (Hassell, "Commanding General's Doghouse," *TD* 12.4 [June 1987], 101-102).

42   The American Red Cross "girls" were sent to the military base to boost morale and provide recreational activities. Other females working at the base included Canadian and American military nurses and a few members of the Royal Air Force Women's Division (Carr, 252-253). In 1945, a squadron of American Women's Auxiliary Corps was posted to Goose

Bay. The women worked in many different offices (Hassell, 103). Labrador women were employed in the large base laundry.

43 Celesta Gerber Acreman, *For the Love of Labrador—My Story* (St. John's: Robinson-Blackmore, [1998?]), 26.

44 McFarlane, 39.

45 "Needlework Guild Column," *ADSF* 41.2 (July 1943), 59.

Chapter 8

1 Millicent Blake Loder, *Daughter of Labrador* (St. John's: Harry Cuff, 1989), 39-42. Loder's wage was 50 cents a month. In addition to their household duties, the girls fished, hunted, and picked berries.

2 Ruth P. Byerly, "Summer Nursing in Labrador," *American Journal of Nursing* (May 1946), 302.

3 BM to Everybody, June 2, 1944, BMG Papers.

4 W.A. Paddon, *Labrador Doctor: My Life with the Grenfell Mission* (Toronto: James Lorimer, 1989), 24.

5 Dr. Harry Paddon's son, Dr. Anthony Paddon, told a story about an unnamed lieutenant governor visiting Labrador and when introduced to "old Pastine," an Innu elder, explained that he was the "Representative of the Great White Father." Pastine replied, "Me want Dr. Paddon" (Paddon, "Life with Father … and the Grenfell Ships," *Dateline Labrador* 2.3 [July 1967], 23).

6 The list for the entire Grenfell Mission volunteer and paid staff was published every year in *ADSF*. "Our Staff," *ADSF* 42.3 (October 1944), 76-77.

7 *Instructions and Information for Staff Members* (n.d.), 1, RPA, IGA, MG 63.2138.

8 BM to Everybody, June 2, 1944, BMG Papers.

9 BM to Everybody, June 2, 1944, BMG Papers.

10 Florence Michelin, "Florence Goudie RN," *TD* 18.4 (July 1993), 32-37.

11   John Parsons and Burton K. Janes, *The King of Baffin Land, W. Ralph Parsons, Last Fur Trade Commissioner of the Hudson's Bay Company* (St. John's: Creative, 1996), 67.

12   Grenfell cloth was tightly woven cotton fabric manufactured at the Haythornthwaite Mill in Burnley, England. It was light and durable and shed water. Grenfell's name was used by the company though he did not profit from the use of his name (Rompkey, *Grenfell*, 322).

13   Rhoda Dawson, "The Folk Art of the Labrador," *ADSF* 36.2 (July 1938), 39.

14   BM to Everybody, July 15, 1944, BMG Papers.

15   Cyril and Florence Michelin, "Florence and Cyril Michelin 50th Wedding Anniversary," *TD* 21.3 (Spring 1996), 28-29.

16   BM to Everybody, July 15, 1944, BMG Papers.

17   BM to Peoples, July 19, 1944, BMG Papers.

18   Steve Hamilton was an artist from Amherst, Massachusetts, who came to Labrador as a volunteer and stayed several years. He taught art in Yale School. Dick Budgell said students, when given a choice of French or art, "all chose art." The Canadian Officer's mess at Goose Bay once had a mural painted by Hamilton (Eric Budgell, July 6, 2012).

19   Maria Halsey Stryker, "Rag Dolls to Labrador," *ADSF* 31.4 (January 1934), 186.

20   Priscilla Randolph (Randy) Toland Page, interview by author, August 26, 2008.

21   The American Air Force had a 50-foot crash boat with three engines. The RCAF Marine section had three boats: a "Cape Islander" work boat, a 30-foot-long "Cape Cod" boat called *Grebe*, and a 30-foot-long crash boat with two Chrysler 8-cylinder engines. Dick Budgell said the Cape Islander was used to bring people back and forth to North West River, usually on Sunday (Eric Budgell, January 30, 2008).

22   Robert George Gillard worked for the HBC in North West River from 1941 to 1944 as Post Manager (www.gov.mb.ca/chc/archives/hbca/biographical, accessed May 23, 2013).

23   Possibly Palokovich. BM to Everyone, July 29, 1944, BMG Papers.

24   BM to Everybody, July 15, 1944, BMG Papers.

25   Harold G. Paddon, *Green Woods and Blue Waters: Memories of Labrador* (St. John's: Breakwater, 1989), 86-87.

26   Captain Thomas J. Connors had been sailing ships in the Newfoundland coastal service since 1904. His first command was 1912 and he captained nearly every vessel in the fleet before he retired in 1950 (*ENL*, s.v. "Connors, Thomas J.").

27   BM to Everyone, August 9, 1944, BMG Papers.

28   Diary, August 3, 1944, BMG Papers. The Earl of Athlone became Governor-General of Canada in June 1940. He hosted conferences in Quebec on two occasions with Mackenzie King, Winston Churchill, and Franklin D. Roosevelt to discuss Allied war strategy (www.gg.ca/document.aspx?id=14615, accessed June 22, 2009).

29   BM to Everybody, August 9, 1944, BMG Papers.

30   BM to Everybody, August 9, 1944, BMG Papers.

31   Diary, September 19, 1944, BMG Papers.

32   Diary, August 25 & 26, 1944, BMG Papers. Dick Budgell recalls going to North West River in the crash boat with his brother George, who was in the RCAF Marine Section. They brought a Dr. Bell to see Clayton Montague, who was very sick. After the doctor examined the boy, he asked Dick and George if they had been anywhere else in the community, and they said no. The doctor said, "We'd better get out of here because this place could be quarantined" (Eric Budgell, July 6, 2012).

33   Diary, September 6, 1944, BMG Papers.

34   Diary, September 11, 1944, BMG Papers.

35   Diary, September 13, 1944, BMG Papers.

36   Harry L. Paddon, "With the Trappers to Muskrat Falls," *ADSF* 33.4 (January 1936), 147.

37   BM to Everybody, October 8, 1944, BMG Papers.

38   Lee White, "Battle Dress & Sealskin Boots," *TD* 12.4 (June 1987), 91-93.

39   Diary, October 31, 1944, BMG Papers.

40   Diary, November 12, 1944, BMG Papers.

41   Diary, November 22, 1944, BMG Papers.

42   Diary, December 5-8, 1944, BMG Papers.

43   Diary, December 15 & 16, 1944, BMG Papers. Jane Chaulk and Jessie Goudie were expert needlewomen.

44   Merrick, *Northern Nurse* (New York: Scribner's, 1942), 32.

45   Merrick, *Northern Nurse*, 231.

46   Rompkey, ed., *The Labrador Memoir of Dr. Harry Paddon 1912-1938* (Montreal & Kingston: McGill-Queen's University Press, 2003), 241.

47   Rompkey, *Labrador Memoir*, 234.

48   Dr. W.A. Paddon said that after the war "x-ray equipment was built into the dispensary, and we went after the problem of tuberculosis in Labrador hammer-and-tongs, x-raying everyone annually and treating all the cases we found as vigorously as possible" (Paddon, "Life with Father," 26).

Chapter 9

1   North West River, Newfoundland and Labrador Census for 1945, RPA.

2   BM to Everybody, February 17, 1945, BMG Papers.

3   Lester Burry, "Memories of Labrador," in *The Book of Newfoundland*, v. 4, edited by Joseph R. Smallwood (St. John's: Newfoundland Book Publishers [1967] Ltd., 1967), 58.

4   Hector Swain, *Lester Leeland Burry: Labrador Pastor & Father of Confederation* (St. John's: Harry Cuff Publications, 1983), 38-40. Barbara Groves did not mention having a radio receiver on the trapline during the two winters she spent with Russell. Dick Budgell said heavy radio receivers and batteries would not have been taken by trappers who were portaging their supplies to traplines a distance away from the Grand River (Eric

Budgell, July 6, 2012).

5   W.A. Paddon to Charles Curtis, September 8, 1942, RPA, IGA, MG 63.1966.

6   Rompkey, *Grenfell*, 285.

7   Paddon, *Labrador Doctor*, 75.

8   Russell Groves, May 22, 2003.

9   BM to One and All, December 31, 1944, BMG Papers.

10 BM to Mother, April 8, 1945, BMG Papers.

11 Diary, July 4, 1945, BMG Papers.

12 W.A. Paddon to IGA Board, June 23, 1945, RPA, IGA, MG 63.1966.

13 Curtis to Cecil Ashdown, September 19, 1945, RPA, IGA, MG 63.1967.

14 Mina Paddon to Cecil Ashdown, February 9, 1946, RPA, IGA, MG 63.1966.

15 Paddon, *Labrador Doctor*, 76-82. The hospital in North West River closed in 1983, after a bridge was built across North West River, making it possible for people to drive to the hospital in Happy Valley-Goose Bay.

16 Priscilla Randolph Toland Page, August 26, 2008.

Chapter 10

1   BM to Mother, October 13, 1945, BMG Papers.

2   Greater Yellowlegs is a large, long-legged shorebird, also called twillick, nansary, and auntsary (*Dictionary of Newfoundland English* [*DNE*], s.v. "twillick").

3   Diary, September 19, 1945, BMG Papers.

4   Diary, September 23, 1945, BMG Papers.

5   BM to Mother, October 26, 1945, BMG Papers.

6   BM to Mother, October 26, 1945, BMG Papers.

7   Diary, November 18, 1945, BMG Papers.

8   BM to Mother, December 3, 1945, BMG Papers.

9   Hazel Hoyles's husband, Vernon, was the school principal.

10 Many patients who went sent from Labrador to the hospital in St. Anthony never came home. Ernest Goudie was buried in the United Church cemetery in St. Anthony. A marker on his grave reads, "Erected by His Fellow Trappers of North West River Labrador to the Memory of Ernest E. Goudie died March 3, 1946 Aged 27 years."

11 BM to Mother, January 30, 1946, BMG Papers.

12 "Staff Selection Notes," *ADSF* 43.4 (January 1946), 119.

13 Diary, March 10, 1946, BMG Papers.

14 Diary, March 25, 1946, BMG Papers.

15 Diary, April 6, 1946, BMG Papers.

16 BM to Mother, April 26, 1946, BMG Papers.

17 Diary, April 16, 1946, BMG Papers.

18 Diary, May 3, 1946, BMG Papers.

19 Diary, May 5-13, 1946, BMG Papers.

20 BM to Mother and Harriet, May 21, 1946, BMG Papers.

21 Diary, July 1, 1946, BMG Papers.

Chapter 11

1   McLean described his party as "half starved, half naked and half devoured" when they arrived at Fort Nascopie, seven weeks after they left Fort Chimo and a few days before they saw the falls. John McLean, *John McLean's Notes of a Twenty-Five Years' Service in the Hudson's Bay Territory*, edited by W.S. Wallace (Toronto: The Champlain Society 1932; facsimile, New York: Greenwood Press, 1968), 229.

2   Hugh Stewart, "A.P. Low (1861-1942)," *Arctic* 39.3 (September 1986),

275, and *The Bottle of Churchill Falls* (St. John's: The Department of Labrador Affairs, 1968), 2.

3   Philip Smith, *Brinco: The Story of Churchill Falls* (Toronto: McClelland & Stewart, 1975), 47.

4   Smith, 8-16. As British prime minister, Churchill had given Newfoundland premier Joseph Smallwood encouragement and important introductions to investors interested in potential Labrador hydroelectric development.

5   *Lower Churchill Hydroelectric Generation Project ...* (St. John's: Newfoundland and Labrador Hydro, 2006), 8-9.

6   *The Bottle*, 2.

7   Merrick, *True North* (New York: Scribner's, 1933), 229.

8   *The Bottle*, 3.

9   John Michelin, "To the Grand Falls," *TD* 1.2 (December 1975), 48.

10   Alexander Forbes, *Northernmost Labrador Mapped from the Air* (New York: American Geographical Society, 1938), 133.

11   Harold G. Crowley, "To Grand Falls by Air," *ADSF* 30.4 (January 1933), 172-173.

12   Crowley, 173.

13   Andrew Brown and Ralph Gray, "Labrador Canoe Adventure," *National Geographic* (July 1951), 95.

14   On modern maps, the river is Minipi, but some Labrador residents prefer Mininipi, another anglicized version of the Innu name. Innu call the lake that drains into the river Minai-nipi. In English, it would be Burbot Lake, named for the freshwater fish. The river is Minai-nipiu-shipu; in English it would be Burbot Lake River (Peter Armitage, e-mail to author, May 19, 2013; www.innuplaces.ca/list.php?lang=en, accessed May 19, 2013).

15   John Blake, "Trapper and Guide," *TD* 25.3 (Spring 2000), 39-41.

16   Horace Goudie, "A Night in the Ashes," *TD* 4.3 (1979), 24.

17   Brown and Gray, 95.

18   Horace Goudie, *Trails to Remember* (St. John's: Jesperson, 1991), 43.

19   Brown and Gray, 95.

20   Randle Holme, "A Journey in the Interior," 195.

21   Portaging Round the First Falls, page 95 in "Labrador 1887," in Coll-22, Randle F.W. Holme. Archives and Special Collections, Memorial University.

22   Henry G. Bryant, "A Journey to the Grand Falls of Labrador," *Bulletin of the Geographical Club of Philadelphia* 1.2 (1894), 55.

23   Barbara and Nora were the second and third women to put their names in the bottle. The Hubbard she mentioned was Charles J. Hubbard, co-pilot and mechanic of the Forbes flying crew in 1931 and 1932. Barbara may have been thinking of American writer and adventurer Leonidas Hubbard, who starved to death in Labrador in October 1903 in an attempt to reach Ungava Bay by way of the Nascopie and George rivers. His widow, Mina, successfully made the trip with four guides in 1905 (*The Bottle*, 4, and Forbes, *Northernmost Labrador*, 25).

24   Brown and Gray, 94.

25   Jonathan Prince Cilley Jr., *Bowdoin Boys in Labrador* (Rockland, ME: Rockland Publishing, [189?]), 14.

26   Cilley, 50, and Bryant, "The Grand Falls of Labrador," *The Century Magazine* 44.5 (September 1892), 655.

27   Merrick, *True North*, 230.

28   Cilley, 46-47. There are no photos of the canyon or falls in Cilley's book. In a collection of expedition photos on the Maine Memory Network website, a digital museum and archive, there are several of expedition members at the beginning and end of their adventure, some of men posing in sealskin clothing or with guns and paddles (www.mainememory.net/exhibits/exhibits_archive.shtml., accessed May 19, 2013). Cary's and Cole's photographs may have been damaged by moisture, as happened with Bryant and Kenaston.

29   Brown and Gray, 95.

30   Bryant, "The Grand Falls," 655.

31 Also gozzard, American common merganser (*DNE*, s.v. "gizzard").

32 *The Bottle*, 1.

33 *The Bottle*, 8.

34 Smith, 79.

35 Smith, 346-349.

36 Smith, 156.

Chapter 12

1 "Alumni News," *ADSF* 45.1 (April 1947), 24. America House was a not-for-profit retail outlet that sold fine handicrafts. Mrs. Aileen Osbourn Webb, president and founder of the American Craftsmen's Council, opened the shop in 1940. Bella Neyman, "The (America) House That Mrs. Webb Built" (www.themagazineantiques.com/articles/america-house/, accessed February 5, 2013).

2 "Flushing Sews for Laborador's [sic] Frozen Natives," *Long Island Sunday Press*, May 4, 1947.

3 "Demarest Students Hear Talk on Interesting Life in Labrador," *Bloomfield Independent Press*, June 20, 1947.

4 See Kristina Fagan's discussion of the important place Campbell occupies in the literary tradition of Labrador in "'Well done old half breed woman': Lydia Campbell and the Labrador Literary Tradition," *Papers of the Bibliographical Society of Canada* 48.1 (Spring 2010), 49-76.

5 Lydia Campbell, "Sketches of Labrador Life by a Labrador Woman," *The Evening Herald*, December 7, 1894.

6 Campbell, "Sketches," December 7, 1894.

7 Arminius Young, *A Methodist Missionary in Labrador* (Toronto: S. and A. Young, 1916), 18.

8 The HBC post journals show that traders often performed marriages, baptized babies, and officiated at services on Sunday and special occasions.

9   Campbell, "Sketches," December 10, 1894.

10   Margaret Campbell Baikie, *Labrador Memories: Reflections at Mulligan* (Happy Valley-Goose Bay, Labrador: Them Days, n.d.), 35.

11   Flora Baikie, "I Likes to Go Fishing," *TD* 1.4 (June 1976), 12.

12   The Baptist chaplain on the military base was probably waiting to hear if it was legal for him to perform the ceremony. Marriage law in Newfoundland "extended the right to all those ministers with publicly recognized congregations and chapels" and the Baptists did not have a church in Newfoundland until 1953 (*ENL*, s.v. "Baptist Church" and "Marriage," and Trudi Johnson, "A Matter of Custom and Convenience: Marriage Law in Nineteenth Century Newfoundland," *Newfoundland Studies* 19.2 [2003], 282-296).

13   Diary, August 31, 1947, BMG Papers.

14   Diary, September 14, 1947, BMG Papers.

Chapter 13

1   Horace Goudie, "Lobstick Lake Was My Trapping Place," *TD* 25.3 (Spring 2000), 19.

2   Goudie, *Trails*, 41.

3   Gerald White, "I Became a Grand River Trapper When I Was Fifteen," *TD* 25.3 (Spring 2000), 10.

4   Goudie, *Trails*, 21.

Chapter 14

1   Raoul Thevenet's comments were made in a sworn affidavit included in the evidence considered by the British Privy Council in the boundary case. Voluntary Statement of Raoul Thevenet, of Northwest River, Lake Melville. No. 1424, in the Privy Council (Great Britain), in the Matter of the Boundary between the Dominion of Canada and the Colony of Newfoundland on the Labrador Coast, July 21, 1921, vol. 8, 3739.

2   Blake, "Trapper and Guide," 39.

3   A.G. Frith and G. Budgell, "Labrador Life—Indians," *The Honker* (Mid-Summer 1945), 2.

4   Thevenet, 3741.

5   In 1970, when he was over 80 years of age, Mestokosho told the story of his life to anthropologist Serge Bouchard. Bouchard, *Caribou Hunter: A Song of a Vanished Innu Life*, translated by Joan Irving (Vancouver: Greystone Books, 2006), 137.

6   Bouchard, 57.

7   Bouchard, 41.

8   Bouchard, 68-71.

9   Fr. Edward J. O'Brien, later Monsignor O'Brien, went to Labrador every year from 1921 to 1946. He had prematurely grey hair and was known to the Innu as Father Whitehead. His many photographs and moving pictures of the people are in provincial and national archives.

10   John E. Keats, "Establishment of Mission at Davis Inlet," *TD* 10.3 (March 1985), 11.

11   Hayward Parsons, "Hudson's Bay Company & Relief," *TD* 10.3 (March 1985), 13-14.

12   Edward J. O'Brien, "Starvation," *TD* 10.3 (March 1985), 20-21.

13   Joe Rich, "Keeping in Touch," *TD* 10.3 (March 1985), 26.

14   Bouchard, 131.

15   Tanner, "Outlines," 713.

16   Max McLean, "Max McLean North West River—1989," *TD* 14.3 (April 1989), 26.

17   John Montague, "Trappin' Was Our Life," *TD* 18.4 (July 1993), 62-63.

18   White, "Grand River Trapper," 9-15. Not every trapper adjusted to the solitary life. Dick Budgell remembered a version of "The Trapper's Alphabet" song, composed by North West River trapper Judson Blake, with

a line referring to a man who "is never alone, so he wraps up his game bag and he's on the way home." Budgell said a man would be embarrassed to be known for not wanting to be alone (Eric Budgell, July 6, 2012). Another version of the song is in a typed song sheet dated October 1959, in "Saturday Sing-Song at Mr. & Mrs. Sid's," and "The Alphabet Song" has this line: "'D' is for Donald who sits home all [the] time," BMG Papers.

19   Goudie, *Trails*, 58.

20   Bouchard, 35.

Chapter 15

1   Merrick, *True North*, 257.

2   Isaac Rich, "Returning Home," *TD* 1.1 (August 1975), 9.

3   Blake, "Trapper and Guide," 38.

4   John Michelin, "Trappin' Yarn," *TD* 4.2 (1978), 23.

Chapter 16

1   In 1983, Byron (Fiddler) Chaulk told researcher Debbie Michelin that "The Trapper's Song" by "an old trapper," Douglas Best of Mud Lake, "was the only trapper's song that [he] used to hear [his] parents sing. It was a favorite of everyone around the area" (Byron Chaulk, "I Got a Knack for Putting Words Together," *TD* 21.2 [Winter 1996], 9). The song lyrics were included in an article by Marjorie Wheeler ("A Crowd of Jolly Trappers," *ADSF* 46.4 [January 1949]), but the title was not given and the songwriter was not credited. Two photos by Barbara Mundy Groves were published with this article.

2   Goudie, *Trails*, 64.

Epilogue

1   Diary, March 24, 1949, BMG Papers.

BIBLIOGRAPHY

Published Sources

A Brick for Labrador. London: Grenfell Association of Great Britain and Ireland, [1930?].

Acreman, Celesta Gerber. *For the Love of Labrador—My Story*. St. John's: Robinson-Blackmore, [1998?].

Affidavit of Joseph Michelin. No. 1619. In the Privy Council (Great Britain). In the Matter of the Boundary between the Dominion of Canada and the Colony of Newfoundland in the Labrador Peninsula. Volume 8. September 10, 1909.

Ames, Randy. "Land Use in the Rigolet Area." In *Our Footprints Are Everywhere: Inuit Land Use and Occupancy in Labrador*, edited by Carol Brice-Bennett, Alan Cooke, and Nina Davis, 279-308. Nain, Labrador: Labrador Inuit Association, 1977.

Baikie, Margaret Campbell. *Labrador Memories: Reflections at Mulligan*. Happy Valley-Goose Bay, Labrador: Them Days, n.d.

The Bottle of Churchill Falls. St. John's: The Department of Labrador Affairs, 1968.

Bouchard, Serge. *Caribou Hunter: A Song of a Vanished Innu Life*. Translated by Joan Irving. Vancouver: Greystone Books, 2006.

Brice-Bennett, Carol, Alan Cooke, and Nina Davis, eds. *Our Footprints Are Everywhere: Inuit Land Use and Occupancy in Labrador*. Nain, Labrador: Labrador Inuit Association, 1977.

Budgell, Richard and Michael Staveley. *The Labrador Boundary*. Happy Valley-Goose Bay: Labrador Institute of Northern Studies, Memorial University of Newfoundland, 1987.

Burchill, Dora Elizabeth. *Labrador Memories*. Victoria, Australia: The Shepparton News Publishing Co., 1947.

Burry, Lester. "Memories of Labrador." In *The Book of Newfoundland*, v. 4, edited by Joseph R. Smallwood, 58-66. St. John's: Newfoundland Book Publishers (1967) Ltd., 1967.

Carr, William Guy. *Checkmate in the North: The Axis Planned to Invade America*. Toronto: MacMillan, 1945.

Cilley, Jonathan Prince, Jr. *Bowdoin Boys in Labrador*. Rockland, ME: Rockland Publishing, [189?].

Dunmore, Spencer. *Wings for Victory: The Remarkable Story of the British Commonwealth Air Training Plan in Canada*. Toronto: McClelland & Stewart, 1994.

Forbes, Alexander. *Northernmost Labrador Mapped from the Air*. New York: American Geographical Society, Special Publication No. 22, 1938.

——. *Quest for a Northern Air Route*. Cambridge: Harvard University Press, 1953.

Gosling, W.G. *Labrador: Its Discovery, Exploration and Development*. New York: John Lane Company, 1911.

Goudie, Horace. *Trails to Remember*. St. John's: Jesperson, 1991.

Grenfell, Wilfred. *Forty Years for Labrador*. London: Hodder and Stoughton, 1934.

Hadley, Michael. *U-Boats against Canada: German Submarines in Canadian Waters*. Montreal: McGill-Queen's University Press, 1985.

Hiller, J.K. "Moravian Land Holdings on the Labrador Coast: A Brief History." In *Our Footprints Are Everywhere: Inuit Land Use and Occupancy in Labrador*, edited by Carol Brice-Bennett, Alan Cooke, and Nina Davis, 83-93. Nain, Labrador: Labrador Inuit Association, 1977.

Jordan, Richard H. "Inuit Occupation of the Central Labrador Coast since 1600 AD." In *Our Footprints Are Everywhere: Inuit Land Use and Occupancy in Labrador*. Edited by Carol Brice-Bennett, Alan Cooke, and Nina Davis, 43-48. Nain, Labrador: Labrador Inuit Association, 1977.

Kennedy, David M. *The American People in the Great Depression: Freedom from Fear: Part I*. New York: Oxford University Press, 1999.

KOINE, Connecticut College Yearbook, 1933.

Leach, MacEdward. *Folk Ballads and Songs of the Lower Labrador Coast*. Ottawa: National Museum of Canada, Anthropological Series No. 68, Bulletin 201, 1965.

Laverty, Paula. *Silk Stocking Mats: Hooked Mats of the Grenfell Mission*. Montreal & Kingston: McGill-Queen's University Press, 2005.

Loder, Millicent Blake. *Daughter of Labrador*. St. John's: Harry Cuff, 1989.

Lower Churchill Hydroelectric Generation Project. Project Registration Pursuant to the Newfoundland and Labrador Environmental Protection Act. St. John's: Newfoundland and Labrador Hydro, 2006.

MacArthur, Burke. *United Littles: The Story of the Needlework Guild of America*. New York: Coward-McCann, 1955.

McLean, John. *John McLean's Notes of a Twenty-Five Years' Service in the Hudson's Bay Territory*. Edited by W.S. Wallace. Toronto: The Champlain Society, 1932; facsimile, New York: Greenwood Press, 1968.

Merrick, Elliott. *True North*. New York: Scribner's, 1933.

——. *Northern Nurse*. New York: Scribner's, 1942.

——. *Green Mountain Farm*. New York: MacMillan, 1948.

Neary, Peter. *Newfoundland in the North Atlantic World, 1929-1949*. Montreal and Kingston: McGill-Queen's University Press, 1988.

O'Brien, Patricia, ed. *The Grenfell Obsession: An Anthology*. St. John's: Creative, 1992.

Paddon, Harold G. *Green Woods and Blue Waters: Memories of Labrador*. St. John's: Breakwater, 1989.

Paddon, W.A. *Labrador Doctor: My Life with the Grenfell Mission*. Toronto: James Lorimer, 1989.

Parsons, John and Burton K. Janes. *The King of Baffin Land: W. Ralph Parsons, Last Fur Trade Commissioner of the Hudson's Bay Company*. St. John's: Creative, 1996.

Post, Emily. *Etiquette*. New York: Funk & Wagnalls, 1945.

Rompkey, Ronald. *Grenfell of Labrador: A Biography*. Toronto: University of Toronto Press, 1991.

Rompkey, Ronald, ed. *The Labrador Memoir of Dr. Harry Paddon 1912-1938*. Montreal & Kingston: McGill-Queen's University Press, 2003.

Smith, Philip. *Brinco: The Story of Churchill Falls*. Toronto: McClelland & Stewart, 1975.

Swain, Hector. *Lester Leeland Burry: Labrador Pastor & Father of Confederation*. St. John's: Creative, 1983.

Toland, Harry. *A Sort of Peace Corps: Wilfred Grenfell's Labrador Volunteers*. Bowie, MD: Heritage Books, 2001.

Voluntary Statement of Malcolm McLean of Carter Basin, Lake Melville. No. 1425. In The Privy Council (Great Britain). In the Matter of the Boundary between the Dominion of Canada and the Colony of Newfoundland on the Labrador Coast. Volume 8. July 19, 1921.

Voluntary Statement of Raoul Thevenet, of Northwest River, Lake Melville. No. 1424. In The Privy Council (Great Britain). In the Matter of the Boundary between the Dominion of Canada and the Colony of Newfoundland on the Labrador Coast. Volume 8. July 21, 1921.

Young, Arminius. *A Methodist Missionary in Labrador*. Toronto: S. and A. Young, 1916.

Online Articles

"Amtrak's Downeaster." www.american-rails.com/downeaster.html.

Anderson, Duncan. "D-Day Beachhead." www.bbc.co.uk/history/worldwars/wwtwo/dday_beachhead_01.shtml.

"Bowdoin College Scientific Expedition to Labrador." www.mainememory.net/exhibits/exhibits_archive.shtml.

Collins, Paul. "Sinking of the Caribou." www.heritage.nf.ca/law/caribou_sinking.html.

——. "Other U-Boat Encounters." www.heritage.nf.ca/law/uboat.html.

"Connolly, Henry." www.gov.mb.ca/chc/archives/hbca/biographical.

Davies, William H.A. "Notes on Esqimaux Bay and Surrounding Country." Paper presented to the Literary & Historical Society of Quebec, February 19, 1842. Published in *Transactions* 4.1 (1855). www. morrin.org/transactions/docsfromclient/books/130/130.html.

"The Earl of Athlone." www.gg.ca/document.aspx?id=14615.

"Gillard, Robert George." www.gov.mb.ca/chc/archives/hbca/biographical.

Higgins, Jenny with Luke Callanan. "Goose Bay." www.heritage.nf.ca/law/goose_base.html.

"Minai-nipi." www.innuplaces.ca/list.php?lang=en.

Neyman, Bella. "The (America) House That Mrs. Webb Built." www.themagazineantiques.com/articles/america-house/.

Peel, Bruce. "Connolly, Suzanne." www.biographi.ca.

Unpublished Sources

"A Few Facts about the Grenfell Missions of Newfoundland and Labrador," 1937. Centre for Newfoundland Studies, Memorial University Libraries (CNS). File.

Ashdown, Cecil and T.A. Greene. *Report of the Commission Appointed by the Directors of the International Grenfell Association, April 13, 1935, to Confer with the Commission of Government for Newfoundland and Survey Conditions on the Coast of Newfoundland and Labrador.* New York: November 26, 1935. The Rooms Provincial Archives, St. John's (RPA), IGA, MG 63.1951.

Barbara Mundy Groves Papers. Private collection of Marjorie Groves.

Bryant, Henry. *My Financial Adventures.* January 1930. Unpublished manuscript. Private collection of Anthony Bryant.

Goudie Family Tree. Genealogical research compiled by Bernie Heard for Labrador Metis Nation, now NunatuKavut, (n.d.). Happy Valley-Goose Bay, Labrador.

Mundy and Bryant Papers. Private collection of Peter Mundy.

Correspondence between Barbara Mundy and Dr. Wilfred Grenfell, Cecil Ashdown, and Vera Grenfell (1935-1942). RPA, IGA, MG 63.2959.

Correspondence from Charles Curtis to W.A. Paddon (1942), W.A. Paddon to IGA Board (1945), and Mina Paddon to IGA Board (1946). RPA, IGA, MG 63.1966.

Correspondence from Charles Curtis to Cecil Ashdown (1945). RPA, IGA, MG 63.1967.

Curtis, Charles. *Report of the Superintendent of the Board of Directors of the International Grenfell Association, November 1950.* RPA, IGA, MG 63.113.

Instructions and Information for Staff Members. New York: International Grenfell Association, (n.d.). RPA, IGA, MG 63.2138.

Mundy, Barbara. *The Twentieth Annual Report of the Coast-to-Coast Labrador Branch of the Needlework Guild of America.* New York, 1940. RPA, IGA, MG 63.227.

"No. 476, Interview with Dr. Grenfell on Trade Matters, February 1, 1901." *Moravian Missions Documents [1768-1921].* CNS, Microfilm 513, reel 4.

North West River. Newfoundland and Labrador Census for 1945. RPA.

Parish Record of United Church, Labrador, 1932-33. RPA.

Post Journal of North West River, 1836-1851. Hudson's Bay Company Archives at Archives of Manitoba, Winnipeg (HBCA). B.153/a/1-11, Reel 1M105.

Tamblyn, H.W. and John Adams Brown. *The Grenfell Mission: A Survey, Analysis and Recommendations.* New York: February 4, 1938. RPA, IGA, MG 63.2031.

Thirteenth Census of the United States. Montclair Township, Essex Country, New Jersey. 1910. National Archives and Records Administration.

"To the Brethren of the Mission Board, London, October 1930." *Records of the Moravian Mission in Labrador [1764-1944].* Public Archives of Canada, Ottawa, 1960. CNS, Microfilm 511, reel 8.

Among The Deep-Sea Fishers (ADSF) **Articles**

A.G.G. "The Boston Fair." 30.1 (April 1932).

"Alumni News." 33.4 (January 1936).

——. 38.2 (July 1940).

——. 41.1 (April 1943).

——. 45.1 (April 1947).

Crowley, Harold G. "To Grand Falls by Air." 30.4 (January 1933).

Curtis, Charles S. "St. Anthony in 1932." 31.1 (April 1933).

Dawson, Rhoda. "The Folk Art of the Labrador." 36.2 (July 1938).

"Financial Report of the International Grenfell Association." 37.1 (April 1939).

"Glasgow to St. Anthony with the Scots." 33.4 (January 1936).

Gould, Albert T. "The New Cluett." 39.3 (October 1941).

Grenfell, Sir Wilfred. "Varick Frissell." 29.2 (July 1931).

——. "The Land Vision of a Sailor." 30.3 (October 1932).

——. "Sir Wilfred's Letter." 30.4 (January 1933).

——. "Dr. Harry Locke Paddon." 37.4 (January 1940).

Hamilton, Elisabeth and Shirley S. Smith. "All Offerings Gratefully Received." 39.1 (April 1941).

Kivimaki, Anna. "Hard Winter Ahead." 37.3 (October 1939).

Merrick, Elliott. "Escape to the North." 30.3 (October 1932).

"Needlework Guild Column." 31.2 (July 1933).

——. 31.4 (January 1934).

——. 37.4 (January 1940).

——. 41.2 (July 1943).

——. 41.4 (January 1944).

"Our Staff." 42.3 (October 1944).

Paddon, Harry L. "With the Trappers to Muskrat Falls." 33.4 (January 1936).

"Report of the Staff Selection Committee." 26.2 (July 1928).

——. 27.2 (July 1929).

——. 33.2 (July 1935).

Sanger, Lilian Schieffelin. "A Temporary Industrial Shop in New York." 29.2 (July 1931).

"Schedule of Sir Wilfred's Lecture Tour Abroad, Autumn of 1928." 26.3 (October 1928).

"Sir Wilfred's 1929 Lecture Tour." 26.4 (January 1929).

"Staff Selection Notes." 43.4 (January 1946).

Stryker, Maria Halsey. "Rag Dolls to Labrador." 31.4 (January 1934).

Toop, John R. "An Incident at Northwest River Recalled." 31.3 (October 1933).

Wheeler, Marjorie. "A Crowd of Jolly Trappers." 46.4 (January 1949).

Young, Kathleen. "Labrador Calling." 40.1 (April 1942).

———. "Our Staff." 39.2 (July 1941).

New York Times (*NYT*) **Articles**

"The Late Henry Keep—The Millionaire's Will." September 14, 1869.

"Garments for the Poor." November 20, 1891.

"The Needlework Guild." February 21, 1892.

"Mrs. Schley's Bequests." July 1, 1900.

"Copartnership Notices." January 1, 1908.

"Notes of Social Activities." April 18, 1928.

"Miss Rodman Entertained." December 1, 1929.

"Operas That Will Serve Charity." October 26, 1930.

"In Grenfell's Labrador." November 7, 1930.

"Open Shop Tonight to Aid Grenfell Work." March 24, 1931.

"Grenfell Makes Plea for Labrador People." April 25, 1931.

"Stock Exchange News." September 27, 1931.

"5 Girls, 3 Jobless, Live on $33 a Week." November 15, 1931.

"For Grenfell Units." November 6, 1932.

"Mundy on Excelsior Bank Board." November 15, 1932.

"Many Bazaars." November 28, 1932.

"2,000,000 Children's Jobs Sought for Adults." November 28, 1932.

"Charities to Gain by Flower Show." March 19, 1933.

"Award to Mrs. Mundy." January 5, 1934.

"Grenfell to Explain Work in Labrador." April 7, 1935.

"Needle Guild's Jubilee." April 21, 1935.

"Two Fashion Shows for Charity." March 29, 1936.

"Social Service Auxiliary of Stony Wold to Give Benefit Luncheon and Style Show." February 20, 1938.

"Many Offer Help in Grenfell Work." December 11, 1938.

"*Parsifal* Will Aid Grenfell Mission." February 25, 1940.

"Wilfred Grenfell of Labrador Dead." October 10, 1940.

"Mundy-Burt." January 4, 1944.

"Obituary, Floyd W. Mundy, 77, Securities Executive." November 17, 1953.

Them Days (*TD*) Articles

Baikie, Flora. "I Likes to Go Fishing." 1.4 (June 1976).

Blake, John. "Trapper and Guide." 25.3 (Spring 2000).

Chaulk, Byron (Fiddler). "I Got a Knack for Putting Words Together." 21.2 (Winter 1996).

Davis, Mercer. "The Days Leading up to Confederation." 27.2 (Winter 2002).

Davis, Robert. "42 Years on the Goose." 12.4 (June 1987).

Fry, Eric. "Search for the Goose." 12.4 (June 1987).

Goudie, Horace. "A Night in the Ashes." 4.3 (1979).

———. "Lobstick Lake Was My Trapping Place." 25.3 (Spring 2000).

Hassell, Col. B.R.J. "Commanding General's Doghouse." 12.4 (June 1987).

Keats, John E. "Establishment of Mission at Davis Inlet." 10.3 (March 1985).

McFarlane, W.J. "First Commanding Officer Report: Sept. '41-Mar. '42." 12.4 (June 1987).

McGrath, Tom M. "Ferry Command Begins." 12.4 (June 1987).

McLean, Max. "Max McLean North West River—1989." 14.3 (April 1989).

Merrick, Elliott. "War Comes to Hamilton Inlet." 12.4 (June 1987).

Michelin, Cyril and Florence. "Florence and Cyril Michelin 50th Wedding Anniversary." 21.3 (Spring 1996).

Michelin, Florence. "Florence Goudie RN." 18.4 (July 1993).

Michelin, John. "To the Grand Falls." 1.2 (December 1975).

——. "Trappin' Yarn." 4.2 (1978).

Montague, John. "Fur Traders." 4.3 (1979).

——. "Trappin' Was Our Life." 18.4 (July 1993).

O'Brien, Edward J. "Starvation." 10.3 (March 1985).

Parsons, Hayward. "Hudson's Bay Company & Relief." 10.3 (March 1985).

Rich, Arthur. "My Grandfather Came from England." 26.4 (Summer 2001).

Rich, Isaac. "John Montague." 23.4 (Summer 1998).

——. "Returning Home." 1.1 (August 1975).

——. "We Grabbed the Chance." 12.4 (June 1987).

Rich, Joe. "Keeping in Touch." 10.3 (March 1985).

Roosevelt, Elliott. "Report to Washington, D.C." 12.4 (June 1987).

"The War Years." 12.4 (June 1987).

White, Gerald. "I Became a Grand River Trapper When I Was Fifteen." 25.3 (Spring 2000).

White, Lee. "Battle Dress & Sealskin Boots." 12.4 (June 1987).

Other Published Articles

"And They Grew and They Grew." *The Honker* (Christmas 1945).

Brown, Andrew and Ralph Gray. "Labrador Canoe Adventure." *National Geographic* (July 1951).

Bryant, Henry G. "The Grand Falls of Labrador." *The Century Magazine* 44.5 (September 1892).

——. "A Journey to the Grand Falls of Labrador." *Bulletin of the Geographical Club of Philadelphia* 1.2 (1894).

Byerly, Ruth P. "Summer Nursing in Labrador." *American Journal of Nursing* (May 1946).

Campbell, Lydia. "Sketches of Labrador Life by a Labrador Woman." *The Evening Herald*, December 6, 7, and 10, 1894.

Davis, Robert. "Memories of the 'Other' Labrador." *Dateline Labrador* 2.2 (June 1967).

"Demarest Students Hear Talk on Interesting Life in Labrador." *Bloomfield Independent Press*, June 20, 1947.

"Eleven College Boys and Girls Sail to Work with Grenfell Mission." *The Boston Herald*, June 27, 1935.

Fagan, Kristina. "'Well done old half breed woman': Lydia Campbell and the Labrador Literary Tradition." *Papers of the Bibliographical Society of Canada* 48.1 (Spring 2010).

"Flushing Sews for Laborador's [sic] Frozen Natives." *Long Island Sunday Press*, May 4, 1947.

Frissell, Varick. "Explorations in the Grand Falls Region of Labrador." *The Geographical Journal* 69.4 (April 1927).

Frith, A.G. and G. Budgell. "Labrador Life—Indians." *The Honker* (Mid-Summer 1945).

Grenfell, Wilfred. "Story of Labrador Medical Mission." *Empire Club of Canada Addresses*. Toronto: The Empire Club of Canada, 1923.

——. "Newfoundland and Labrador." *Journal of the Royal Society of Arts* 82.4250 (May 4, 1934).

——. "Warm Hearts in Labrador." *The Rotarian* 47.1 (July 1935).

——. "Labrador—Lesson in Humanity." *The Rotarian* 53.6 (December 1938).

Holme, Randle. "A Journey in the Interior of Labrador, July to October 1887." *Proceedings of the Royal Geographical Society and Monthly Record of Geography* (April 1888).

Johnson, Trudi. "A Matter of Custom and Convenience: Marriage Law in Nineteenth Century Newfoundland." *Newfoundland Studies* 19.2 (2003).

Kivimaki, Anna. "Nursing with the Grenfell Mission." *American Journal of Nursing* 37.6 (June 1937).

McLean, Melvin D. "The Epic of Goose." *The Honker* (Christmas 1945).

——. "North West River." *The Honker* (Christmas 1945).

Neary, Peter. "The Diplomatic Background to the Canada-Newfoundland Goose Bay Agreement of October 10, 1944." *Newfoundland Studies* 2.1 (Spring 1986).

Paddon, Anthony. "Life with Father ... and the Grenfell Ships." *Dateline Labrador* 2.3 (July 1967).

Stewart, Hugh. "A.P. Low (1861-1942)." *Arctic* 39.3 (September 1986).

Tanner, Vaïnö. "Outlines of the Geography, Life and Customs of New-foundland-Labrador." *Acta Geographica* 8.1 (1944).

Interviews by Author

Blake, Sylvia. October 10, 2007.

Budgell, Eric (Dick). October 1, 2007, January 30, 2008, and July 6, 2012.

Chaulk, Derrick (Dick). September 14, 2007.

Chaulk, Morris. September 28, 2007.

Dyson, Gerald. January 27, 2008.

Groves, Russell. May 22, 2003.

Mundy, Peter. June 7 & 8, 2008.

Page, Priscilla Randolph (Randy) Toland. August 26, 2008.

ABOUT THE AUTHOR

Anne Budgell grew up on military bases all over Canada until her parents returned home to Labrador in 1966. Budgell's first trip to Newfoundland was in 1967 to attend Memorial University. She had a long career as a radio and television journalist with CBC in Newfoundland and Labrador, retiring in 2007.

She credits her parents with instilling in her an interest in Labrador

Ned Pratt photo

and its history. Her father, George, grew up in Rigolet, the son of Hudson's Bay Company factor George Budgell from Fogo Island and Phyllis Painter of Sandwich Bay. Her mother, Ruby, grew up in North West River, the daughter of trapper Murdock McLean from Kenemich and May Baikie of Moliak. Ruby was proud to say she was born in a log house on the Nascopie River. George could try to top it with his story of being born on the coastal vessel *Seneff*.